Marietta Fauntleroy Hollyday Gibson

Mrs. Charles H. Gibson's Maryland and Virginia Cook Book

Marietta Fauntleroy Hollyday Gibson

Mrs. Charles H. Gibson's Maryland and Virginia Cook Book

ISBN/EAN: 9783744763677

Printed in Europe, USA, Canada, Australia, Japan

Cover: Foto ©Andreas Hilbeck / pixelio.de

More available books at **www.hansebooks.com**

MRS. CHARLES H. GIBSON'S

Maryland and Virginia Cook Book.

CONTAINING NUMEROUS VALUABLE RECEIPTS FOR

AID IN HOUSEKEEPING.

Prepared and Tested by

MRS. CHARLES H. GIBSON,

Of Ratcliffe Manor, Easton, Talbot County,

MARYLAND.

BALTIMORE:
JOHN MURPHY & COMPANY,
1894.

To My Mother,

Mrs. ANNE HOLMES POWELL,

A practical housekeeper for fifty years, and to whom I am indebted for so much valuable information, is this book most affectionately dedicated.

MARIETTA P. GIBSON.

Ratcliffe Manor, Talbot Co., Md.,
December, 1894.

PREFACE.

IN the selection and arrangement of the recipes contained in this volume, the compiler has chosen those known to her, from actual and long experience, to be the best and most economical. Every one knows how desirable and important it is to both health and comfort, that the food for the daily use of a family and its guests should be properly prepared. Physicians will tell you that all food which is not properly prepared and cooked is both indigestible and unhealthy, and is often the source of many of the ailments we complain of. The recipes in this book have been selected with the greatest care, and will aid all housekeepers in preparing wholesome food and tempting delicacies for their daily requirements. In other words, it is the "art of cooking made easy." A fair trial of them will convince anyone that the wide field embraced within this book comprises all that is useful and valuable, both to the lady of the house and her cook, who, if unskilled, will find the assistance herein rendered of great comfort. Most of the recipes are my own, or such as I have used for years, and taken from old books that have never been printed, and were known only to some of the best housekeepers in Maryland and Virginia. Those who have contributed to fill these pages are known to me as excellent housekeepers, whose recipes I am glad to add to my own.

In placing my book before the public I feel that I have a right to claim a like indulgence to those who, before me, have given to the world the benefit of their experience, and I feel confident that my "Cook Book," being the result of an experience of twenty years, will meet with a just reward.

"THE AUTHORESS."

RATCLIFFE MANOR, TALBOT CO., MD.
  December, 1894.

CONTENTS.

RULES FOR BREAD AND CAKE MAKING.

YEAST.

TABLE OF WEIGHTS AND MEASURES.

BREAD.

	PAGE.
Potato Rolls	7
Brandon Corn Bread	7
Batter Bread	8
Drop Biscuit	8
Crumpets	8
Flannel Cakes	8
Quick Biscuit	8
Ratcliffe Rusks	9
Rusks	9, 10
Bath Rusks	9
Ratcliffe Rolls	10
Brentford Rolls	10
Ratcliffe Loaf Bread, No. 1	11
Spoon Rolls	11
Puffets	11
White of Egg Muffins	11
Cream Muffins	11
Water Muffins	12
Muffin Bread	12
Muffins	12, 13, 20, 22
Delicious Corn Waffles	12
Turks' Heads	13
Washington's Breakfast Cakes	13
Journey Cake	13
Bachelor's Loaf	13
Soft Brown Bread	13
Brown Bread	14, 21
Gems	14
Rice Waffles	14
Hominy Waffles	14
Quick Waffles	14
Waffles	15
Half-Meal Griddle Cakes	15
Potato Cakes	15
Sally Lunn	15, 16
Sally Lunn without Yeast	16
Irish Lunn	16
Graham Bread	16, 21
Maryland Biscuit	17
Bread Cakes	17
Aunt Clarissy's Corn Slappers	17
Mush Bread	17
Tea Bread	17
Milk Toast	18
Rice Cakes	18
Rye Drop Cakes	18
Muffin Loaf	18
French Bread	19
Bonny Clabber Cakes	19
Washington's Breakfast Bread	19
Milk Rising Bread	19
Bread Muffins	19
Potato Muffins	20
Tea Cakes	20
Suet Cakes	20
Orange Cake	20
Bran Bread	21
Rye Bread	21
Rye Bread (Steamed)	22
Buckwheat Cakes	22, 24

	PAGE.		PAGE.
Virginia Rice Bread	23	Broiled Squirrels	36
Fried Corn Mush for Breakfast,	23	How to Cook Rabbits	36
Oatmeal Porridge	23	Indian Curry	37
Graham Biscuit	24	How to Cook Wild Ducks	37
Minute Biscuit	24	To Cure Hams and Other Meat,	38
Crumpets (Sweet)	24	Ratcliffe Manor Sausage	38
Boston Brown Bread	24	No. 1 Veal Cutlets	38
		Breaded Chops	38
MEATS.		Stewed Kidneys	39
Roast Fillet of Veal	25	Stuffed Breast of Veal (for the Stuffing)	39
Broiled Veal Cutlets	26	Veal Croquettes	39
Beef Hash	26	Liver and Bacon	40
To Cook Liver	26	Broiled Liver	40
Boiled Mutton	26	Irish Stew	40
Boiling or Stewing	27	Sheep's Head Hash	40
Mutton Cutlets	27	To Bake or Roast a Quarter of Lamb	41
To Broil Ham	27	Baked Hash	41
To Glaze a Cold Ham	27	Corned Beef Hash	41
A Quick Way to Broil Steak	27	Frizzled Beef	41
Giblet Pie with Oysters	28	Curry of Mutton	42
Virginia Brunswick Stew	28	Liver with Brown Sauce	42
English Meat Pie	28	Sweetbreads à la Crème	42
Fried Chicken, Maryland Style,	29	Sweetbreads Fried	43
A Nice Hash	29		
Fricasseed Chicken	29	SOUPS.	
Broiled Chicken	30	Mock Turtle Soup	45
Baked Ham	30	Okra Soup...........................45,	48
Pompey's Head	30	Gumbo Soup	45
Calf's Head...................30,	34	Ratcliffe Crab Soup. No. 1	46
Tenderloin of Beef	31	Potato Soup	46
Beef Stew (with Tomatoes)	31	Bean Soup	46
Boiled Ham	32	Asparagus Soup	47
Baked Calf's Head	32	Ratcliffe Asparagus Soup. No. 1,	47
Chicken Fricassee	32	Vegetable Soup	47
Veal Cutlets	33	Corn Soup..........................48,	54
Fillet of Beef	33	Tomato Soup	48
Beefsteak with Mushrooms	34	Veal Soup	49
Beef a la Mode	34	Dried Pea Soup	49
Beefsteak Pie	35	Catfish Soup	50
To Grill a Calf's Head	35	Plain Oyster Soup	50
Calf's Heart	35	Crab Soup	50
Haricot of Mutton	36		
Shoat Cutlets	36		

CONTENTS.

	PAGE.
Stock, or Pot au feu	51
A "No. 1" Oyster Soup	51
Turtle Bean Soup	52
Canned Tomato Soup	52
Clear Soup	52
Suet Dumplings	53
Tomato Bisque	53
Bouillon No. 1	53
Veal Stock	54
Cream of Celery Soup	54
Pea Soup	55
Caramel Coloring for Soup	55

FISH AND SHELLFISH.

To Fry Fish	57
Planked Shad	57
Shad Roe Croquettes	57
Broiled Shad	58
Baked Shad	58
Boiled Rock	59
Baked Sturgeon	59
To Fry Perch	59
Codfish and Potato Stew	59
Fish a la Creme	60
Halibut Steak	60
Fried Shad	60
Chowder	61
Clam Chowder	61
Oyster Fritters	62
Broiled Oysters	62
Stewed Oysters	62
Scalloped Oysters	63
Oyster Sauce for Fowls	63
Pickled Oysters	63, 65
Panned Oysters	63
Crab Cakes	64
Boiled Crabs	64
Soft Crabs	64, 66
Fricasseed Oysters	64, 65
Fried Oysters	65
Devilled Crabs	65
Crab Croquettes	66

VEGETABLES.

	PAGE.
A Kitchen Time Table	67
Lima Beans	67
Boiled Peas	68
Baked Salsify	68
Corn Fritters	68
Curled Savoy Cabbage Cooked like Cauliflower	68
To Boil Rice Dry	68
Hints for Roasting Potatoes	69
Corn Pudding	69
Spinach	69
Baked Tomatoes (whole)	69
Stewed Tomatoes	70
Boston Baked Beans	70
Potatoes Baked with Beef	70
Saratoga Potatoes	71
Beets	71
Macaroni with Cheese	71
To Cook Cranberries	72
Fried Egg-Plant	72, 73
Fried Parsnips	72
Cymlings	72
Cauliflower	73
Baked Cabbage	70
Turnips	73
Hot Slaw	74
Green Corn Pudding	74
Corn Fritters	74
Boiled Potatoes	74
Baked Egg-Plant	75
Scalloped Tomatoes	75
Potato Fritters	75
Green Corn (Boiled)	75
Macaroni Milanese	75
Stewed Potatoes	76, 77
Fried Salsify	76
Stewed Salsify	76
Broiled Tomatoes	76
Stuffed Tomatoes	77
Sweet Potatoes	77

CONTENTS.

	PAGE.		PAGE.
Stewed Onions....................	77	Sauce Hollandaise...............90,	91
Hominy Croquettes..	78	Espagnole Sauce.....................	91
Rice Croquettes.....................	78	Mushroom Sauce.....................	91
Southern Way of Cooking Rice Dry....................................	78	Roux....................................	92
		Drawn Butter........................	92
Stewed Macaroni....................	79	Horse-Radish Sauce...............	92
Baked Cymlings.......	79	Onion Sauce.................	93
Boiled Rice, Savannah Style....	79	Egg Sauce.............................	93
Broiled Mushrooms................	80	Apple Sauce...........................	93
Hashed Brown Potatoes..........	80	Fish Sauce.............................	93
		Celery Sauce..........................	94
Eggs.		Common Sauce......................	94
Omelet..................................	81	Olive Sauce............................	94
Omelet (with Bread-crumbs)...	81	Wine Sauce for Meat...............	94
Devilled Eggs........................	81	Parsley Sauce.........................	94
Omelet (with Parsley).............	82	Pudding Sauce.......................	94
Baked Eggs...........................	82	Wine Sauce...........................	95
Dropped Eggs.......................	82	Cold Sauce............................	95
Egg Toast.............................	82	Butter Sauce.........................	95
Omelet Soufflée.................83,	86	Sauce for Boiled Fish and Cauliflower................................	95
Boiled Eggs...........	83		
Breakfast Dish of Eggs...........	83	Mayonnaise Dressing..............	96
Fried Eggs.....	84	White Sauce.........................	96
Breaded Eggs........................	84	Chestnut Sauce......................	97
Omelet with Chipped Beef......	84	Shad Roe Sauce.....................	97
Plain Omelet.................84,	85	Tartare Sauce........................	97
Cheese Omelet, No. 1.............	85	A Rich Sauce.........................	97
Rum Omelet.........................	85	Strawberry Sauce..........	98
Egg Timbales........................	85	Sauce for a Burning Plum Pudding............................	98
Poached Eggs........................	86		
Egg Cutlets for Summer..........	86	Cold Slaw Dressing.................	98
		English Cream Salad Dressing,	98
Sauces and Dressings for Salads.		Lettuce Dressing....................	99
		Fish Mayonnaise................	98
Brown Celery Sauce................	89	Dressing for Lobster Salad.......	99
Sauce for Roasted or Boiled Fowl..................................	89	White Wine Sauce..................	100
		Hard Sauce............................	100
Onion Sauce for Mutton..........	89	Montrose Sauce.....................	100
Chicken Sauce.......................	89	Vanilla Sauce.........................	101
Sauce for Roast Venison.......90,	93		
Maitre d'Hotel Butter.............	90	**Side Dishes and Salads.**	
Mint Sauce...........................	90	Croquettes............................	103
Tomato Sauce.......................	90	Potato Croquettes..................	103

CONTENTS.

	PAGE.
Veal Croquettes	104
Tongue Toast	104
Potato Salad	104, 108, 110
Chicken Terrapin	104
Chicken Salad	105
Welsh Rarebits	105, 111
Terrapin, Philadelphia Style	105
Terrapin, Maryland Style	106
Sweetbreads	106
Fried Sweetbreads	107
Chicken Croquettes	107, 108, 112
Imitation Terrapin	108
Lobster Salad	108
Cottage Cheese	109
Oyster Patés	109
Crab Salad	109
Crab Croquettes	110
Broiled Pigeons	110
Cream Salad Dressing	110
Tomato Salad	110
Fruit Salad Dressing	111
Fruit Salad	111
Cheese Straws	111
Lobster a la Newburgh	111
Lobster Patties	112
Beef Sauté	112
Cheese Pudding (Philadelphia style)	112
Stuffed Potatoes	113
Filling for Patties	113

ICES.

Orange Water Ice	115
Caramel Ice Cream	115
Orange Ice Cream	115
Parker's Ice Cream	115
Chocolate Ice Cream	116, 120
Grape Sherbet	116
Frozen Pudding	116
Tutti Frutti	117
Orange Ice	117
Strawberry Ice Cream	117
Lemon Ice Cream	118

	PAGE.
Pineapple Ice	118
Lemon Sherbet	118
Frozen Custard	118
Ice Cream	118, 119
Plombiere	119
Peach Ice Cream	119
Iced Jelly	119
Caramel Cream	119
Almond Cream	119
Bisque Glace	120
Coffee Ice Cream	120
Strawberry Acid	120
Strawberry Water Ice	121
Roman Punch	121
Frozen Punch	121
Apple Ice Cream	121

DESSERTS.

Pig's Feet Jelly	123, 124
Calf's Foot Jelly	123, 124
Cream Jelly	124
Lemon Jelly	124
Strawberry Jelly	125
Syllabub	125
To Make Jelly without Boiling	125
Orange Jelly	125
Quince Jelly	126
Jelly Made of Cooper's Isinglass	126
Blanc Mange, No. 1	126
Chocolate Blanc Mange	126
Irish Moss Blanc Mange	127, 131
Isinglass Blanc Mange	127
Blanc Mange	127, 128
Snow Pudding	127
Trifle	127, 131
Rice Flummery	128
Danish Blanc Mange	128
Rice Blanc Mange	129
Bird's Nest Blanc Mange	128
Velvet Cream	129
Apple Float	130
Apple Meringue	130
Apple Soufflée	130

CONTENTS.

	PAGE.
Floating Island	130
Mock Gooseberry Fool	131
Tapioca Jelly	131, 132
Tipsy Pudding	132
Chocolate Custard	132, 138, 139
Cold Custard	132
Ambrosia	133
Oranges with Transparent Jelly	133
Irish Cream	133
Bavarian Cream	133
Chocolate Cream	133
Almond Custard	134
Almond Snowballs	134
Lemon Cream	134, 136
Boiled Custard	135
Swiss Cream	135
Velvet Cream	135
Spanish Cream	135, 136, 137
Stone Cream	136
Italian Cream	136, 137
Snow Rice Cream	136
Snow	137
Cream Custard	138
Baked Custard	138
Burned Custard	138
Charlotte Russe	139, 140
Custard without Eggs	139
Manioca Cream	140
Fruit Jelly	141

PUDDINGS AND PIES.

Batter Pudding	143
Sweet Potato Pudding	143, 160, 167
Irish Potato Pudding	143, 160
Cocoanut Pudding	143, 167
Buttermilk Pudding	143
Jeff Davis Pudding	144
Delmonico's Pudding	144
Plum Pudding	144, 156, 165, 167
Chocolate Pudding	144
Lemon Pudding	145, 159
Potato Pudding	145, 148, 152, 168
Baked Whortleberries	145

	PAGE.
Currant Pie	145
Cottage Pudding	145, 146, 152
Cream Cake Pudding	146
Apple Pudding	146, 148, 160, 166
Indian Meal Pudding	146
Tyler Pudding	146
Sweetmeat Pudding	147
Sponge Pudding	147, 161
Boiled Rice Pudding	147
Prune Pudding	147
Carrot Pudding	148
Blackberry Pudding	148
Tapioca Pudding	148, 157
Custard Pudding	149
Rice Méringue	149, 156, 170
Orange Pudding	149
Velvet Pudding	149
Baked Apple Dumplings	150
Apple Sago	150
Florentine Pudding	150
Boiled Pudding	150
Meringue Pudding	151, 168
Meringues	151
Whortleberry Pudding	151, 164
1, 2, 3, 4 Pudding	152
Apple Charlotte	152
Dandy Jack Pudding	152
Bread Pudding (Boiled)	153
Baked Bread Pudding	153
Sweet Apple Pudding	153
Cardinal Richelieu's Pudding	154
Ground Rice Pudding	154
Dried Peach Pudding	154
Apple Float	154
Apple Trifle	154
Float	155
Peach Cobbler	155
Peach Pudding	155, 164
Baked Plum Pudding	155
Rice Pudding	156
Bird's Nest	156
Strawberry Tapioca	157
Baked Batter Pudding	157

CONTENTS.

	PAGE.
German Tarts	158
Queen's Pudding	158
Molasses Pudding	158
Brown Betty	158
German Puffs	159
Black Plum Pudding	159
English Plum Pudding	159
Plum or Suet Pudding	160
Plain Baked Pudding	161
Cracker Pudding	161
Pumpkin Pies	161, 166, 167
Fritters	161
Pancakes	161, 162, 164
Bell Fritters, No. 1	161
Thickened Milk Fritters	162
French Fritters	163
Apple Fritters	163
Corn Fritters	163
German Fritters	163
City Pudding	164
Winter Pudding	164
Lemon Pie	165
Omelet Soufflée	165
Omelet au Rhum	165
Boiled Roly-Boly Pudding	166
Quince Pudding	166
Thickened Milk Pudding	166
Cream Pudding	167
Boiled Apple Dumplings	168
Baked Pears	168
Balloons	168
Potato Pudding	168
Baked Custard	169
Mince Meat	169
Plain Family Paste	169
Puff Paste	169
Nice Paste for Dumplings	170

CAKES.

Measures for Cake	171
Cocoanut Pound Cake	171
Cocoanut Cakes	172, 177, 195
Kisses	172, 182

	PAGE.
White Cake	172
Mountain Ash Cake	172
Icing	172, 196, 197
Sugar Cake	173, 179, 189, 199
Sunshine Cake	173
Icing for Cake	173
White Fruit Cake	173
Gingerbread	173, 175, 188, 189, 194, 195, 197
Chocolate Cake	174, 176, 192
Lemon Butter	174, 187
Black Cake	174, 180, 183, 184
Spice Cake	174, 190
Ginger Crackers	174, 189
White Mountain Cake	175, 184
Fig Cake	175
Tea Cakes	175
Custard for Cake	175
Lady-Fingers	176
Pound Cake	176, 195
Sugar Gingerbread	176
Gingersnaps	177, 181
Cup Cake	177
Orange Cake	177, 186, 199
Doughnuts	177, 182, 186, 191
Tucker's Cake	178
Lady Cake	178
Ormskirk Gingerbread	178
Jumbles	178, 179, 182
Soft Gingerbread	178, 180, 187, 189, 195
Scotch Cake	179
Sponge Cake	179, 198
Pound Cake Gingerbread	179
Ginger Cake	179
Raisin Cake	180
Cheap Plain Cake	180
Coffee Cake	180, 191
Superior Ginger Loaf	180
Bride's Cake	181
Hard Ginger Cake	181
Starch Cake	181
Cold Water Cake	181

CONTENTS.

	PAGE.
Cocoanut Jumbles	181
Rice Sponge Cake	182
Crisp Gingerbread	182
Macaroons	182
Cocoanut Drops	183
Queen of Cakes	183
Minnie's Premium Cake	183
Florence Jumbles	184
Fruit Cake	184, 188, 194
Ginger Pound Cake	184, 188
Ice Cream Cake	184
Albany Cake	185
Lemon Jelly Cake	185
Strawberry Shortcake	185, 193
Drop Jumbles	186
French Buns	186
Cocoanut Cakes or Balls	187
Gold Cake	187
Silver Cake	187, 190
Soda Cake	187
Jelly Twist	187
Marble Cake	188
Gingernuts	189
Angel's Food Cake	190
Nice Cake for the Yolks	190
Crullers	191, 198
Straws	191
Lemon Cake	191
Apple Cake	192
Horse Cake	192
Corn Meal Cake	192
Cocoanut Balls	192
Chocolate Eclairs	193
Pineapple Shortcake	193
Florida Cake	194
Butter Sponge	195
French Loaf Bread	195
Boiled Icing	196
Chocolate Icing	197
Cookies	198
Drop Ginger Cakes	198
Light Gingerbread	198
Quick Doughnuts	198

	PAGE.
Nut Cake	199
A Delicious Cake	199

PRESERVES.

Quince Jelly and Marmalade	201
Preserved Quinces	201
Orange Marmalade	201
Green Tomato Preserve	202
Melon Marmalade	202
Brandy Peaches	202
Green Citron Preserve	202
Watermelon Rind Preserve	203
Watermelon Rind Jam	203
Preserved Apples	203
Grape Jam	204
Raspberry Preserve	204
Plum Jelly	204
Apple Jelly	204
Hodge-Podge	205
Preserved Figs	205
Cantaloupe Preserve	205
Preserved Strawberries	206, 208
Preserved Pineapple	206
Currant Jelly	206, 207
Crab Apple Jelly	206
Gooseberry Jelly	207
Blackberry Jam	207
Chopped Apple Preserve	208
Green Tomato Jam	208
Peach Cakes	208
Home-Made Raisins	209
Candied Oranges	209
Peach Leather	209
Conserved Peaches or Pears	209

PICKLES AND CATSUPS.

General Directions for Making Pickles	211
Ragout Pickle	212
Chopped Tomato Pickle	212
Damson Pickle	212
Walnut Pickle	212, 221
Green Tomato Pickle	213, 221, 223

CONTENTS.

	PAGE.
Green Tomatoes Pickled without Boiling	213
Pickled Damsons	213
Martynia Pickle	213, 221
Peach Mango	214
Pickled Onions	214, 220
Yellow Pickle	214, 215, 220
Pickled Cucumbers	215
Green Cucumber Pickle	215
Peach Pickle	216
French Pickle	216
Ripe Cantaloupe Pickle	216
Boiled Cabbage Pickle	216
Chowchow Pickle	217, 218, 228
No. 1 Oil Mangoes	217
Oil Pickle	218
Sweet Cantaloupe Pickle	218
Pickled Cherries	219
Pickled Walnuts	219
To Mango Cucumbers	219
Pepper Mangoes	221
Rough and Ready Pickle	222
Chilli Sauce	222
Cucumber Sweet Pickle	222
Ripe Cantaloupe Mangoes	223
Hyden Salad	223
To Pickle Nasturtions	224
Tomato Catsup	224, 225, 226, 227, 228
Cucumber Catsup	224, 225, 227
Walnut Catsup	225, 226
Cold Tomato Catsup	225
Pepper Sauce (Pickled)	226
Tomato Catsup or Soy	226
Green Tomato Catsup	227
Cold Cucumber Pickle	228
Tomato Pickle	228
Onion Pickle	229
Cucumber or Gherkin Pickle	229
Very Fine Chowchow	230

WINES.

Wine of First and Sec'd Quality	231
Blackberry Wine	237, 241
Currant Shrub	237, 242
Geranium Cordial	237
Punch	237
Fish House Punch	238
Philadelphia Fish House Punch	238
English Claret Cup	238
Blackberry or Dewberry Cordial	237
Raspberry Vinegar	239
Currant Wine	239, 241
Superior Punch	239
Champagne Punch	239
Ratcliffe Punch	239, 244
Egg-Nogg	240, 244
One Gallon Roman Punch	240
Grape Wine	240
Strawberry Wine	241
Blackberry Cordial	241, 243, 245
Beer	242
Egyptian Punch	242
Ginger Beer	242
Cherry Bounce	242
Roman Punch	243
Claret Peach Cordial	243
Ginger Pop	243
Apple Toddy	243, 246
Cobblers	244
Egg and Milk Punch	244
Milk Punch	245
Fruit Cordial	245
Bitters	245
Regent Punch	245
Claret Punch	246
Lemon Brandy	246
Seligson's Half and Half	246
Seligson's Champagne Cocktail	247
Seligson's Frappéd Café Royal	247

MENUS.

Home Breakfast	249
Summer Breakfast	249
Winter Home Breakfast	249
Ratcliffe Manor Breakfast	249
Breakfast	250

CONTENTS.

	PAGE.
Luncheon	250, 252
Luncheon for Spring	250
Lenton Luncheon	251
Luncheon for Six People	251
Lunch for Brain-Workers	252
Afternoon Tea	252
Christmas Dinner	253
Eastern Shore Home Dinner	253
Home Dinner for Winter	253
Spring Dinner	254
Summer Dinner	254
Dinner	254, 255
Colonial Dinner	255
Thanksgiving Dinner	255
Friday Dinner	256
Cardinal Dinner	256
Supper after the Theatre	256
Supper	256, 257
Home Tea	257
Diet for Invalids	257

COFFEE AND TEA, ETC.

To Make Coffee with Milk	259
Cuban Coffee	259
Tea	259
How to Make Chocolate	259
Chocolate (for One)	260
Good Boiled Coffee	260
French Coffee	260

INVALIDS.

Chicken Broth	261
Irish Moss Jelly	261
Sago	261
Beef Tea	261
To Prepare an Uncooked Egg	262
Panada	262, 263
Iceland Moss	262
Egg Water	262
Barley	263
Lemon Sponge	263
Corn Meal Gruel	263
Grape Juice	263

CANDY.

	PAGE.
Molasses Candy (Taffy)	265
Molasses Candy	266, 271
Cocoanut and Chocolate Caramels	266
Barley Sugar, and Burnt Almonds	267
Caramels	268, 269
Cocoanut Caramels	269, 271
Chocolate Caramels	269, 270
Taffy	270
Everton Taffy	270
Chocolate Candy	270
Cream Candy	270
White Taffy Candy	271
Plain Candy	271
Chocolate Drops	271
Sugar Candy	272

CURING, CANNING, ETC.

Beef Brine	273
Pickle for Butter	273
To Cure Shad	273
To Cure Beef Hams	273
To Cure Pork Hams	274
Sausage Meat	274, 280
To Preserve Butter for Winter	275
To Cure Beef	275
To Cure Bacon	275
Important to Butter Makers	276
Beef Pickle	276, 279
Canned Salmon	276
Canned Tomatoes and Okra for Soup	276
To Seal Preserves	277
To Can Tomatoes	277
To Prepare Rennet	277
Tomatoes for Broiling	277
To Clean Calf's Head and Feet	278
How to Make Vinegar	278
Horseradish Vinegar	278
How to Mix Mustard	278

CONTENTS. xvii

	PAGE
Recipe for Preserving Corn	279
To Preserve Oranges Whole	279
To Prepare Syrup for Preserves	279
To Keep Game from Tainting	280
To Brown Flour	280
The Best Mode of Keeping Butter	280
To Cure Corn for Winter Use	281
To Cure Pig's Feet for Souse	281
To Make Lard	282

MISCELLANEOUS RECIPES.

	PAGE
How to Cook a Husband	283
Tomatoes	284
Sicilian Sorbetto	284
Biscuits Tortoni	284
Indelible Ink	285
Cologne	285, 298
Remedy for Poison	285
Opodeldoc	285
Colic Drops	286
Staining Floors	286, 297
Restoring Colors	286, 294
Mucilage for Envelopes	286
To Cure a Felon	286, 291
Small-Pox Remedy	287
Boneset for a Cough	287
To Cook Puddings in Boiling Water	287
Cleansing Laces	287
Soft Soap	288
Washing China, Glass, or Silver	288
Hard Soap	288, 289
Hard Soap (without Boiling)	289
Gathered Breast	289
Cough Mixture	289, 291, 296
To Extract Salt from Lard	290
An Experiment	290
Pretty Centre Piece	290
To Clean White Satin Slippers	290
Cosmetic Soap	290
Lip Salve	291
Poison Oak Cure	291

	PAGE
Lemon for a Cough	291
Scalds or Burns	291
Cure for a Cold	291
Items	292, 293
Three Ways of Cleaning Black Silk	292
Tricophorus for the Hair	292
To Set Colors in Calicoes	293
Paint for Pavements	293
Floor Polish	293
Cure for Thrush	293
Hop Poultice	294
Camphor Ball	294
To Remove Spots from Carpets	294
To Take Mildew out of Linen	294
To Remove Spots in Furniture	295
To Destroy Bed-Bugs	295
To Restore Color to Ivory-Handled Knives	295
Essence of Verbena	295
Croup Mixture	295
To Cure Freckles	295
Cure for Rheumatism, etc	295
Remedy for Diphtheria	296
For Whooping Cough	296
Chalk Mixture	296
For Ear Ache	296
To Cure a Consumptive Cough	296
Sore Eyes	297
Prickly Ash	297
Tonic to Prevent Chills	297
To Curl Tumbled Feathers	297
To Clean Straw Matting	297
To Make the Best Tea	298
To Clean Black Lace	298
To Stop the Flow of Blood	298
Antidotes to Poison	298
Hair Tonic	298
To Whiten and Soften the Hands	299
For Children Teething	299
Maids of Honor	299
Butterless Sauce	300

CONTENTS.

	PAGE.
Cold Cream Sauce	300
Everyday Sauce	300
Foaming Sauce	301
Helps for Housewives	301
Beignets d'Abricots	305
Greengages Glaces	305
Fruit Charlotte	305
Remedy for Rheumatism	306

SUNDRIES.

Peaches in the Chafing-Dish	307
Corn Meal Pudding Bread	307
Wild Ducks	307
Stewed Sweetbreads	307
Best Tea Punch	308
How to Crown Soups	308
General Directions for Boiling	308
Pumpkin Preserve	308
Tomato Marmalade	309
Parfait Aux Fraises	309
Strawberry Ice Cream	309
Felicia's Apples	309
Stuffed Peppers	310
Boned Turkey	310
Galantine of Turkey	310
Orange Omelette	311
Omelette Soufllée	312
Barbecued Ham	312

	PAGE.
Chinese Eggs	312
Sauted Oysters	312
Curry of Oysters	312
Lobster Newburg	313
Baked Tomatoes with Corn	313
How to Prepare Potatoes	313
Baked Sweetbreads	313
How to Broil a Beefsteak	314
Fried Beefsteak	314
Pineapple Pudding	315
Shaddocks for Luncheon	315
Timbale of Beef	315
Sardine Fritters	315
Sausage Rolls	316
Prune Pudding	316
Fig Layer Cake	316
Nut Drops	317
Eclairs	317
Rum Fruit	318
Salmon Sandwich	318
Sardines	318
Lima Beans	319
Amateur Surgery	319
Miscellaneous	320
Cure for Corns or Bunions	321
Complexion Wash	321
Whitewash	321

MRS. CHAS. H. GIBSON'S COOK BOOK.

RULES FOR BREAD AND CAKE MAKING.

It requires experience to become a good bread-maker. You must know when the bread has risen enough. Of course this depends upon the weather. In warm summer weather, bread made up at twelve o'clock in the day is ready for tea by seven o'clock. In winter, set it to rise, if for breakfast, by eight o'clock in the evening, and put it away, covered, in a warm place. In the morning, work it over again, and set it to rise for at least an hour and a half before breakfast, setting it near the fire, and letting it rise to the top of the pan. If for tea, make it up by eight o'clock in the morning in winter, and work it over about four in the afternoon. If you have too much dough for breakfast take out a piece before the second rising, and put it on ice until wanted to rise again. Potatoes will always improve bread. For baking, the oven should be rather hot and the doors closed, except when necessary to look at the bread. Any sudden draught on the oven affects the baking of bread or cake. These rules apply equally to pastry. For cake, always beat eggs separately and cream the butter thoroughly. When cream of tartar, or soda, or yeast powder is used, the oven should be heated very hot; if these ingredients are not used, have slow heat. Whenever a recipe calls for soda use some acid, either sour milk or cream of tartar, with it. Soda should always be dissolved in something, either milk or water, and cream of tartar sifted with the flour. It is always well to sift flour twice. A little ammonia will improve cake, making it lighter. To test when a cake is done, run a dry broom straw down into it. If the straw comes out perfectly dry the cake is done; but if it is the least moist, or if any particles stick to it, it is not done. For loaves, always put thin, greased paper in the bottom and sides of the pan. In summer time, before making cake, put the eggs on ice, to keep them cool and fresh, otherwise they will not beat up light.

For icing, always use pulverized sugar, beat very slowly, and a long time.

Eggs should always be beaten thoroughly; the whites to a stiff froth, and the yolks to a light color. The fresher the eggs, the better they will beat up.

HOW TO MAKE YEAST, No. 1.

Steep an eighth of an ounce of pressed, or a small handful of loose hops in a quart of boiling water for about five minutes. Strain the boiling infusion upon half a pint of flour, stirred to a smooth paste with a little cold water. Mix well, boil a minute; then add one ounce of salt and two ounces of white sugar. When lukewarm stir in a gill of liquid yeast or an ounce cake of compressed yeast dissolved in warm water. Let stand twenty-four hours, stirring occasionally, then cover closely, and set in a cool place. Yeast made in this manner will keep sweet for two weeks in summer, and much longer in winter, and can be used at any time during that period for starting a fresh supply of yeast, as well as for making bread.

DRY YEAST.

Take half a pint of meal, and mix it with water about as warm as is used to make up light bread or rolls. Make it about as stiff as corn bread for kitchen use; add half a cake of yeast. It will lighten in just the same time as other yeast.

Use it wet if preferred, or stir more meal in it; let it stand a few hours more, and make it into cakes to dry.

MRS. CHARLES H. GIBSON'S VERY BEST HOP AND POTATO YEAST.

Take four large or eight small potatoes, wash clean, leaving on the skin, let them lie in cold water for half an hour, then put on to boil with three quarts of *boiling* water, and one dessert spoonful of compressed hops, or a small handful of loose hops. Let all boil until the potatoes are done, then pour the water off, remove the skins, take out the hops, and mash the potatoes very smooth, adding the water the potatoes and hops has been boiled in. If much water has boiled away, add more boiling water, so as to have nearly three quarts. Let this mixture cool, then add one teacup of white sugar, one of salt, one teaspoonful of powdered alum, and three cakes of Warner's Compressed Yeast, dissolved in lukewarm water; or one teacupful of good liquid yeast, but I much prefer Warner's Compressed Yeast. Set it in a pan or earthen jar, with a cover on it, by the fire in winter, to rise, away from the fire in summer. When it has risen well, which it ought to do by 6 o'clock in the afternoon in summer if made up by 10 A. M. (in winter it takes longer), stir well and bottle. This yeast will keep on ice two weeks in warm weather and longer in cold.

DUTCH YEAST.

Take two quarts of water, put in a handful of hops, and let them boil twenty minutes. Have ready four large potatoes well mashed. Strain the hop liquor, and pour it on the potatoes. Add one teacup of Indian meal and one teacup of flour. Set it on the fire, and let it boil a few minutes. Then let it cool, and when it is milk warm put in one tablespoonful of sugar, one of salt, and half a pint of yeast. The next day bottle it tight. Be particular to stir it all the time it is on the fire.

POTATO YEAST, No. 2 (without Hops).

Take four large *old* potatoes, peel and let them lie in cold water half an hour; then grate the potatoes into two pints of boiling water; add one-half teacupful of granulated sugar and two large tablespoonsful of salt. Boil for ten minutes, stirring all the time. When cool, set to rise, adding either one cake of compressed yeast dissolved in milk-warm water or one teacupful of potato yeast, if perfectly sweet.

THE HOUSEWIFE'S TABLE OF WEIGHTS AND MEASURES.

The following is a very valuable housewife's table, by which persons, not having scales and weights at hand, may readily measure the articles wanted to form a recipe without the trouble of weighing, allowance to be made for extraordinary dryness or moisture of the article weighed or measured:

Twenty-four large tablespoonsful are one pint.
Seven large tablespoonsful are one gill.
Four large tablespoonsful are half a gill.
Two gills are half a pint.
Two pints are one quart.
Four quarts are one gallon.
A common sized tumbler holds half a pint.
A common sized wineglass is half a gill.
A claret wineglass is one gill.
A tablespoonful is half an ounce.
Forty drops are equal to one teaspoonful.
Four teaspoonsful are equal to one tablespoonful.
Two teaspoonsful are equal to one dessert-spoonful.
Twelve tablespoonsful are half a pint.

TABLE OF WEIGHTS AND MEASURES.

One pint liquid is one pound.
Four cups of flour—one quart or one pound.
Three cups of corn meal—one pound.
One cup of butter—half pound.
One pint of butter—one pound.
One tablespoonful of butter—one ounce.
One solid pint chopped meat—one pound.
Two cups granulated sugar—one pound.
One pint granulated sugar—one pound.
One pint brown sugar—thirteen ounces.
Wheat flour—one pound is one quart.
Indian meal—one pound two ounces are one quart.
Butter—when soft, one pound is one pint.
Lard—one pound is one pint.
Loaf sugar—broken, one pound is one quart.
White sugar—powdered, one pound one ounce are one quart.
Best brown sugar—one pound two ounces are one quart.
Ten eggs are one pound.
Flour—eight quarts are one peck.
Flour—four pecks are one bushel.

BREAD.

POTATO ROLLS.

Four large potatoes boiled, and mashed through a cullender, one quart of flour, three ounces of butter, three eggs beaten light, one coffee cup full of yeast, one teaspoonful of salt, one of white sugar.

Sift the flour. Put it in the bowl it is to rise in. Mash the potatoes while hot into it, and work them in with the butter, until quite smooth. Add the eggs, then the salt and sugar, and the yeast. Knead well on the board, as you do bread, and set it to rise. In summer, set it at twelve o'clock for tea; in winter, at eleven o'clock. About an hour before tea, turn it out on the board dredged with flour. Don't work it at all, but flour lightly, and roll it out, half an inch thick. Cut in round cakes, and set it to rise in the pan they are to be baked in without touching. Bake like rolls. They are done in fifteen minutes.

BRANDON CORN BREAD.

Take two teacups of small hominy. Boil it well, and while hot, stir in a tablespoonful of butter. Beat four eggs very light, stir them into the hominy, add gradually a pint of milk and half a pint of white corn meal. The batter should be about as thick as boiled custard.

Bake for one hour in a deep pan, to allow for rising, and with a good deal of heat at the bottom. Either rice or hominy can be used in this recipe.

BREAD.

BATTER BREAD.

Five eggs, one quart of milk, one pint of flour, as much meal as will make it a thick batter; one spoonful of lard.

DROP BISCUIT.

One quart of flour, one pint of sour cream or buttermilk. Three eggs, half a teacup of melted butter, one teaspoonful of soda, in the cream. Stir well together and drop with a spoon into a pan.

CRUMPETS.

One quart of warm milk made into a batter, with the yolks of three or four eggs. A piece of butter the size of a walnut, a little salt, about two spoonsful of good yeast. Beat well together and set to rise over night for breakfast. The batter must be rather thicker than pancake batter. The griddle for baking made pretty hot, and well greased.

They are quite good made of bread in the morning, if you make it of the proper consistency, with warm milk and eggs. Set it in a warm place, and they will soon rise, and require no extra yeast. The more they are beaten the better.

FLANNEL CAKES.

Five eggs, one pint of milk, one and one-half pints of flour, one spoonful of butter, and two of yeast. Set to rise.

QUICK BISCUIT.

One quart sifted flour, one teaspoonful salt, one-half pint milk, one large spoonful lard, two heaping teaspoonsful of Royal Baking Powder or a half-teaspoonful of soda and one teaspoonful of cream of tartar.

Put the baking powder, or cream of tartar and soda, and salt into the flour and sift it again. Then rub into this, the lard. Now see that the oven is very hot (400° Fahr.).

Grease the pans and get the cutter and rolling pin. Have everything ready before you put in the milk, then add the milk and knead up quickly. Roll out on the board one inch thick, cut with a small round cutter, put quickly into the pans and then into the oven. Bake twenty minutes. Remember, to have them a success, handle as little and make as rapidly, as possible.

Make Rye Biscuit as above, except use one pint of rye flour and one pint of wheat flour, instead of one quart wheat flour.

RATCLIFFE RUSKS.

Two teacupsful of potatoes, mashed through a cullender, four eggs beaten light, one teacupful butter, one of milk, two of yeast, one pound white sugar, and flour enough to work it out. Warm the butter and milk together. Lastly add the yeast, and set to rise at night. Work it out next morning into rolls. Set it to rise before baking. Cover with white of egg, sugar and cinnamon. If compressed yeast, use one-half cake.

RUSKS.

Two quarts flour, six eggs, three-quarters of a pound sugar, one-half pound butter, one pint milk. Flavor with cinnamon or nutmeg. White of egg, sugar and cinnamon over the top. One teacup liquid yeast, or one-half cake compressed.

BATH RUSKS.

Seven eggs, one pound sugar, one ounce butter, one pint new milk warmed with the sugar. Make into a batter the consistency of flannel cakes, with one cup of yeast, or one-half cake compressed yeast. Let it rise six hours. Make a dough not very stiff. Set to rise again, and make into rolls. Egg, sugar and cinnamon on top. Flavor with nutmeg or cinnamon. This quantity will take about five pints of flour, and makes a great amount.

RUSKS.

Two pounds ten ounces of flour, one pound of sugar, ten ounces of butter and lard mixed, yolks of two eggs, white of one, one pint milk, one and a half cups of yeast, or one-half cake compressed yeast, two nutmegs. Rub the sugar and butter into the flour, then beat the eggs, yeast, milk, nutmegs, a little salt, and a half pint of mashed potatoes in the middle of the flour, and leave it to rise all night. In the morning work it up with two ounces of flour, which should be left out at night, and put it in rolls to rise a second time in the oven.

RATCLIFFE ROLLS.

Two quarts of flour, one pint boiled milk (but it must only be lukewarm when used). One tablespoonful of butter, one dessert-spoonful of sugar, a small teacupful of home-made hop yeast, or one-half cake compressed yeast, and a little salt. Sift the flour twice, put it in a bowl, make a hole in the centre, and place the sugar, butter, milk and yeast there. Mix all thoroughly with the flour, and knead it well for fifteen minutes, then set it to rise. Next morning knead it again, and make it out in turnover rolls. Do not let them touch in the baking pan.

BRENTFORD ROLLS.

Make a sponge with a pint of milk, and set to rise at night. Then take three pints of flour, a teacupful of white sugar, one quarter pound butter, and one egg. Mix these in the flour, and then work in the sponge. Knead it for twenty or thirty minutes, then make into rolls. Put them in pans, let them rise two or three hours, then bake in a quick oven. Lard will do instead of butter. One-half cake of compressed yeast, or one teacupful of liquid yeast. *Very nice.*

RATCLIFFE LOAF BREAD, No. 1.

One and a half pounds of flour, two large spoonsful of liquid yeast or one-half cake of compressed yeast, one large potato boiled and mashed smooth, piece of lard size of an egg. Mix with cold water in summer, and lukewarm water in winter. Make in loaves; work well at night and again in morning.

SPOON ROLLS.

Six eggs well beaten, one quart of flour, four tablespoonsful of yeast, or one-quarter cake of compressed yeast, or enough butter and milk warmed together to make a thick batter. Beat all well. Drop it in the oven with a spoon, or what is better, bake in small pans with a quick heat. *Very nice.*

PUFFETS.

Two pints flour, one pint milk, two eggs, a piece of butter the size of an egg, one teaspoonful of soda, and two of cream of tartar, or two teaspoonsful of Royal Baking Powder. Sift the cream of tartar in the flour, and dissolve the soda in the milk. Beat the butter and eggs together, then add the flour and milk. Bake in muffin rings in a quick oven.

WHITE OF EGG MUFFINS.

Whites of eight eggs beaten stiff. A full pint of flour. Milk enough to make the batter as thick as batter pudding. Add a little salt, and bake quickly.

CREAM MUFFINS.

One quart flour, three eggs, one cup of cream. A piece of butter the size of an egg. Milk enough to make a thick batter, one teaspoonful of soda dissolved in the cream, if sour. If not, add two teaspoonsful of cream of tartar just before baking, or two teaspoonsful of Royal Baking Powder.

WATER MUFFINS.

Stir four tablespoonsful of fresh yeast, or one-quarter cake of compressed yeast, in one pint of milk-warm water, add a small teaspoonful of salt, then stir in gradually as much flour as will make a thick batter. Cover it, and set it to rise. When it is light, heat the griddle, grease it, and put on the rings. Put in each ring a spoonful of batter, and bake over a quick fire.

MUFFIN BREAD.

Three pints flour, half pint of milk and half pint of warm water mixed, one-half cake of yeast, or if liquid yeast use one teacupful, and a little salt. Mix all together at night, leaving out one pint of flour, to be added in the morning when it is light. Then set it aside for the second rising. When risen, bake.

MUFFINS.

One quart of warm milk, half pound of butter, and six eggs well beaten. Work the flour in till it is stiff enough for a spoon to stand up in. Half pint of good yeast, or one-half cake compressed yeast. After they have risen in the morning, do not beat the batter up. Dip the spoon in cold water, and take up as much batter as will nearly fill the rings. Let them rise a little before baking, and do not bake too long, or they will be hard. This is enough for a large company.

DELICIOUS CORN WAFFLES.

One teacup of flour; one teaspoonful Royal Baking Powder; one and a half cups of cold boiled rice; one and a half tablespoonsful of melted butter; one-half teaspoonful of salt; four well beaten eggs; one pint of milk; mix rice and butter, then milk and flour, and last the eggs; beat well together. Grease the waffle-irons with butter, fill them three-fourths full and bake brown.

TURKS' HEADS.

One pint flour, one pint milk, two eggs, a lump of butter the size of an egg, and a little salt. Mix the flour and butter, then add the milk, and lastly the eggs. They must be beaten very light.

MUFFINS.

One quart flour, two eggs, one quart buttermilk, a very small piece of butter, a little salt, and a large teaspoonful of soda. Bake at once.

WASHINGTON'S BREAKFAST CAKES.

One pound flour, one pint new milk, three eggs, one tablespoonful of butter, and a half cupful of yeast, or one-quarter cake of compressed yeast. Beat them well together, and set them to rise.

JOURNEY CAKE.

One quart sifted corn meal, a piece of lard the size of an egg, a little salt, and warm water enough to mix it, so you can spread it on the board. Bake before a hot fire. If you have no board for the purpose, and no *open* fire, bake in biscuit tins, smoothing it thin with the hand.

BACHELOR'S LOAF.

Take three eggs beaten light, add one pint of rich milk, three quarters of a pound of corn meal, one half teacupful of flour, and a spoonful of butter or lard. Grease the tins, and bake quickly.

SOFT BROWN BREAD.

Two pounds coarse brown flour, one quarter pound of white flour, two large spoonsful of yeast, a little salt, and a teacupful of boiled grits, a piece of lard or butter the size of an egg. Make it up with tepid milk and water. Bake slowly in loaves when light. If compressed yeast, use one-half cake.

BROWN BREAD.

Two pints of brown flour, half pint of corn meal, half pint of white flour, one teacupful of yeast, or quarter cake of compressed yeast, a piece of lard the size of an egg, and a pinch of salt. Mix with warm water, and add a tablespoonful of black molasses. Set it to rise at night, and bake in a hot oven.

GEMS.

One pint new milk, one pint flour, one egg beaten very light. Mix well, and fill the irons nearly full after they have been heated and greased. Put them to bake at once in a quick oven. They are very nice made of graham flour. Good for dyspeptics.

RICE WAFFLES.

Two eggs beaten very light, one and a half pints of flour, one quart of new milk, one pint of boiled rice, one tablespoonful of butter, and a little salt. Add the flour to the eggs gradually while beating them, and let the batter stand for half an hour before baking. Teaspoonful of Royal Baking Powder just before baking.

HOMINY WAFFLES.

Take two teacupsful of hot hominy, and add one teaspoonful of butter. When cold, add one teacupful of flour, salt, as much milk as will make a stiff batter, and three eggs well beaten. Mix well, adding half teaspoonful of soda and one teaspoonful of cream of tartar, or one large teaspoonful of Royal Baking Powder.

QUICK WAFFLES.

One pint of milk, three eggs beaten very light, enough flour to make a thick batter, salt, one teaspoonful of Royal Baking Powder.

WAFFLES.

Take three eggs, a teacupful of boiled rice, with a small lump of butter stirred in a pint of flour, and a pint of new milk. Beat very light.

HALF-MEAL GRIDDLE CAKES.

Two pints of flour, two pints of white corn meal, four eggs well beaten, a piece of butter the size of an egg, a teacupful of home-made yeast, or one-half cake of compressed yeast, and water enough to make a batter.

POTATO CAKES.

Two pounds of Irish potatoes mashed through a cullender. While warm, add one spoonful of lard, a dessert-spoonful of salt, one pound of sifted flour. Knead it well. Roll them out and bake on a griddle. Prick them with a fork.

SALLY LUNN.

One and a half pints of flour, one quarter of a pound of butter, one teacupful of sugar, one pint milk, three eggs, two teaspoonsful of Royal Baking Powder to be put in the last thing. Bake one hour and a half in a slow oven.

SALLY LUNN.

One quart flour, one-quarter pound of butter, two eggs, one teaspoonful salt, half a teacupful of sweet milk, and sufficient flour to mix the dough to a proper consistency. Make it up about nine o'clock in the morning in winter, and eleven o'clock in summer. Work it over at about four o'clock, and make it in a round shape into pans, and bake for seven o'clock tea. Butter it before sending to table.

SALLY LUNN WITHOUT YEAST.

Beat three eggs separately, two pints of flour, a lump of butter the size of an egg, one teaspoonful soda, two teaspoonsful of cream of tartar. Make it up with sweet milk to a batter, and bake quickly. Instead of cream tartar and soda use two teaspoonsful of Royal Baking Powder.

SALLY LUNN.

Four cups of flour, two of white sugar, one cup of milk, quarter of a pound of butter, four eggs, two teaspoonsful of cream of tartar, one of soda, or two teaspoonsful of Royal Baking Powder, one nutmeg.

SALLY LUNN.

To one and a half pounds of flour add six eggs, beaten separately, one pint of new milk, two teacupsful of white sugar, one cup butter, one of yeast. Beat all together. Grease the tins well and bake slow. Give six hours to rise.

IRISH LUNN.

Take one pint of milk (made milk-warm), add quarter of a pound of butter, six eggs beaten light, one teaspoonful of salt, two tablespoonsful of sugar, a wineglass of rose water, and half a cup of yeast, or one-quarter cake compressed yeast. Then add flour enough to make a stiff batter, put it to rise, grease the pans, and bake in a hot oven.

GRAHAM BREAD.

Two pints of graham flour, a little meal, quarter of a pound of white flour, a small piece of lard, a little salt. For bread, add a teacupful of yeast, make it with milk-warm water, and set it to rise over night. Bake in a loaf for breakfast. For biscuits, a large iron spoonful of lard, roll out, prick with a fork, and bake quickly.

MARYLAND BISCUIT.

One and a half pounds of flour, quarter of a pound of lard, a pinch of salt. Mix enough milk and water to make a stiff dough. Beat the dough with an axe for half an hour, until the dough is soft, or until it breaks when pulled. Machines come for the purpose, which facilitate the operation. Form into small biscuits, prick with a fork several times, and bake quickly.

BREAD CAKES.

Soak a pint of stale bread (crumbled) in a pint of sweet milk, over night. Next morning strain it through a cullender and add three eggs well beaten, four tablespoonsful of flour, a little salt, one teaspoonful of Royal Baking Powder. Bake them on a griddle.

AUNT CLARISSY'S CORN SLAPPERS.

One pint sifted corn meal, scald it, half a teacup of sifted flour, one egg, a piece of butter or lard the size of an egg, a little salt, about half a pint of milk and water mixed, enough to make a very thin batter. Grease the griddle well, and have it very hot. Bake quickly. Rice or grits is very nice mixed in.

MUSH BREAD.

One pint of mush; while hot, beat into it a piece of butter the size of an egg; let cool. Then beat into the mush the yolks of four eggs, and one pint of milk. Grease a baking dish; just before you are ready to put into the oven, whip the whites and beat into the batter. Bake quickly and serve immediately.

TEA BREAD.

One quart of flour, four large potatoes boiled and mashed, three eggs beaten separately, one teacupful of yeast, or one-quarter cake compressed yeast, one of butter and lard mixed, one teaspoonful salt, one tablespoonful sugar, no water or milk.

Work it well. Put the butter or lard in the flour, then mash the potatoes, mix with the eggs and other ingredients. Pour all into the flour and set to rise.

MILK TOAST.

Boil one quart of milk and stir into it three ounces of butter, mixed with one teaspoonful of corn-starch and one salt spoonful of salt. Let the whole boil five minutes. Have ready a few slices of toast, pour the milk over them, and send it to the table hot. This is generally a breakfast dish, but is nice for supper also.

RICE CAKES.

Soak half a pound of rice over night. Next morning boil it soft, drain and add quarter of a pound of butter, and let it get cool. When cold stir in one quart milk. Beat six eggs, sift half a pint of flour. Stir the eggs and flour alternately into the rice and milk. Beat well, and bake on a griddle. Butter them and serve hot. Two teaspoonsful Royal Baking Powder.

RYE DROP CAKES.

One pint of milk, three eggs, one tablespoonful of sugar, one salt spoonful of salt. Stir in the flour until about the consistency of pancakes (about three cups). Beat the whites of the eggs separately, and add them the last thing. This makes the cakes lighter. Bake in buttered cups or saucers half an hour.

MUFFIN LOAF.

One quart of boiled milk, one ounce of lard put in the milk while it is hot. Four eggs, well beaten, added to the milk when cold. Sift in flour, till it is a little thicker than muffin batter. After the flour is well mixed add one-half a cake of yeast. In warm weather, make it up at eleven o'clock in the morning for tea. It must be put in the *shape* to rise one hour before baking.

FRENCH BREAD.

Take six pounds flour and put it on the board. Make a hole in the middle, in which put two teacups of yeast, or one cake compressed yeast. Make the dough with warm water, not very stiff. Work it up well, adding two ounces of salt dissolved in a little warm water. Cover and set it in a warm place to rise. The quality of the bread depends on this part of the operation. Having left the dough one or two hours (according to the season) knead it again, and leave it as before for two hours. In the meanwhile heat the oven, divide the dough into eight loaves, bake in Vienna bread pans, and put them in the oven as quickly as possible.

BONNY CLABBER CAKES.

Break one egg into a dish, put in one pint of bonny clabber, one pint of flour, with a little salt. Add one teaspoonful of soda.

WASHINGTON'S BREAKFAST BREAD.

Five pints of flour, one pint of new milk, three eggs, one spoonful of butter, two spoonsful of yeast, or one-half cake compressed yeast. Beat all well together, and set to rise. When light, bake.

MILK RISING BREAD.

To one pint of new milk add enough boiling water to make it warm. Beat in as much flour as will make a thick batter. Sprinkle a little dry flour over it, and set it to rise for about two hours, then add flour enough for rolls or loaves.

BREAD MUFFINS.

Make the dough up at night, as you would for loaf-bread. In the morning work well and break off in pieces a little larger than for biscuits. Roll rather thin and set to rise an hour and a half, bake on the *top* of the stove, and turn over as you would other cakes. They will bake in a very few minutes.

POTATO MUFFINS.

Four eggs, one cup butter and lard mixed, one pint mashed potatoes, one cup yeast, or one-half cake compressed yeast, one tablespoonful of sugar, flour sufficient to make a stiff batter, then let it rise, and make it into a dough as stiff as you would for light biscuit. Let it rise again, then make into muffins in pans, or cut it out and set it to rise. Bake in a quick oven. These are delicious for tea.

TEA CAKE.

Take light dough, roll it about an inch thick, stick raisins over it. Make a mixture of cinnamon, butter and sugar, and spread in a thin layer over the dough. Note.—I generally set the dough to rise after rolling and placing in the pans, then cover with the raisins and the mixture. Put it in the stove and bake as bread. Cut into squares. *Very nice.*

MUFFINS.

One pint milk, three eggs, a little salt. Make a batter about as thick as sponge cake batter, with flour. Beat the whites very light. This cake is to be baked as muffins for breakfast. One teaspoonful of Royal Baking Powder.

SUET CAKES.

Chop suet fine, pour over it scalding water, let it stand until cool enough to work in the flour. Knead in flour lightly, roll it thin, cut them out, and bake them quickly. Serve up hot. One teaspoonful of salt.

ORANGE CAKE.

One quart flour, one cup butter, four eggs, two spoonsful yeast, or one-half cake compressed yeast, or one-half teacup of liquid yeast. Make in a stiff batter the night before with milk. Next morning add a teacupful of meal finely sifted. Beat it well, and pour it in cups to rise.

BRAN BREAD.

Rub one teaspoonful of salt, and *very thoroughly* two teaspoonsful of cream of tartar, in one quart of bran flour; then add two scant tablespoonsful of molasses, and mix in sufficient new milk to make a stiff batter. Dissolve one teaspoonful of soda in two tablespoonsful of cold water, and stir in thoroughly and quickly. Bake slowly one hour. This will keep fresh and moist three days, and is relished by those who cannot eat graham bread prepared in other ways.

BROWN BREAD.

To two quarts of corn meal allow a teacupful of boiling water, one quart graham flour, four tablespoonsful of strong hop yeast, or one-half cake compressed yeast, one tablespoonful of salt, one teacupful of molasses, and one quart of lukewarm water. Scald one quart of the corn meal with the boiling water, add the lukewarm water, and then stir in gradually the other quart of meal and the graham flour, add the other ingredients, the yeast last, and set it to rise. When light bake in a quick oven.

GRAHAM BREAD.

To two pounds of graham flour allow one pint of milk, one pint of water, one wineglass of molasses, one teaspoonful of salt, and two tablespoonsful of liquid strong yeast, or one-half cake compressed yeast. Beat the yeast, molasses, soda and salt in lukewarm water and milk. Stir in the flour until too stiff to use a spoon. Knead and bake as usual.

RYE BREAD.

Make a rather stiff mush of corn meal, boiling it long and well; salt to taste. When milk-warm stir in yeast in just the proportion for wheat sponge. In cool weather this must be done over night, and in the morning, when light, work in as much rye flour as the sponge will hold. Do not get it too stiff, for it will adhere to the hands, even when stiff enough, and unlike wheat dough its stickiness is not a sign of the need of more flour. Let the dough rise, and do not attempt to mould it, but pour into well buttered tins.

RYE BREAD (Steamed).

Half a pint rye meal unsifted, one pint of sifted corn meal, the same quantity of sour milk, half a gill of molasses, one teaspoonful salt, and a large tablespoonful of soda, dissolved in a little warm water. Stir well together, adding the soda last. Steam it for four hours.

BUCKWHEAT CAKES.

Make a thin mush of corn meal, cooking it ten minutes; let it become perfectly cool before putting the cakes to rise. In mixing the cakes take a pint of the mush to a quart of buckwheat flour; add water and yeast as in ordinary cakes made of buckwheat. Making a mush of the corn meal prevents the raw taste there always is when the meal is put in uncooked.

BUCKWHEAT CAKES.

Half a cake of yeast, one tablespoonful of salt, and one of brown sugar; one teacup of flour or meal, one quart of buckwheat. Mix all with warm water, and beat well when you make them. Stir one tablespoonful of molasses in before baking, after beating down the batter.

MUFFINS.

The nicest muffins are made in this simple fashion : Early in the morning take a piece of light bread dough, and thin this to the consistency of batter by adding sweet milk. After beating it till smooth let it rise all together for an hour, then upon a buttered griddle drop the batter from a spoon, and as soon as it is lightly brown turn it over. To be served up hot, and torn open, not cut open.

VIRGINIA RICE BREAD.

Take one teacup of rice and boil it well. This will, when boiled, make one pint. Stir into the rice while warm one spoonful of lard or butter, and some salt. Take three eggs, beat whites and yolks separately, one pint of milk, half a pint of meal. Mix the yolks and milk together, add the rice, and last of all the whites. Butter the dish and put the batter in, filling the dish as full as it will hold, as it bakes better.

FRIED CORN MUSH FOR BREAKFAST.

Corn mush is made by sprinkling corn meal into well-salted boiling water (a pint of corn meal to three pints of water) and cooking it well. But corn meal mush is much lighter, and when fried for breakfast, browns better, by cooking it as follows. Put one quart of water on to boil. Stir a pint of cold milk with one pint of corn meal and one teaspoonful of salt. When the water boils pour in the mixture gradually, stirring all well together. Let it boil for half an hour, stirring often, to prevent it from burning. To have it fried for breakfast it must be thoroughly cooked and made the day before. When cold, slice it, dip each slice in beaten egg (salted) and bread or cracker crumbs, and fry in boiling hot lard.

OATMEAL PORRIDGE.

Take one heaping cup of oatmeal to one quart of boiling water and one teaspoonful of salt. Boil twenty minutes. The water should be salted and boiling, and the meal sprinkled in with one hand, while it is lightly stirred in with the other. When all mixed let it boil, but only stir it occasionally to keep it from burning at the bottom and to mingle the grains two or three times, so that all may be evenly cooked. If much stirred the porridge will be starchy or waxy, and poor in flavor.

BUCKWHEAT CAKES.

One quart buckwheat, one quarter of a pound graham flour, one pint sifted corn meal, one iron spoonful white flour, a little salt. Mix with two iron spoonsful of yeast, and tepid milk and water to a thick batter. Beat well, and set to rise twelve hours before it is to be used. Add two spoonsful dark molasses, to make them bake a nice brown. Use either one-half cake compressed yeast, or one-half teacup of liquid yeast.

GRAHAM BISCUIT.

Three cups of graham and one of white flour, three cups of milk, two tablespoonsful lard, one of white sugar (heaping), one salt spoon of salt, one teaspoonful soda, and two of cream of tartar. Mix and bake as you do soda biscuit.

MINUTE BISCUIT.

One pint sour milk or buttermilk, one teaspoonful soda, two of melted butter, and flour to make a soft dough, just stiff enough to handle. Mix, roll and cut out quickly, with as little handling as possible, and bake in a quick oven.

CRUMPETS (Sweet).

One pint raised dough, three eggs, three tablespoonsful butter, and half a cup of white sugar. When the bread has passed its second rising, work into the above-named quantity the butter (melted), then the eggs and sugar, beaten together till very light. Bake in muffin rings for about twenty minutes.

BOSTON BROWN BREAD.

Three cups brown flour, three of rye flour, one of corn meal, one cup molasses, four sweet milk, two teaspoonsful of soda. Mix all together; salt enough to season. Bake one hour; if the loaves are pretty thick, bake a little longer.

Nan Day's Biscuit

Sift together several times
1 quart flour
1 teaspoonful salt
1 tablespoonful sugar
2 heaping teaspoonfuls Royal baking powder
Add 3 large tablespoonfuls of shortening (Crisco
 + rub into the flour.
Add enough milk to make dough as soft as
 can be handled. (Handle as little as possible
Take a little dough at a time + roll lightly
Cut out - Brush tops with melted butter &
Bake quickly in a hot oven. It takes from
 7 to 15 minutes to bake

Health bread -

1 cup whole wheat flour
2 "   Ralston's bran
1 "   sour milk
½ "   seeded raisins
½ teaspoonful of soda stirred in the milk
½ "   salt -
 Mix + bake in a slow oven 1 hour.

Bran Bread (Mrs I. Stringham)

2 eggs -
4 cups bran flour
2 "   white   "
2 "   milk
1 "   molasses
3 teaspoons baking powder
1 "   salt
1 saltspoon soda dissolved in
1 tablespoon of hot water + stirred into the
 molasses - Bake 1 hour in 2 brick

MEATS.

ROAST FILLET OF VEAL.

Take out the bone of the joint, make a deep incision between the fillet and the flap, then fill it with stuffing, made as follows: Two cupsful of bread-crumbs, half a cupful of chopped pork, peel (grated) of half a lemon, a little of the juice, summer savory, thyme or any herb to taste. Or it may be filled with a veal stuffing as follows : Half a pound of bread (without the crust) in tepid water, then squeeze it dry. Put three ounces of butter into a stew-pan, and when hot stir in a small onion, minced; color it slightly. Then add the bread, three tablespoonsful of parsley chopped fine, half a teaspoonful of powdered thyme, a little grated nutmeg, pepper, salt, and a gill of stock. Stir it over the fire till it leaves the bottom and sides, then mix in two eggs. After stuffing bind the veal into a round form, fasten it with skewers and twine, sprinkle over it pepper and salt, and cover it with buttered paper. Be careful not to put the meat too near the fire at first. Baste well and often. Just before it is done remove the paper, sprinkle over it a little flour, and rub over it a little butter. This will give a frothy appearance to the surface of the meat. When done, put the pan of gravy on the fire, add a little flour, some boiling water, and when cooked, some lemon juice. Strain it, remove the grease, and pour it around the roast. Fry some pieces of ham cut in diamond shape; place these in a circle around the roast, alternately, with slices of lemon.

MEATS.

BROILED VEAL CUTLETS.

Rib cutlets should always be trimmed, and the bone scraped at the end, so that it will look smooth and white. Broil them on a moderate fire, basting them occasionally with butter, and turning them often. Dish them in a circle with tomato sauce.

BEEF HASH.

Chop the cold cooked meat very fine, use half as much meat as of cold boiled potatoes, also chopped. Put a little boiling water and butter into a saucepan; when it boils again put in the meat and potatoes, well salted and peppered. Let it cook well, stirring occasionally, not enough to make a purée or mush of it. It is not done before there is a coating at the bottom of the pan from which the hash will free itself without sticking. The hash must not be at all watery, nor yet too dry, but so that it will stand quite firm on well trimmed and buttered slices of toast. Chicken, turkey, corn beef or veal hash may be made in the same manner.

TO COOK LIVER.

Fry in a sauté pan some thin slices of breakfast bacon, and when done put them on a hot dish. Fry then thin slices of liver in the same fat, which have previously been thrown into boiling water, for only a *moment*, and then sprinkled with flour. When well done on both sides serve them and the bacon on the same dish, and garnish them with slices of lemon.

BOILED MUTTON.

This should be quite fresh. Put it in well-salted boiling water, and keep it boiling until the meat is thoroughly done. The rule is to boil it a quarter of an hour for each pound of meat. Caper sauce should be served with this dish, either in a sauce-boat or poured over the mutton. Garnish with parsley.

MEATS.   27

BOILING OR STEWING.

For boiling, stewing or braising, inferior pieces of meat may be used and made very good—but remember, 1st: Be sure the water is boiling when you pour it over the meat. 2d: Stand it on the back part of the range where it will simmer. Never boil. Allow forty minutes for every pound of meat. Add salt when meat is half done.

MUTTON CUTLETS.

Trim them well, scraping the bones. Roll them in a little melted butter or oil, season, and broil them, or they are nice rolled in egg and bread-crumbs and fried. If broiled serve them round a bed of mashed potatoes, or with tomato sauce. They are very nice with almost any kind of vegetable, such as peas or string-beans, in the centre of the dish, with the cutlets in a circle around.

HOW TO BROIL HAM.

Slice the meat as thin as possible, then put it into a pan of cold water, set it on the stove, and let it come to a boil. Then have the griddle hot, and broil the ham, adding a little cayenne pepper.

TO GLAZE A COLD HAM.

After the ham is boiled and cold cover it with the well-beaten yolk of an egg. Sprinkle with cracker or grated stale bread, then cover again with sweet cream, and bake until brown.

A QUICK WAY TO BROIL STEAK.

Have a nice tenderloin steak, pound it until thin. Put it in a dry, hot skillet if you have no broiler. Have ready in a meat dish a heaping tablespoonful of butter, one teaspoon of salt, a good deal of pepper, and a little water. Set this in front of the stove. As the juice cooks out of the steak, pour it in the dish, then turn it, and brown on the other side. Saturate the steak well with the gravy and serve very hot.

GIBLET PIE WITH OYSTERS.

Take the giblets of two full-grown chickens or a large turkey, stew them until nearly done, then cut them up in pieces an inch in size. Have ready a pan lined with rich paste, into which pour the giblets mixed with a quart of oysters. Put in also enough of the oyster liquor to make the pie very juicy. Add flour to thicken slightly, with butter, pepper and salt, and bake until the pastry is a light brown.

VIRGINIA BRUNSWICK STEW.

For a large family take three gallons water, to which add two chickens which have been cut up and one pound fat bacon, also cut very fine. As soon as the chickens are sufficiently cooked for the meat to leave the bones, take them out and extract all the bones. Return the meat to the water, then add half a gallon of Irish potatoes boiled and mashed, one and a half pints green corn cut off, one pint green butter-beans, one quart skinned tomatoes, and a good sized loaf of light bread. Season with black and red pepper, salt and butter. The bread must not be put in till the stew is nearly done. As soon as it begins to thicken it must be stirred constantly until it is done. If it should be too thick add more water. Much depends on the judgment of the person who makes it. When properly made no one is able to detect any of the ingredients. Squirrels are a very good substitute for chicken.

ENGLISH MEAT PIE.

Chop any kind of cold meat very fine. Season with the grated rind and juice of a lemon, a little nutmeg, red and black pepper, salt, a teaspoonful of dry mustard, a little onion and parsley. Two raw eggs with a little rich gravy or butter.

Grate bread-crumbs on top, covered with lumps of butter. Bake it and garnish it with hard-boiled eggs.

FRIED CHICKEN, MARYLAND STYLE.

Have the chickens killed the day before they are to be eaten and put on ice. Cut the chicken in seven pieces, have them wiped dry, then flour lightly, season high with pepper and salt. Have your lard boiling hot, then put the chicken in, turning carefully, let it soak well, then take it out, and put in a pan to keep hot. Then have some flour browned, and add to the gravy in the pan with a good cup full of cream or rich milk with some parsley chopped, let it thicken, and serve it in a gravy dish. Make *Mush* cakes, fry separately, serve on the dish with the chicken.

A NICE HASH.

A small piece of cold turkey, chicken or veal, two or three hard boiled eggs, two or three well boiled potatoes, a lump of butter the size of an egg, salt and pepper to taste; chop all very fine, and put it on the fire to heat thoroughly, but *not* to cook. The butter should be allowed to melt through the hash thoroughly, and then serve it very hot. A little sweet cream may be an improvement, but it is not necessary. It is better and more delicate with a greater quantity of eggs and potatoes than meat. It is very nice baked hash brown.

FRICASSEED CHICKEN.

Cut up the chickens, wash them, and let them remain in water half an hour in order to make them white. Drain them and put them in a saucepan with a pint of fresh water. Season them with pepper and salt, place them on the fire, and let them stew half an hour. Then take two tablespoonsful of flour and two ounces of butter, stir them together till quite smooth, and add this to the chickens with half a pint of cream. Boil till the chickens are tender. A little mace or onion parsley may be added if desired.

BROILED CHICKEN.

Clean them nicely, cut them down the back, and break the breastbone with a rolling-pin. Wash and wipe them dry. Place them on a gridiron over bright coals; cover them with a sheet of tin and turn them several times. When done they should be brown on both sides. Take them up, season with pepper and salt, and baste them with butter. Serve very hot.

RECIPE FOR BAKED HAM.

Take a new ham, parboil it until it is tender enough to be skinned easily. Then stick cloves all over the top about an inch apart. Mix a pint of wine and quarter pound of sugar, and baste the ham repeatedly with it while it is baking. Do not pour it all over at once, but a few spoonsful at a time. Bake two or three hours. When cold it is excellent for broiling.

POMPEY'S HEAD.

Three pounds of uncooked round of beef minced up, some very fat ham, and a large slice of bread; season with onions, thyme, parsley, ground cloves, salt and pepper, and one egg; mix all well and form into a large ball bound around with strips of cloth to keep it in shape. These can be removed before dishing the beef. Put in an oven with a little water and slices of bacon, or a spoonful of lard; cook slowly, baste often. When taken up make the gravy of browned flour. Grate on bread-crumbs before taking off the fire.

CALF'S HEAD.

One head and liver. Boil liver until done and head until the bones can be pulled out. Cut it in pieces no larger than walnuts, chop two white onions and mix it with half a teaspoonful of powdered nutmeg or mace; same of allspice, one heaping tablespoonful black pepper, salt to taste, quarter pound butter, one wineglass of sherry wine, the same of brandy. Mix all and put it in a dish. Grate bread-crumbs on top and spread some of the butter over to brown it. Bake.

TENDERLOIN OF BEEF.

To serve tenderloin as directed below, the whole piece must be extracted before the hind quarter of the animal is cut out. This must be particularly noted, because not commonly practised, the tenderloin being usually left attached to the roasting pieces in order to furnish a tidbit for a few. Wash the piece well, put it in an oven, add about a pint of water, and chop up a good handful of the following vegetables, as an ingredient of the dish, viz.: Irish potatoes, carrots, turnips, and a large bunch of celery. They must be washed, peeled and chopped up raw, then added to the meat; blended with the juice they form and flavor the gravy. Let the whole slowly simmer, and when nearly done add one teaspoonful of pounded allspice. To give richness to the gravy, put in one tablespoonful of butter. If the gravy should look too greasy skim off some of the melted suet. Boil also a lean piece of beef, which when perfectly done, chop fine, flavoring with a small quantity of onion, besides pepper and salt to the taste. Make into small balls, wet them on the outside with egg, roll in grated cracker or fine bread-crumbs. Fry these balls a light brown. When serving the dish put them around the tenderloin, and pour over the whole the rich gravy. This is a dish fit for an epicure.

BEEF STEW (with Tomatoes).

Slice three pounds lean beef and seven moderate sized tomatoes with one onion. Cut up the tomatoes very small, and chop the onion fine. Stew slowly, add salt, a few cloves, and just before it is done, a little butter and half a gill of catsup.

HOW TO BOIL A HAM.

It is always best to wash a ham the evening before the day it is to be cooked, and let it soak in water all night. In the morning cover it well with water, and keep it boiling until ready to dish up dinner. If the bone on the under side comes out easily the ham is done. You may remove the outside skin or not. The prettiest way of serving a ham is to take off the skin after it is thoroughly boiled, to grate bread-crumbs thickly over the top, and brush the whole over with the yolks of eggs. Then put it into an oven, and let it brown thoroughly. If while boiling it is found necessary to add more water to the ham, be sure that the water is boiling, for cold water will inevitably make the meat tough.

BAKED CALF'S HEAD.

Boil the head after being well cleaned until all the bones may be easily drawn out. Lay the pieces of meat on a dish and cut them into small pieces. Season with cayenne pepper, mace, cloves, nutmeg, parsley, onions, sweet marjoram and a little thyme, a small bit of each chopped up fine; salt to taste. Lay some lumps of butter over it, and as much butter as will cover it. Then put it in the oven, and when baked tender take the meat out, adding half a pint of Madeira wine, a teacup of walnut catsup, and three or four eggs beaten up with butter to the gravy, which must then be thickened over the fire. Keep stirring it while thickening, and then pour it over the meat, which is now ready to be served.

CHICKEN FRICASSEE.

Take two chickens, cut them up, and lay them in a skillet with two thin slices of ham, two small eschalots, and a few blades of mace. Then season the fowls with pepper and salt. Add a little water. When about half done add half a pint of cream and a lump of butter the size of a walnut rolled in flour. Keep the fricassee constantly stirring till done.

VEAL CUTLETS.

Cut the veal an inch thick. Beat the yolks of two eggs, and rub the meat with it. Throw over it grated bread, parsley, thyme, grated nutmeg, and pepper and salt. Stir into the gravy, after the cutlets are taken out, butter and pepper. Fry brown and well. Lemon peel improves them.

TO TRIM A FILLET OF BEEF.

All the skin and fat must be removed from the top of the fillet, from one end to the other; then the rib bones are disengaged. The fat adhering to the side opposite the ribs is only partially removed. Then the sinewy skin covering the upper meat of the fillet must be removed in strips, proceeding by slipping the blade of the knife between the skin and the meat. This is a very simple process, yet it requires great precision. The upper part of a trimmed fillet must be smooth, not furrowed by hollows occasioned by wrong movements of the knife. The skin being removed, both extremities of the fillet are rounded. The fat inside of the rib is the only portion allowed to adhere to the meat. The larding of the meat is applied to its upper surface.

TO COOK A FILLET OF BEEF.

After it is trimmed and larded put it into a small baking pan, in the bottom of which are some chopped pieces of pork and beef suet. Sprinkle some salt and pepper over it, and put a large ladleful of hot stock in the bottom of the pan, or it may be simply basted with boiling water. The oven should be very hot, and half an hour before dinner put the beef in. Baste it often, supplying a little hot stock if necessary.

BEEFSTEAK WITH MUSHROOMS.

Take one quart of fresh mushrooms, skin and wash them carefully through several waters, and put them in a stew-pan with no more water than that which adheres to them. Season with salt and pepper, and dredge through them a dessertspoonful of flour, stirring very lightly; when half done add two ounces of fresh butter. Broil one or more steaks, which when done place on a well-heated dish and season with salt and pepper, basting them with butter. Then pour the mushrooms over, and serve hot.

CALF'S HEAD.

Wash and boil a nice head until it is tender. Take out the brains as soon as it is washed and the chops divided from the skull. Have ready one quart beef gravy; add spices and walnut catsup to your taste. Cut the head up, put it in the gravy and stew it a short time. Add two tablespoonsful of butter rubbed in brown flour. Add a little wine last of all. Bake in a dish and garnish with pastry cakes and hard-boiled eggs. Put all on a dish with forcemeat balls and brain cakes.

BEEF A LA MODE.

Take the bone from a round of beef, and fill the space with a forcemeat made of the crumbs of a stale loaf, four ounces of marrow, two heads of garlic chopped with thyme and parsley, some nutmeg, cloves, pepper and salt, mix it to a paste with the yolks of four eggs beaten, stuff the lean part of the round with it, and make balls of the remainder. Sew a strip of linen over it strong and wide enough to keep it round and compact. Put it in a vessel just large enough to hold it, add one pint red wine, cover it with sheets of tin or iron, set it in a brick oven properly heated and bake it three hours. When done skim the fat from the gravy, thicken it with brown flour, add some mushroom and walnut catsup and serve it up garnished with fried forcemeat balls. It is good eaten cold with salad, or with vegetables around it in the gravy.

BEEFSTEAK PIE.

Cut up some nice steaks, and stew them till done; put a puff paste in the dish, lay in the steaks with a few slices of boiled ham. Season the gravy very high, pour it in the dish, put on the lid of paste, and bake it.

TO GRILL A CALF'S HEAD.

Clean and divide it, take out the brains and tongue, boil it tender, take the eyes out whole, and cut the flesh from the skull in small pieces. Take some of the water in which it was boiled, for gravy, put to it salt, cayenne pepper, a grated nutmeg, with a spoonful of lemon pickle; stew it till it is well flavored, take the jowl or chop, remove the bones, and cover it with bread-crumbs, chopped parsley, pepper and salt, and set it in an oven to brown. Thicken the gravy with the yolks of two eggs, and a spoonful of butter rubbed into two of flour. Stew the head in it a few minutes, put it in the dish, and lay the grilled chop on it. Garnish it with brain cakes and broiled sweetbreads.

CALF'S HEART.

Take the heart and liver from the haslet, and cut off the windpipe; boil the lights very tender, and cut them in small pieces. Take as much of the water they were boiled in as will be sufficient for gravy, add to it a large spoonful of white wine, one of lemon pickle, some grated nutmeg, pepper and salt, with a large spoonful of butter mixed with one of white flour. Let it boil a few minutes, put in the minced lights, and set it by till the heart and liver are ready. Cut the ventricle out of the heart, wash it well, and lard it all over with narrow strips of middling. Fill the cavity with good forcemeat, and put it in a pan on the broad end, that the stuffing may not come out. Bake it a nice brown. Slice the liver an inch thick, broil it, set the heart upright in the middle of the dish, make the minced lights hot, pour the mince around it, lay the broiled liver on, and garnish with bunches of fried parsley. It should be served up extremely hot. This is a very nice dish.

HARICOT OF MUTTON.

Take the nicest part of the rack, divide it into chops, with one bone in each, beat them flat, sprinkle salt and pepper on them and broil them nicely. Make a rich gravy out of the inferior parts, season it well with pepper, a little spice, and any kind of catsup you like. When sufficiently done strain it, and thicken it with butter and brown flour; have some carrots and turnips cut into small dice and boiled till tender, put them in the gravy, lay the chops in and stew them fifteen minutes. Serve them up garnished with green pickle.

TO MAKE SHOAT CUTLETS.

Take the skin from the hind quarter, and cut it in pieces, prepare them the same as veal cutlets; make a little nice gravy with the skin and the scraps of meat left, thicken it with butter and brown flour, and season it as you like.

BROILED SQUIRRELS.

Clean and soak them to draw out the blood. Wipe them dry and broil them over a hot, clear fire, turning often. When done, lay them in a hot dish, and cover with melted butter, seasoned with pepper and salt. Use at least a tablespoonful for each squirrel, and let it lie five minutes between two hot dishes, before serving.

TO COOK RABBIT FOR BREAKFAST.

Take a nice fat rabbit, cut it open and sprinkle it with a little salt and pepper and some flour. Have ready some lard, boiling hot, and put the rabbit in it. Fry till it is a nice brown. Then take a spoonful of brown flour and add a little hot water. Mix the flour with a small lump of butter and stir it in the gravy. Season very high. Place the rabbit on the dish, pour the gravy over it, and serve very hot. Cream instead of water for the gravy is better.

INDIAN CURRY.

Cut up an onion very fine and brown it in a tablespoonful of lard or butter; add a tablespoonful of curry powder made into a paste, put it on the fire and stir it until thoroughly cooked, being careful not to scorch it. Then add the meat— chicken, rabbit or mutton, as you prefer—and stir in a cupful of stock of boiling water; then cover it with stock or boiling water, and let it boil slowly until the meat is tender. To thicken the gravy add three boiled and mashed potatoes. If you wish it very hot add a little Worcestershire sauce. Serve with rice boiled dry all around the dish.

HOW TO COOK WILD DUCKS.

After cleaning and preparing the ducks place them in a very hot oven, and cook them eighteen or twenty minutes. Wild ducks should never be stuffed. To retain the wild juicy flavor which is so delightful they should always be underdone. In order to test when they are done (which of course depends upon the size of the duck and the heat of the oven), stick a fork into them, and if the red juice runs out they must be cooked a little longer. Serve with gravy from the ducks. No flour is used with them at all. Serve with celery, fried hominy, or currant jelly.

SAUSAGE.

Twenty-five pounds of meat, seven pounds of fat; one-half pound of salt, eighteen tablespoonsful of sage, seven of black pepper, six of fresh thyme, or dried if you can't get fresh, one teaspoonful of red pepper.

TO CURE HAMS AND OTHER MEAT.

One bushel of salt (Ashton the best), two pounds of sugar, one-quarter pound black pepper, tablespoonful of cayenne pepper. This quantity is for one thousand pounds of meat. Rub it well on the hams, let them lie with skins down, and put an extra handful of the mixture on the top of each ham; at the end of three weeks rub this well into the hams. If the weather is cold, let them remain this way for six weeks; if mild, for five weeks, at the end of which time hang up with tar rope, and smoke every day for four weeks with hickory, and cedar wood mixed. Cure breakfast bacon and shoulders the same way.

RATCLIFFE MANOR SAUSAGE.

Fifty-one pounds of lean pork, twenty-four pounds of chine, fat cut separately, three-quarters of a pound of salt, four ounces of black pepper, six ounces of sage (country sage the best), two teaspoonsful of cayenne pepper, one ounce of thyme, one-half ounce of sweet marjoram, two teaspoonsful of saltpetre.

No. 1. VEAL CUTLETS.

Have the cutlets cut thin, then season with salt and pepper; beat up two eggs for a good-sized dish, and dip the cutlets in the egg; then roll in stale bread-crumbs or grated cracker, and have your lard boiling hot; put the cutlets in the lard and fry brown. Of course they must be turned. Then remove the cutlets, and add half pint of cream or rich milk, with a large tablespoonful of brown flour, to the gravy, and season with parsley, thyme and nutmegs. Let the gravy just come to the boiling point. If you have no cream or milk, use water with a good-sized lump of butter.

BREADED CHOPS.

Broil French chops ten minutes, turn them very often, take them from the broiler, baste with melted butter, season with salt and pepper; let them stand ten minutes; dip them in beaten eggs, roll in bread crumbs, and fry in boiling fat. Fill the bottom of a meat dish with tomato sauce, slip the paper quillings over the end of the bones, and arrange the chops nicely in the sauce. Garnish with parsley, and serve very hot.

STEWED KIDNEYS.

Have the kidneys perfectly fresh; split them in half; trim with a sharp knife, very carefully, the sinews and fat that are inside. Now cut the kidneys in small pieces, put in a pan, cover with cold water, stand on a moderate fire and bring almost to a boiling point. Drain this water off, cover with fresh cold water and heat again; do this three times. Do not let it boil, or the kidney will be tough and hard. Put a tablespoonful of butter in a frying pan, stir until brown; add one tablespoonful of flour, one-half pint of boiling water or stock; stir constantly until it boils. Now add one tablespoonful of Worcestershire sauce, one tablespoonful of mushroom catsup, salt and pepper, and the kidney. Stir again until the kidney is thoroughly heated, take from the fire, add four tablespoonsful of sherry, and serve immediately.

STUFFED BREAST OF VEAL (for the Stuffing).

One cup of bread crumbs, one teaspoonful of sweet marjoram, one-quarter pound salt pork, one teaspoonful of thyme, one of salt, two dashes of pepper. Chop the pork fine, add it and all the ingredients to the bread crumbs. Wipe a breast of veal with a damp cloth, make long gashes through the ribs, and fill with the stuffing. Place it in a baking pan, and roast the same as the loin.

VEAL CROQUETTES.

Veal croquettes are made the same as chicken croquettes—using chopped veal, leaving out the sweetbreads (calf's brains added in their place), and if carefully made, good judges can scarcely discover the difference.

LIVER AND BACON.

One pound of calf's liver, one-half pound of bacon, one-half teaspoonful of salt, one tablespoonful of flour, a dash of black pepper. Cut the liver into thin slices and scald it; wipe dry. Cut the bacon into as many thin slices as you have of liver; put the bacon into a frying-pan and fry until brown; take it out, put on a heated dish and keep it warm. Dust the liver with flour, salt and pepper, and fry it in the bacon fat. When a nice brown, arrange it on the heated dish with a slice of bacon on each slice of liver. Add the flour to the fat remaining in the pan; mix; add one-half pint of boiling water; season with salt and pepper; pour it around the liver and serve.

BROILED LIVER.

Cut the liver into slices and scald it; wipe it dry, season with salt and pepper, broil over a clear fire, first on one side then on the other. It will take about five minutes. When done spread lightly with butter and serve on a heated dish.

IRISH STEW.

Three pounds of the neck of mutton, four good sized onions, four potatoes cut into dice—salt and pepper to taste, four quarts water. Cut the meat into small pieces, cover with the water—which should be boiling, add the onions sliced, and simmer gently for three hours. Half an hour before the meat is done add the potatoes, season with salt and pepper, and if you like it the beaten yolk of an egg. Dumplings may be added the same as in stew of beef with dumplings.

SHEEP'S HEAD HASH.

Clean a sheepshead, same as calf's head, put it on to stew with the liver and heart well washed, add one onion, and simmer gently one and one-half hours. When done, take out and stand away to cool. When cold take the meat from the head, chop it with the heart and liver very fine. Put them into a stewpan, add one large tablespoonful of butter, one pint water or liquor in which they were boiled, salt and pepper, stew up once, and serve with squares of toast around the dish.

TO BAKE OR ROAST A QUARTER OF LAMB.

Wipe the meat with a damp towel, place it in a baking pan, dredge it with pepper. Put one teaspoonful of salt in the bottom of the pan, add one cup of water to baste with, when it evaporates use its own drippings. Lamb must be basted every ten minutes, and baked fifteen minutes to every pound in a very hot oven. Mint sauce, green peas, and asparagus tips, should be served with spring lamb.

BAKED HASH.

One quart cold cooked chopped beef, two eggs, one pint chopped uncooked potatoes, salt and pepper. Put the chopped potatoes in a pan with one pint of water. Let them stew five minutes, then add the meat and enough water to make the moisture required. Stew ten minutes longer. Take from the fire, add the beaten eggs, one teaspoonful of salt and three dashes of pepper. Turn it into a baking dish and bake twenty minutes in a quick oven.

CORNED BEEF HASH.

One pint cooked corned beef chopped fine, one pint cold boiled potatoes chopped fine, one tablespoonful of butter, three dashes pepper, one cup of stock or water, one teaspoonful of onion juice. Mix the meat and potatoes together, put them in a frying pan, add the stock, butter, onion juice and pepper. Stir constantly until it boils. Serve on buttered toast.

FRIZZLED BEEF.

Chip dried beef very thin. To every half pound allow a large tablespoonful of butter and one tablespoonful of flour. Melt the butter in a frying pan, then add the meat, and stir over the fire for about two minutes, or until the butter begins to brown; dredge in the flour, stir again; then add the milk and a little pepper, stir again until it boils, then serve.

CURRY OF MUTTON.

One pint finely-chopped mutton, one-half cupful of rice, one tablespoonful Curry Powder, two quarts boiling water, one tablespoonful of butter, one of flour, salt to taste. Wash the rice, put it in boiling water; let it boil thirty-five minutes, drain in a cullender. Put the butter in a frying pan; when melted, add the flour, and stir until smooth; add one-half pint boiling water; let it boil up once, then add meat curry and salt. Stir ten minutes. Now heap it in the centre of a meat dish and put the rice around. Brush all over with beaten egg and place in the oven to brown.

LIVER WITH BROWN SAUCE.

One pound calf's liver, two slices of bacon, one tablespoonful of Worcestershire sauce, one tablespoonful of mushroom catsup, one tablespoonful of flour, one-half pint boiling stock or water. Cut the liver in slices, cover with boiling water, let it stand five minutes to draw the blood. Take it out and wipe dry. Dredge with flour, salt, and pepper. Fry out the bacon, then put the liver in the hot bacon fat, fry brown on one side then the other. Place it on a hot dish with the bacon, cut in small pieces, add the flour to the fat in the pan, stir until brown; add the boiling stock or water, stir again until it boils, then add the sauce, catsup and salt to taste. Pour it over the liver, and serve.

SWEETBREADS À LA CRÈME.

One pound of sweetbreads, five mushrooms, one tablespoonful of flour, one tablespoonful of butter, one-half pint of cream; parboil the sweetbreads as directed, pick them to pieces, rejecting all the fine membranes; chop rather fine; also the mushrooms. Melt the butter; when melted, add the flour, mix until smooth; add the milk, stir constantly until it boils, add the mushrooms and sweetbreads, stir over the steam of the teakettle for five minutes, add one-half teaspoonful of salt, and a dash of white pepper, serve in silver shells or little paper cases.

SWEETBREADS FRIED.

Wash, trim, and parboil the sweetbreads fifteen minutes. Then cut them in nice pieces, dip them first into egg, then in bread crumbs; fry in boiling fat. Serve with cream sauce.

SOUPS.

MOCK TURTLE SOUP.

Parboil a calf's head, scrape the hair off, split it open and take out the brains, then put the head back in the pot, with one and a half gallons of water; add liver and haslet, a bunch of thyme, and a large slice of middling; let it boil till the bones come out; take these out, and season the soup to taste. Put in one tablespoonful of allspice, a good pinch of cloves, the same of mace, four tablespoonsful of pounded pepper and salt. Thicken it. Slice the head and liver, put it all back and let it simmer until done. Fry the brains in butter, and put them in the soup. Boil hard eggs and put in one yolk to each plateful; cut in small pieces.

OKRA SOUP.

Take two dozen okra pods. When they are tender slice them and put on to boil five hours before dinner in one and a half gallons of water. Then add four sliced onions, one and a half pods of red pepper; let them simmer two hours; then add two dozen tomatoes with a pint of lima beans, two young cymbelines, and half a dozen ears of corn. An hour after add a pound of fresh meat or chicken, and a few thin slices of fat bacon. Just before serving up add a cup of cream and a piece of butter the size of an egg.

GUMBO SOUP.

Take any kind of cold meat—cold roast beef is the best—and cut it in small pieces. Put these and the bones into a pot, with as much water as you will need, early in the day.

Let it boil slowly, keeping it well skimmed. In the meantime take, of young corn, gumbo, and tomatoes, equal parts, and cut them fine. A little onion, just enough to taste, also chopped celery and salt to taste. Put these in the pot with the meat, and let all boil very slowly. Have ready some brown flour, brown sugar, a little wine or vinegar, a large lump of butter seasoned with pepper, mustard and spice. Make these into a paste. Remove the bones from the pot before thickening with the paste.

RATCLIFFE CRAB SOUP. No. 1.

One quart of picked crab, discarding all fat. Take one pint of water, add four pieces of mace, one onion cut in half, so it can be taken out (not served with the soup), three blades of parsley, a little red pepper and salt. When it boils, add the crab, with one large iron spoonful of butter mixed with two tablespoonsful of flour. Stir in the crab, then add one quart of cream or rich milk. Let it come to a good boil; serve hot. Milk must be very fresh and sweet.

POTATO SOUP.

Take one quart of milk, and add as much cold-boiled potatoes mashed through a cullender as will make it the consistency of a thick custard; a large iron spoonful of butter, pepper and salt to taste. If preferred, a little chopped parsley gives a nice flavor. Very simple, but very nice.

BEAN SOUP.

Take any quantity of black beans you wish; soak them over night, then boil them until thoroughly done. Press them through a cullender, retaining the flour only; add thyme, a little butter, pepper, salt, parsley and sweet marjoram. Let it boil well. A short time before serving add forcemeat balls, a sliced lemon, hard-boiled eggs and wine to taste. If you desire, add half a pound of pork, the same of beef, and one or two onions. The proportions are, one pint of beans to one gallon of water.

ASPARAGUS SOUP.

Take four large bunches of asparagus, scrape them nicely, cut off one inch of the tops, lay them in water, chop up the stalks and put them on the fire with a piece of bacon and a large onion cut up, with pepper and salt. Add two quarts of water, boil until the stalks are quite soft, press them through a sieve, strain the water, and put it into the pot. Cut up a chicken with the tops of the asparagus, and boil all until done. Thicken it with flour, butter and milk.

RATCLIFFE ASPARAGUS SOUP. No. 1.

Wash and cut up in small pieces one large bunch of asparagus and one onion. Put on the fire with three pints of water, one pound of any kind of white meat, chicken preferred (veal very good), pepper and salt. Just before serving, add one large spoonful of butter, creamed in same quantity of flour, and one quart of rich milk with the cream in it. Boil up quickly. Strain and serve hot.

A DELICIOUS VEGETABLE SOUP.

What remains of a roast will serve very well for a basis if you have no piece of fresh uncooked meat. Let the vessel in which the soup is to be made be provided with a close cover, and allow yourself plenty of time, so that the soup need only simmer for five or six hours, but never boil hard. As the water evaporates, add more, but always let it be boiling after the first, which should be poured cold over the meat. Add vegetables as you like—for instance a quart of ripe tomatoes scalded and peeled, but if you have not so many, a few will make their impression; a large handful of green corn, cut from the cob; another of young, tender okra, and another of Irish potatoes, peeled and cut small; lastly a handful of small lima beans. Season cautiously with salt and pepper, remembering that more can easily be added at table. In this kind of soup a pod of red pepper, not broken, is preferable to black pepper. Stir the soup frequently, lest the vegetables stick to the bottom and burn. Skim carefully and dish up hot. In the far South, where this soup is made to perfection, they let the vegetables cook so thoroughly as to form an indistinguishable mass, and strain it, so that the flavor is left without the substance.

CORN SOUP.

To each quart of young corn, cut from the cob, allow three pints of water. Boil until the grains are tender. Take two ounces of sweet butter mixed smooth with one tablespoonful of flour. Stir the butter into the soup and let it boil ten or fifteen minutes longer. Just before taking out of the pot, beat up an egg and stir it in with pepper and salt to taste.

OKRA SOUP.

To one gallon of water, cut up two double handsful of okra. Half an hour afterwards add one handful of lima beans, pieces of tender squashes, some fresh meat or a fowl boiled till well done. One hour before you take it up, put in five large tomatoes, or a pint of small ones, peeled and sliced, and when almost done put in a lump of butter rolled in flour. Season with salt and pepper. Do not let it be too thick. Put it on early and let it simmer only.

TOMATO SOUP.

Take seven or eight medium-sized tomatoes, three pints of broth, four or five stalks of parsley, two of thyme, salt, pepper, a teaspoonful of peppercorns, a bay leaf, two onions, three cloves, three or four cloves of garlic, quarter of a pound of rice, one tablespoonful of butter, one ounce of sugar and three slices of bread. Put the tomatoes in boiling water for a few seconds, then take them off, drop them into cold water, and skin them. Then put them in a saucepan and set them on a moderate fire, with the broth, parsley, salt and pepper, and the following spices tied in a linen bag: thyme, peppercorns, bay leaf, onions and cloves. When cooked, the whole is turned into a cullender (except the spices in the bag) and forced through with a potato-masher, except the tomato seeds; then the strained juice and pulp are mixed with the rice; after it has been boiled the butter and sugar are added. The whole is simmered for about half an hour and turned into a soup-dish. While it is simmering the slices of bread are cut into dice and fried with a little butter and put into the soup tureen before pouring the mixture therein. Cover it for two minutes and serve. Excellent.

VEAL SOUP.

Put a knuckle of veal into three quarts of cold water, with a small quantity of salt, and one small tablespoonful of uncooked rice. Boil slowly, hardly above simmering, four hours, when the liquor should be reduced to half the quantity; then remove from the fire. Into the tureen put the yolk of one egg, and stir into it a teacupful of cream, or in hot weather new milk. Add a piece of butter the size of a hickory nut; on this strain the soup boiling hot, stirring all the time. Just at the last beat it well for a minute.

DRIED PEA SOUP.

Take one quart split peas, put them in three quarts of very soft water, with three onions chopped, and a little pepper, and salt; boil them two hours. Mash them well, and pass them through a sieve. Return the liquor to the pot, thicken it with a large piece of butter mixed with a tablespoonful of flour; put in some slices of nice salt pork, and a large teaspoon of celery seed pounded. Boil it until the pork is done, and serve it up. Have some toasted bread cut into dice and fried in butter, and put these in the tureen; then pour the soup over.

CATFISH SOUP.

Take two large or four small catfish that have been caught in deep water, cut off the heads, and skin and clean the bodies. Cut each in three parts, and put them in a pot with one pound lean bacon, one large onion cut up, a handful of parsley chopped small, some pepper and salt; pour in a sufficient quantity of water, and stew them till the fish are quite tender, but not broken. Beat the yolks of four fresh eggs, add to them a large spoonful of butter, two of flour, and half a pint of rich milk. Make all these warm and thicken the soup; take out the bacon, and put some of the fish in the tureen; pour in the soup, and serve it up.

PLAIN OYSTER SOUP.

Strain the oysters. Take the liquor if it is perfectly fresh: if not, throw it away and use one pint of water instead. Add a small onion, three blades of mace, some celery chopped fine, pepper and salt. Celery salt is the best to use if you have it. Let it come to a boil; then add the oysters. When they have come *just* to a boil, add as much cream and milk as will fill the tureen. Thicken it with flour and butter rubbed together, about two spoonsful of flour and three ounces of butter to a tureen full, and three pints large oysters.

CRAB SOUP.

Take one pint water, add a little onion, three or four blades of mace, a little parsley, cayenne pepper and salt. Let them come to a boil. Then add one quart picked crabs, one quart rich milk and cream half and half, one-quarter pound butter rubbed into a tablespoonful flour. Stir all into the crab. Let it come to a good boil and send it hot to the table.

STOCK, OR POT AU FEU.

In ordinary circumstances beef alone, with some vegetables, will make a good broth or stock, in the proportions of two and a half pints of cold clear water to every pound of bones and meat; the bones and meat should be of about equal weight. It makes the soup more delicate to add chicken or veal. Good soup can be made also by using the trimmings of fresh meat, bits of cold cooked beef, or the bones of any meat or fowl. In the choice of vegetables, onions (first fried or sauté and a clove stuck in), parsley and carrots are used, as these will keep. Turnips, parsley and celery should be employed more sparingly. The soup bunch at market is generally a very good distribution of vegetables. Nothing is more simple than the process of making stock or broth. Remember not to let it boil for the first half hour; then it should simmer slowly and steadily for four or five hours. Skim frequently, as the scum, if allowed to remain, gives an unpleasant flavor to the soup. Use salt sparingly, putting in a little at first, and seasoning at the last moment. Many a good soup is spoiled by an injudicious use of seasoning. Some add a few drops of lemon juice to a broth. If wine or catsup is added, it should only be at the last moment. Always strain the soup; small scraps of meat or sediment look slovenly in a soup. About fifteen minutes before dinner each day, you can add what vegetables you like, to vary the soup.

A "NO. 1" OYSTER SOUP.

To make a tureen of rich oyster soup take three pints of good oysters and wash them through two waters, then put them into a stewpan with a pint of water and one small onion (not cut small), six blades of mace, two stalks of celery cut fine. Let it come to a boil, then strain out the oysters. Have ready one quart roast oysters, quarter pound fresh butter, two tablespoonsful of flour rubbed together very smooth. Then add three pints of rich cream and milk half and half. (Morning's milk must be used as older milk will curdle.) Then let it come to a good boil, season with a little cayenne pepper and salt, place the roast oysters in the tureen very hot and pour the soup over them. This is the best oyster soup made.

TURTLE BEAN SOUP.

Soak one quart of beans over night, then drain off the water. Add fresh water and let them boil up once; drain them through a cullender. Then put them into more water with a knuckle of veal, cold beef or mutton (about two pounds of meat). Boil it five hours, then strain the whole through a sieve, mashing the beans so that all but the skins will go through. Put it on again, let it boil, flavor with salt and pepper. Cut a lemon into slices and boil two eggs hard. Chop them up and put them into the tureen with a cup of wine (if you desire it), and then pour in the soup.

CANNED TOMATO SOUP.

Make a strong soup seasoned with an onion, a little parsley, pepper and salt and half a can of tomatoes. Let them boil in the soup for an hour, then strain it and thicken with a little flour and butter. For a large family use a whole can of tomatoes and more seasoning.

CLEAR SOUP.

Take one large beef shank, split the bones, and slightly roast the meat. To this put six quarts of water, one can tomatoes, one bunch celery chopped fine, two or three blades of mace and a bunch of soup herbs. Boil all together for six or eight hours. Then strain it through a cullender and set it aside until next day. After the soup becomes cold be careful to remove all grease. Then set it on the stove until it becomes warm, when clear it with the whites of three eggs well beaten. Before sending to table add a small quantity of red pepper. If it is of too light a color stir in a spoonful of burnt sugar, one teaspoonful of Tournades or Kitchen Bouquet.

SUET DUMPLINGS.

One pound flour, half a pound chopped suet, one teaspoonful salt, quarter of a teaspoonful of pepper. Moisten with water until it is a stiff paste. They may be made into balls and are used in savory pies, hash stews or soups.

SUET DUMPLINGS.

One quart flour, one quart suet, a little salt. Mix with one pint of milk. Roll into balls and drop them in boiling water. They float on top when they are done.

TOMATO BISQUE.

One can of tomatoes. Let them come to a boil, pass through a cullender, then through a fine strainer. Put back in the pot, add a small teaspoon of bread soda to the tomatoes, stir in one tablespoonful of corn starch or cracker powdered very fine, moistened to a paste with a little water, one quart of rich new milk. Let come to a boil, then stir into the tomatoes. Add one teaspoonful of sugar and salt.

BOUILLON NO. 1.

Three pounds of lean beef, two pounds of liver, one gallon cold water. Put on with one can of tomatoes, one pod of red pepper, two carrots, two small turnips, bunch of celery, two onions. All of the vegetables, but tomatoes, to be fried brown. Let it boil well for ten minutes, then put on the back of stove to simmer for five hours. Skim constantly; strain through a tin strainer. Set in a cool place until the grease rises, then skim well and strain through a bag. Put back on the fire with the whites of two eggs well beaten (also shells), two tablespoonsful of browned sugar. Season with Sherry wine and nutmeg. Let boil slowly about twenty-five minutes, strain again through a clean bag. It is then ready for use. One teaspoonful of Tournades or Kitchen Bouquet to color it.

VEAL STOCK.

Two knuckles of veal, five quarts of cold water, one tablespoonful of salt, one onion, one carrot, one bay leaf, one turnip, stalk of celery, sprig of parsley, four cloves, one blade of mace. Wipe the knuckles with a damp towel and have the bones cracked. Put them into a soup kettle with cold water and salt. Place on a moderate fire and bring slowly to a boil; skim. Now simmer for four hours. Clean the vegetables, and add them, and all the ingredients, to the soup, and simmer one hour longer. Strain and it is ready for use.

CREAM OF CELERY SOUP.

Three roots of celery, one quart of milk, one tablespoonful of butter, two tablespoonsful of flour, one pint of water, salt and pepper to taste, one small onion. Wash celery and cut in small pieces. Cover it with water and boil thirty minutes; then press it through a cullender. Put the milk on to boil in a farina boiler; add to it the water and celery that have been pressed through the cullender, also the onion. Rub the butter and flour together and stir into boiling soup, and stir constantly until it thickens. Add salt and pepper.

CORN SOUP.

One pint of grated corn, three pints of boiling water or veal stock, one pint hot milk, three tablespoonsful of butter, two of flour, yolks of two eggs. Put the cobs from which you have removed the corn in the water or stock and boil slowly half an hour. Remove them and put in the corn and boil till very soft, then press it through a sieve. Season and let simmer while you rub the butter and flour together, add these to soup and stir until it thickens. Now add boiling milk, cook one minute, add eggs well beaten and serve immediately.

PEA SOUP.

Shell one-half peck of green peas, wash pods and put in soup kettle with plenty of cold water, boil until tender, drain and throw away pods. Put the peas into this water and boil them three-quarters of an hour. Take out one cup of peas and wash rest through a sieve, and put back into soup kettle. (The soup should now measure about one pint.) Add three pints of rich milk and the cup of peas, let it come to a boil. Rub one-quarter pound of butter and two tablespoonsful of flour to a smooth paste and stir into soup. Add chopped parsley, and salt and pepper to taste.

CARAMEL COLORING FOR SOUP.

Melt half a pound of brown sugar with one teaspoonful of water. Stir steadily over the five until brown. Add slowly one cup of boiling water, one teaspoon of salt. Boil one minute, when cool, bottle and cork tightly. One tablespoonful will color clear soups.

FISH AND SHELLFISH.

TO FRY FISH.

Perch, brook trout, catfish, and all small fish are best fried. They should be cleaned, washed well in cold water and immediately wiped dry inside and out with a clean towel, and then sprinkled with salt. Use oil if convenient, as it is better than drippings or lard. Never use butter as it is apt to burn. See that the oil or lard is boiling hot before putting in the fish.

PLANKED SHAD.

This is the very best way of cooking shad. The plank should be three inches thick, two feet long, and one-half wide, and of well seasoned hickory or oak. Take a fine shad just from the water, scale, split it down the back, clean it, wash well and at once wipe dry. Dredge it with salt and pepper. Place the plank before a clear fire to get *very hot*. Then spread the shad open and nail it skin side next to the hot plank, with four large headed tacks. Put it before the fire with large end down, in a few minutes turn the board so that the other end will be down. To tell when it is done, pierce with a fork; if the flesh is flaky, it is done. Slide the shad on a hot dish, spread with butter and serve at once. White fish caught in the lakes can be cooked in the same manner.

SHAD ROE CROQUETTES.

Two shad roes, one-half pint cream, yolks of two eggs, one-quarter of a grated nutmeg, one teaspoonful of lemon juice, one tablespoonful of butter, two tablespoonsful of flour, one of chopped parsley, salt and black and red pepper. Wash the roes, put in a saucepan of boiling water; add teaspoonful of salt. Cover and simmer slowly fifteen minutes; then take out, remove skin and mash them. Put cream to boil. Rub butter and flour together, add them to boiling cream and stir until very thick. Add yolks, take from fire and add other ingredients; mix well, turn out on a dish to cool. When cold, form into croquettes; dip in beaten egg, then in bread crumbs, and fry in boiling oil or lard. Serve with sauce Hollandaise.

BROILED SHAD.

Scale, wash and score the shad, then mix together one tablespoonful of salt and one of sugar. Rub this over the fish, and let it remain for two hours. Then wash it again, dry it on a towel, and season with cayenne pepper and salt. Heat the gridiron and butter the bars; broil it gradually, and when one side is well browned turn it. When it is done place it on a dish, baste it with butter, and serve hot. The roe of shad is very nice. Wash it carefully, then parboil it in salt water. When done season with salt and cayenne pepper, dredge with flour, and fry in fresh lard till fine brown both sides. Garnish dish with slices of lemon.

BAKED SHAD.

Clean, score and wash the shad; then season well with salt and cayenne pepper. Put it in a pan and make a stuffing of stale bread, a little butter, salt and pepper, and place it inside the fish. Grate bread-crumbs and put on the outside also. Bake in a quick oven. When well done and brown put it on a dish and add the butter in the pan, and if preferred a little tomato catsup or Worcestershire sauce. Garnish the dish with parsley and slices of lemon.

BOILED ROCK.

Scale, empty and clean the inside thoroughly. Take out the gills, and after washing it in cold water dredge over it a little flour. Put it into a fish-kettle of hot salted water, and if of medium size half an hour will boil it. All fish should be wrapped in a white cloth while boiling. When done and well drained fold it in a napkin, and place it on a dish garnished with lemon and parsley. Eat it with drawn butter, fish-sauce or catsup as preferred. All boiled fish are prepared and served in the same manner.

BAKED STURGEON.

The piece six inches from the tail is the best; six or eight pounds makes a good dish. First immerse it in hot water for an hour or two to get rid of the oil. Cut off the gristle. Make incisions in it and fill with stuffing made of bread-crumbs, thyme, marjoram, pepper and salt, and a little butter. Put this dressing over the fish also. Place the sturgeon in a pan with half a pint of water, and bake it slowly nearly an hour.

TO FRY PERCH.

Clean the fish nicely, but do not take out the roes. Dry them on a cloth, sprinkle with salt, and dredge them with flour; lay them separately on a board. When one side is dry turn them, sprinkle salt, and dredge the other side. Be sure the lard boils when you put the fish in, and fry them with great care till they are a yellowish brown, then they are done. Serve with melted butter or anchovy sauce.

CODFISH AND POTATO STEW.

Soak, boil and pick the fish if salt as for fish-balls. If fresh boil and pick into bits. Add an equal quantity of mashed potatoes, and a large tablespoonful of butter and milk, enough to make it soft. Put it into a skillet and add a very little boiling water, just enough to keep it from burning. Turn and toss it constantly until it is smoking hot but not dry. Add pepper and parsley, and serve it up.

FISH A LA CREME.

Boil a rock or trout, or white fish, any good boiling fish, remove all bones, pick the meat carefully, mix with one pint of cream, one-quarter pound butter, two tablespoonsful of flour rubbed in the butter, little red pepper, salt and little parsley. Put it on, cook it until it is thick. Put it in a dish with some beaten crackers and cream. Bake twenty minutes. Serve all in one baking dish or individual dishes.

HALIBUT STEAK.

Wash and wipe the steaks dry. Beat up two or three eggs, and roll out some Boston or other hard crackers until they are very fine. Dip each steak into the beaten egg, then into the bread-crumbs (when you have salted the fish), and fry in hot fat, lard or nice drippings. Another nice way to cook them is to broil them upon a buttered gridiron over a clear fire, first seasoning with salt and pepper. When done, lay in a hot dish, butter well and cover closely.

FRIED SHAD.

Clean, wash and wipe a fine roe-shad. Split it open, cut each side into four pieces, leaving the head off, also the fins and tail. Sprinkle with salt and pepper and dredge with flour. Have ready a frying-pan of boiling hot lard or drippings; put in the fish and fry it brown, turning it over in five minutes to cook the other side. Fry the roe in the same way. Lay the fish in the centre of the dish and the roe around it. Garnish with lemon, parsley or watercresses. Eat with catsup.

CHOWDER.

Take one pound salt pork, cut it into strips, and soak it in hot water five minutes. Put a layer of this in the bottom of a pot. Cut four pounds of cod or sea bass into pieces two inches square, and lay enough of these on the pork to cover it. Follow with a layer of chopped onions, summer savory and pepper, either black or cayenne. Then a layer of split Boston, Butter, or whole Cream crackers which have been soaked in water till moist through, but not ready to break. Above this put another layer of pork, and so on as before till all the materials are used. Let the upper layer be buttered crackers well soaked. Pour in barely enough cold water to cover all. Cover the pot, stew gently for an hour, watching that the water does not sink below the upper layer; if it does, replenish cautiously from the boiling water in the tea-kettle. When the chowder is thoroughly done, take it out with a perforated skimmer and put it into a tureen. Thicken the gravy with one tablespoon of flour and one of butter. Boil it up and pour it over the chowder. Send sliced lemon, pickle and stewed tomatoes to the table with it, as some prefer these added to the chowder.

CLAM CHOWDER.

Fry five or six slices of fat pork crisp, and chop to pieces. Sprinkle some of the-e in the bottom of a pot, and lay upon them a stratum of clams. Sprinkle with red or black pepper and salt, and scatter over all plenty of bits of butter. Now add a layer of chopped onions, then one of small crackers split and moistened in warm milk. On these pour a little of the hot fat left from the pork, and continue the layers as before. When the pot is nearly full cover with water and stew slowly (the pot closely covered) for three-quarters of an hour. Drain off all the liquor that flows freely, and when the chowder is in the tureen return the gravy to the pot.

Thicken with flour or pounded crackers. Add a glass of wine, some catsup and spiced sauce; boil up and pour it over the chowder in the tureen.

OYSTER FRITTERS.

Drain off the liquor, and to one cupful add the same of milk, three eggs, a little salt and flour enough for a thin batter. Chop the oysters and stir them in the batter. Put in the frying-pan a few spoonsful of lard, or lard and butter mixed. When very hot drop the oyster-batter in by the tablespoonful. Try one spoonful to see that the lard is hot enough and the fritter the right size and consistency. When done to a light brown take them out quickly and send to table hot. Some fry the oyster whole enveloped in batter, having one in each fritter. In this case make the batter thicker than you do in using the chopped oysters.

HOW TO BROIL OYSTERS.

Put the oysters in a cullender and drain all the water from them, then put them in a napkin and wipe them dry. A moderate quantity of cayenne pepper may be put on them if desired. Salt gently, and dip each individual oyster in melted butter. Place them in a double gridiron, the bars of which should be greased to prevent them from sticking. Broil over a brisk fire, basting them with the melted butter while cooking. Serve on a hot dish. Pepper and salt to taste.

STEWED OYSTERS.

Separate the oysters from the liquor. Put the liquor in a stew-pan and add one pint water, a wineglass of cream, a lump of butter the size of an egg, pepper, salt and breadcrumbs to taste. Let them boil together, then add oysters and cook till thoroughly heated.

SCALLOPED OYSTERS.

Take the oysters from the liquor, place some in a baking dish or pan, grate bread-crumbs highly seasoned with pepper and salt, and a few celery seed over them, with some bits of butter. Add another layer of oysters and the seasoning. Then pour over them a glass of wine and another layer of grated bread. Bake till hot through.

OYSTER SAUCE FOR FOWLS.

Plump the oysters for a moment or two over the fire. Then take them out and stir some flour and butter mixed into the liquor; salt and pepper to taste. When it has boiled put in the oysters and add a glass of wine.

PICKLED OYSTERS.

Wash the oysters, then drain them. Put them in a kettle on the fire and cover them with cold water. Take off the scum as it rises, and when they commence boiling throw in to every gallon of oysters one tablespoonful each of black-grain pepper and allspice, one-half the quantity of blade mace. When cold, add salt and vinegar to taste.

PANNED OYSTERS.

Take fifty large oysters, remove every particle of shell which may adhere to them; put them into a cullender, and pour over a little water to rinse them. After letting them drain, put them into a stew-pan with quarter pound of butter, salt, black and red pepper to taste. Put them over a clear fire and stir while cooking. As soon as they commence to shrink, take them from the fire and send to table hot *in a heated* covered dish.

CRAB CAKES FOR BREAKFAST. (Very nice.)

Take the crab after it is picked and season it high with red pepper and salt. Then add butter, and make them in round cakes, using a little flour to hold them together. Then dip them in egg and cracker beaten fine. Fry in hot butter or lard.

BOILED CRABS.

Put the crabs in a large kettle with about one quart hot salted water to a kettle full of crabs and let them steam twenty minutes. Put a cover over the kettle and on it a weight, in order that the steam may not escape. Then take them out, wipe them clean, and if the backs can be easily removed, they are done; if not, steam them longer. Then take off the small claws, the backs, and all between the backs and the inner shell, and throw them away. The large claws may be cracked and sent to the table with the rest of the crab when picked.

SOFT CRABS.

Take off the small claws, wash, wipe and open the crabs, and after removing the spongy part and the sand-bag, season in and outside with salt and pepper. Then close them and fry in fresh butter a light brown on both sides.

FRICASSEED OYSTERS.

Drain one quart of oysters. Heat and strain the liquor, thickening it with corn starch to the consistency of drawn butter. After it has boiled up once add the oysters, and cook them for three minutes. Then take them off the fire, add the juice of half a lemon, a little nutmeg, a lump of butter the size of an egg, and the yolk of one egg stirred in last of all. Eat it while hot.

FISH AND SHELLFISH.

FRICASSEED OYSTERS.

Strain one and a half quarts of oysters, and boil the liquor with a little parsley, and, if you like, a little onion, pepper and salt. Put in the oysters and let them come to a boil. Mix one tablespoonful of butter, with half a spoonful of flour, and stir it in to thicken it. Boil half a pint of milk with the yolk of one or two raw eggs. Put the milk when boiled into the tureen and pour the oysters in.

PICKLED OYSTERS.

Scald the oysters in their own liquor until plump. Then take them out, lay them on a dish, and cover with a cloth two or three double. Strain the liquor through a coarse cloth, then boil it. Season with whole black pepper, salt and a few pieces of mace. When cold add a glass of wine and one of vinegar to every gallon of liquor. Then add the oysters.

FRIED OYSTERS.

Take fine large oysters and drain them well. To one quart have ready three eggs well beaten and seasoned with salt and pepper. Dip the oysters in the eggs, then in pounded cracker until well covered. Have the lard boiling, put in the oysters and be careful not to burn them. Serve on a flat dish. Garnish with slices of lemon. Do not pound cracker too fine.

DEVILLED CRABS.

Have the crabs nicely picked and see that none of the shell is left in them. Then chop them fine and to two dozen crabs, allow one pound of butter, a little cayenne pepper and salt. Have the shells clean and nice, and add a small lump of butter to each one. Fill them with the seasoned crabs, and sprinkle them with a little powdered cracker. Put them in the oven and let them remain until they are a light brown. They may be eaten either hot or cold.

SOFT SHELL CRABS.

Soft crabs are nothing more than hard crabs after shedding their shells. They merely get too large for their shells and slip out. Yet they taste very differently. In twenty-four hours they are hard again; this accounts for the short supply.

TO COOK SOFT SHELL CRABS.

Take the shell and remove all the spongy substance on both sides; remove the *apron* or a small loose shell rising to a point in the middle of the under shell; wash them nicely. I think it safest and best to remove all the fat as it is so delicate it sours in cooking. Fry in butter, adding little salt and cayenne pepper. I prefer them without the backs, but most people do not.

CRAB CROQUETTES.

Pick the meat carefully and chop fine, leaving out the fat. Season with cayenne pepper and salt, and to a dozen croquettes a large iron spoon of butter, a little rich cream; add two well-beaten eggs. Mix all up. Make in forms of croquettes and dip in cracker and egg, and boil in very hot lard. Everything is better boiled than fried in lard. It is best to use a wire frying-basket, so they will not break up.

VEGETABLES.

A KITCHEN TIME-TABLE.
A Schedule Useful in Cooking Summer Vegetables.

Early peas will boil in half or three-quarters of an hour. They are best put on with cold water; add salt when nearly done.

String beans require two hours or more. The first water should always be poured off.

Lima beans will cook in three-quarters of an hour. Put on to cook in hot water.

Asparagus will boil in three-quarters of an hour. Use cold water.

Spinach will boil in fifteen minutes. Use hot water.

Summer beets will boil in one hour. Use hot water.

Winter beets will require three hours. Use hot water.

Corn will boil in twenty minutes. Use hot water.

Onions will boil in one and a half hours. Use hot water.

New potatoes will boil in one-half hour. Use boiling water.

Dried corn must be soaked over night. Allow to cook one hour.

Summer squash is better steamed, as putting it in water makes it too watery. Cook three-quarters of an hour.

Turnips require a long time to cook. If cut thin, they will cook in an hour and a quarter; but if only cut in halves, it will take two hours and a half.

FRENCH WAY OF DRESSING LIMA BEANS.

Boil the beans in the usual way, then pour the water off (not drain dry) and add butter, pepper and salt sufficient to

VEGETABLES.

season them; put them on coals and stew them. Just before they are dished, beat the yolk of an egg very light and stir it in the beans. Do not put them on the fire after the egg is added.

BOILED PEAS.

They should be fresh when cooked and boiled in just enough water to cover them, which should be salted and boiling when the peas are put in. Let them cook only twenty minutes, unless old, and keep the vessel uncovered. Drain off all the water. Pour melted butter over them.

TO BAKE SALSIFY.

Boil the salsify until the skin comes off easily; then slice and put in a baking-dish a layer of sliced salsify and one of bread-crumbs, with pepper and salt, with a thin covering of butter. Repeat the layers until the dish is filled, finishing with bread-crumbs. Then pour in as much milk as the dish will hold, and a good spoonful of butter, put in oven and bake brown. It will be done in half an hour.

CORN FRITTERS.

Grate six ears of corn and mix with two eggs, one spoonful butter, pepper and salt to taste, one tablespoon flour. Fry brown.

CURLED SAVOY CABBAGE COOKED LIKE CAULIFLOWER.

Take hard heads, quarter them, put in to boil with a little salt and a pinch of soda in the water, say half teaspoonful. Let it boil until tender. Drain off and serve with drawn butter.

TO BOIL RICE DRY.

Pick the rice clean and wash it in two cold waters, not draining off the last water until ready to put the rice on the fire. Prepare a saucepan of water with a little salt in it. When it boils sprinkle in the rice. Boil it hard twenty minutes, keeping it covered. Then take it from the fire, pour off the water, and then set the saucepan on the back of the range with the lid off, while the rest of the dinner is being dished, so as to allow the rice time to dry and the grains to separate. Rice, if properly cooked, should be soft and white and each grain should stand alone.

HINTS FOR ROASTING POTATOES.

When you think the potatoes are done take them from the stove, and beat them gently so as to let the steam out, then return them to the oven and let them remain till they are needed. In this way they can be kept hot without injury to the potato.

CORN PUDDING.

Scrape the substance out of twelve ears of tender green corn. (It is better scraped than grated as you do not get the husky particles which you cannot avoid with a grater.) Add the yolks and whites of four eggs beaten separately, one teaspoonful of sugar, the same of flour mixed in a tablespoonful of butter, a small quantity of salt and pepper and one pint of milk. Bake about half an hour or three-quarters.

SPINACH.

It should be cooked so as to retain its bright green color, and not sent to table, as it so often is, of a dull brown or olive color. In order to retain its fresh appearance do not cover the vessel while it is cooking. Boil until tender, drain in a cullender, chop fine, add a lump of butter, a teacupful of rich cream, a teaspoonful of salt and a little black pepper. Serve it hot covered with slices of hard-boiled eggs.

BAKED TOMATOES (whole).

Cut nice, ripe, smooth fruit in two, lay them in a dripping pan in which a small piece of butter has been melted, placing the skin side down. Set over a brisk fire. When the under side is brown take them off the fire. Place them in an earthen baking dish, in which place them skin side down one at a time, being careful not to break them. In each one put a small piece of butter, a little salt and pepper and dredge a small portion of flour over them all. Place in a slow oven and bake them three hours. When done, carefully place one at a time on the dish in which they are to be served, and send them hot to table. This is excellent.

STEWED TOMATOES.

Scald and skin the tomatoes (unless canned), and place them in a stewpan without water. Simmer for half an hour. Add pepper, salt, a large piece of butter, a spoonful of white sugar and very little bread finely grated. Boil up once and serve hot.

BOSTON BAKED BEANS.

Put one and a half pints of medium-sized navy beans into a quart bean pot, fill it with water and let it stand overnight. In the morning pour off the water and cover the beans with fresh water, in which mix one tablespoonful of molasses. Put a quarter pound of pickled pork in the centre, leaving a quarter inch of pork above the beans. Bake them eight hours with a steady fire, and without stirring the beans add a cupful of water every hour but the last two. Earthen pots with narrow mouths are made expressly for baking beans. Cooking them in this manner, without first boiling them, renders each bean perfectly whole, and at the same time thoroughly cooked. When done place the pork in the centre of a dish with the beans around it.

POTATOES BAKED WITH BEEF.

Pare potatoes of equal size and put them in the oven in the same pan in which the beef is baked. Every time the beef is basted baste the potatoes also. Serve them around the beef.

SARATOGA POTATOES.

Have a little plane or cabbage cutter. Take two or three fine large potatoes and pare them. Cut them by rubbing them over the plane into slices as thin or thinner than a wafer. Put them for a few moments in ice water to become chilled. Then test some boiling lard to see if it is of the proper temperature. The slices must color quickly, but the fat must not be so hot as to turn them dark. Have ready some salt and a dish for the potatoes; also a tin plate and a perforated ladle. Throw the slices of cold potato separately into the hot lard; keep them separated till they are of a delicate yellow color. Then skim them out on the tin plate, sprinkle them with salt and put them in the dish. Only fry five or six slices at a time until all are cooked. Two potatoes will make a large dishful.

BEETS.

If they are winter beets soak them overnight; in any case be very careful not to prick or cut the skin before boiling, as they will then lose their color. Put them into boiling water and boil until tender. If they are served hot pour a little melted butter, pepper and salt over them. They are often served cold cut into slices, with vinegar over them, or cut into dice and mixed with other cold vegetables for a winter salad.

MACARONI WITH CHEESE.

Do not wash the macaroni. Throw it, broken into pieces of two or three inches, into boiling, well-salted water. Stir or shake it frequently to prevent its adhering to the bottom of the stewpan. The moment it is quite tender pour it into a cullender and shake off all the water. In the mean time melt about two ounces of butter to a half pound of macaroni, and grate a handful of cheese. When the macaroni is well drained, place a little of it in the bottom of the dish in which it is to be served. Pour over it some of the melted butter, and sprinkle over that a little grated cheese. Continue alternate layers of the three ingredients until all the macaroni is in, placing butter and cheese on top. Put the dish in the oven and let it remain three or four minutes, or long enough for the macaroni to soak the butter and cheese. Then take it out, brown the top with a salamander or hot kitchen shovel, and it is ready to serve. It requires about twenty minutes to boil macaroni. You should try to have it done just the moment of serving, otherwise the cheese will cool and harden.

TO COOK CRANBERRIES.

To one quart cranberries put one teacup of water, and place them on the fire. Cook ten minutes, then add two heaping cupsful of sugar, and cook about ten minutes more, stirring often. Pour them into a bowl or mould, then when cold they can be removed as a jelly. The berries will seem very dry before the sugar is added, but if more water is used they will not jelly. This is an accompaniment to roast turkey.

TO FRY EGG-PLANTS.

Cut the egg-plant early in the morning, about three-quarters of an inch thick, and sprinkle with salt. Put a weight on them; let them stand for some hours. Then have ready eggs beaten up and seasoned high. Dip the egg-plant in the egg, then the cracker dust, and fry in boiling lard. Very fine.

FRIED PARSNIPS.

Scrape and wash them; let them boil until very tender. Press them in a cullender, mash them very fine, season them with pepper and salt, and dredge a little flour over them. Then make them into cakes and fry a light brown.

CYMLINGS.

Cut them in quarters, wash and boil them in salted water until tender. When done put them into a cullender and press out all the water. While warm add a small piece of butter, and season with a little more salt and cream. Put them in a covered dish, and before sending to table sprinkle a little black pepper. These are very nice fried like egg-plant.

FRIED EGG-PLANT.

Cut them in slices about half an inch thick, cover them with salt, and put them in a cullender to let them drain. When well drained wipe them, season them with pepper and salt, dredge a little flour over each, and put them in a pan with some hot butter. Fry them slowly till they are soft and dark brown on both sides. Serve very hot.

CAULIFLOWER.

Choose one that is white. Take off the outside leaves and put it in boiling water with some salt. Skim and boil it slowly, when done take it up in a cullender and press out the water. Put it in a vegetable dish, cover with drawn butter and serve. Boiled cabbage is cooked in a similar manner. The secret of keeping the smell of boiled cabbage from spreading through the house is to put a piece of stale bread in a piece of muslin and place it in the pot with the cabbage, keeping the pot well covered. It can be dressed simply with salt and butter.

BAKED CABBAGE.

Boil in salt and water until tender; then cut up fine in a baking dish, adding butter, pepper and salt, and a little cream and stale bread crumbs or crackers beaten in the top. A very nice dish.

TURNIPS.

Pare and wash them, boil until tender, then take them up in a cullender, press out all the water, put them in a pan, and mash them very fine. Season with salt, butter and a little cream. If they are not sweet add one teaspoonful white sugar. When ready to serve sprinkle a little black pepper over them.

HOT SLAW.

Cut up the cabbage, but not so fine as for cold slaw. Put it in a pan, sprinkle a little salt over it, and half a gill of water. Set it on the stove and cover it close. It must cook one hour. When quite tender put in two ounces of butter and as much vinegar as will make it sufficiently sour. Serve it hot.

GREEN CORN PUDDING.

Grate the corn from twelve large ears of corn, add one quart milk, six eggs, two tablespoonsful melted butter, and a little salt. Bake slowly, and let it brown on top. Beat the eggs separately, mix the corn and yolks together, and stir hard; then add the butter and then the milk slowly. Last of all put in the whites.

CORN FRITTERS.

Allow one egg and a half to every cup of grated corn, and one tablespoonful of cream or milk. Beat eggs very light, add salt to taste, one and a half tablespoons melted butter to every pint of corn. Stir in the milk, and thicken it with a little flour, just enough to hold them together. Add pepper. Allow one tablespoonful of the mixture to every two eggs. Test it a little at first to see if it is right. Fry in cakes in hot lard.

TO BOIL POTATOES.

Let them lie in cold water after being washed. Then pour boiling water over them, as soon as they appear mealy. Pour water off; let them stand a few moments on the back of the stove to dry. Then mash through a potato strainer or serve whole.

BAKED EGG-PLANT.

Boil the egg-plant, pare it and mash it up with a little butter, pepper, bread-crumbs, a small portion of boiled onion and nutmeg if you like. Bake in a shallow dish a few minutes, adding plenty of butter, half a cup of cream or rich milk.

TO SCALLOP TOMATOES.

Peel off the skin from large, full-ripe tomatoes, put a layer in the bottom of a deep dish, and cover it well with grated bread-crumbs. Add pepper and salt and some bits of butter. Put alternate layers of each till the dish is full, having the top layer of crumbs and butter. Bake it a nice brown.

POTATO FRITTERS.

Grate six cold boiled potatoes, add to them one pint of cream or new milk, flour enough to make as stiff as other fritters, the yolks of three or four eggs, then the beaten whites and a little salt. Fry in hot lard or butter. These are delicious.

GREEN CORN (Boiled).

Green corn is too often spoiled by being left too long in the water. Very young corn is cooked in ten minutes, and any that is not tender in twenty minutes is too hard to be eaten at all. Husk the corn, remove the silk, and cut out all imperfect places. Put the ears into an iron pot, fill it with boiling water, cover the pot closely, and let it boil for fifteen minutes. Corn is delicious if boiled in the inside husk, removing it before serving. It can be loosened to take out the silk and drawn up again.

MACARONI MILANESE.

Throw the macaroni into boiling water, allowing it plenty of room for swelling. Add some salt and let it boil for twenty-five minutes. Drain it in a cullender, then put it into a deep earthenware baking dish, in successive layers of macaroni and grated cheese. A little cayenne pepper greatly improves the flavor. Lay on the top slices of fresh butter, a quarter pound being enough for a large dishful. Pour over it enough unskimmed morning's milk to cover the whole, and bake in a regularly heated oven for fifteen or twenty minutes. Serve up quickly, and do not let it become dry by exposure to too intense a heat.

STEWED POTATOES.

Peal and slice the potatoes. Put them into a saucepan, cover with boiling water, and boil until tender; then pour off the water. Roll a large piece of butter in flour and beat it in half a pint of hot milk till smooth. Season with pepper and salt and boil. When boiling, put in the potatoes; stew together for five minutes and serve very hot.

FRIED SALSIFY.

Stew the salsify as usual till very tender, then mash it very fine. Beat up an egg, add one teacupful of milk, a little flour, butter and seasoning of pepper and salt. Make into cakes and fry in boiling lard till light brown.

STEWED SALSIFY.

Wash the roots and scrape off their skins, throwing them as you do so in cold water immediately, otherwise they will turn dark. Then cut transversely into little bits, throw them into fresh water; add a little salt and stew in a covered vessel until tender. Pour off the water; add a small lump of butter, a little pepper and a gill of sweet cream.

BROILED TOMATOES.

Take nice firm tomatoes, slice them about half an inch thick, dip them in corn meal or cracker dust. Season them high with pepper and salt, then fry them in butter. When brown, take them out and lay them on a covered dish. Then take half a teacup of sweet cream and stir it in the spider where the tomatoes were cooked. Stir it well and let it get thoroughly hot, and serve in the covered dish.

STUFFED TOMATOES.

Take good-sized ripe tomatoes. Make a hole in the centre and fill with stale bread-crumbs, butter, pepper and salt. Put it in the stove and bake until done. Serve on a flat dish.

SWEET POTATOES.

Put them in a steamer and let them remain until done, and the skins can be easily removed; then slice them lengthwise, and put them in a baking dish with plenty of butter. Sprinkle a little brown sugar all through them; add a little water in the bottom of the dish and put it in to bake until brown. Serve it in the dish in which it is baked.

STEWED POTATOES (for Breakfast).

Pare, quarter and soak them in cold water for half an hour. Stew them in enough cold salted water to cover them. Before taking them up, and when they are breaking to pieces, drain off half the water and put in a cupful of milk. Boil it three minutes, stirring well; put in a lump of butter the size of an egg, a little salt and a pinch of pepper. Boil up well and put it in a covered dish. Add parsley and onion if one likes it.

STEWED ONIONS.

Top, tail and skin them, lay them in cold water for half an hour or more, then put them in a saucepan with hot water enough to cover them. When half done throw off all the water except about a teacupful. Add a like quantity of milk, a great spoonful of butter, and pepper and salt to taste. Stew gently until tender, then turn into a deep dish. If the onions are strong and large boil them in three waters, throwing away all of the first and second, and keeping a little of the third to mix with the milk.

HOMINY CROQUETTES.

To a cupful of cold boiled hominy add a tablespoon of melted butter, and stir hard, moistening by degrees with a cupful of milk, beating to a soft light paste. Put in a teaspoon of white sugar, and last, a well-beaten egg. Roll into oval balls with floured hands, dip in beaten egg, then cracker-crumbs, and fry in hot lard.

RICE CROQUETTES.

Half a cup of rice, one pint of milk, two tablespoons of sugar, three eggs, a little grated lemon peel, one tablespoon of melted butter and a saltspoon of salt. Soak the rice for three hours in warm water enough to cover it. Drain almost dry and pour in the milk. Stew in one saucepan set in another of hot water, till the rice is very tender. Add the sugar, butter and salt, and simmer ten minutes. Whisk the eggs to a froth, and add them cautiously, taking the saucepan from the fire while you whip them in. Return it to the stove and stir while thickening, not allowing them to boil. Remove the pan and add the lemon peel, then turn it out upon a well-greased dish to cool. When cold and stiff roll with floured hands into shape, dip in beaten egg, then cracker-crumbs, and fry in hot lard.

SOUTHERN WAY OF COOKING RICE DRY.

Pick over the rice, rinse in cold water until perfectly clean, then put in a pot of boiling water. Allow one quart of water to less than a teacup of rice, boil hard seventeen minutes, drain off the water very close, let it steam with the lid off fifteen minutes. When carefully done each grain will be separate.

STEWED MACARONI.

Break the macaroni into inch lengths; stew twenty minutes, or till tender. Have the following sauce ready: Cut half a pound of beef into strips, and stew half an hour in cold water. Then add a minced onion and one pint tomatoes, peeled and sliced. Boil an hour and strain through a cullender after taking out the meat. The sauce should be well boiled down by this time. One pint is sufficient for a large dish of macaroni. Return the liquid to the saucepan; add a large piece of butter, pepper and salt, and stew till ready to dish the macaroni. Drain this well; sprinkle lightly with salt and heap it in a dish. Pour the tomato sauce over it. Cover and let it stand in a warm place ten minutes before sending to table. Send grated cheese around with it.

BAKED CYMLINGS.

Boil the cymlings until tender; then rub them through the cullender. Then season with butter, cream and pepper and salt, and bake in a baking dish. Very nice.

BOILED RICE, SAVANNAH STYLE.

Take one pound of rice, pick it clean, take out all dark grains. Put on the fire in a porcelain-lined pot, three quarts of water with two teaspoonsful of salt; let the water come to a boil. Now wash the rice in three waters. The reason for this is to get rid of the pulverized rice-flour which adheres to the grains. This is a necessity; otherwise the rice never will be dry. Throw the rice in water when it is at full boil. Let the rice boil for twenty minutes rapidly. Put the cover on and drain the water entirely off; cover the pot, shake well, and put on the back of the stove, where it is not too hot, for fifteen minutes. Shake the rice into the dish you wish it served; never use a spoon. Rice should never be glutinous.

BROILED MUSHROOMS.

Take fresh mushrooms, wash and skin them carefully; then put them on a broiler over a hot fire, and when done, pour melted butter and pepper and salt. Serve very hot.

HASHED BROWN POTATOES.

Boil potatoes half-done, cut in pieces size of dice; then put on to stew with cream, butter, pepper and salt, a little onion juice and parsley. Then put in a dish and brown over. Serve hot.

EGGS.

OMELET.

Take six eggs, beat them separately, add a little parsley chopped fine (some small pieces of ham also if desired). Fry in butter on one side only. Put the dish on the omelet, and turn the pan over so as not to break it. Serve immediately.

EGG OMELET.

Six eggs, one teacup of milk, one tablespoonful of butter, and one teaspoonful of flour, one teaspoonful of salt. Beat the whites and yolks separately, warm the milk enough to melt the butter, add this to the yolks. Make the flour into a paste with a little of the milk. Add the whites last. Either bake in a deep dish or in shallow pans, and double it over after it browns.

OMELET (with Bread-crumbs).

Soak a teacupful of bread-crumbs overnight in a cup of new milk. Beat separately the yolks and whites of three eggs. Mix the yolks with the bread and milk, stir in the whites, add salt and make as usual.

DEVILLED EGGS.

Boil hard nine eggs, cut them lengthwise; take out all the yolks; mash it, add cupful of cream, tablespoonful of melted butter, little onion chopped fine or celery seed if you don't like onion, a little parsley chopped fine, pepper and salt. Mix all together, refill the whites with the mixture, add a little beaten cracker. Set in the stove in a pan with a little water to brown.

OMELET (with Parsley).

Beat two eggs, yolks and whites together, until very light. Mix one teaspoonful of corn starch, with a scant half teacupful of milk. When well stirred and smooth pour this over the eggs, and beat all well together for a few minutes; add a little chopped parsley.

BAKED EGGS.

Set in the oven until quite hot, a common white dish large enough to hold the number of eggs to be cooked, allowing plenty of room for each. Melt in it a small piece of butter, and breaking the eggs carefully in a saucer, one at a time, slip them into the hot dish. Sprinkle over them a small quantity of salt and pepper, and allow them to cook four or five minutes. Add a tablespoonful of cream for every two eggs when the eggs are first slipped in the dish.

DROPPED EGGS.

Break the eggs in a saucer one at a time, being careful to keep the yolk from breaking. Have ready in a dripping-pan some boiling water or milk. Into this slide the eggs, letting them cook until set. Take them up in a skimmer, put them on a dish, season with butter, pepper and salt, and if preferred put them on buttered toast.

EGG TOAST.

Take two eggs, one and a half cups milk, and flour enough for a stiff batter. Cut stale bread thin, dip in the batter, and fry brown in butter.

OMELET SOUFFLÉE.

Three tablespoonsful of sugar, beaten yolks of five eggs mixed together, flavored with teaspoonful of vanilla, and a very little salt; beat whites of four eggs stiff, and mix all together. Bake for ten minutes and eat while hot.

OMELET SOUFFLÉE.

Separate the yolks of twelve eggs from the whites. Put the yolks of five in a deep dish with one-half pound sugar, one teaspoonful of vanilla; beat all together for ten minutes. Put the whites of your eggs in a large bowl, and beat them very stiff; then mix them with your yolks and sugar. Butter a dish into which pour the above. Put it in a moderate oven, about twelve minutes; sprinkle sugar on top and serve immediately.

BOILED EGGS.

To try the freshness of eggs, put them into cold water; those that sink are the best. Always let the water boil before putting the eggs in. Three minutes will boil them soft. In four minutes the whites will be completely done, and in eight they will be all hard boiled.

BREAKFAST DISH OF EGGS.

Boil six eggs hard, chop them up in a dish; add bread-crumbs, a good-sized lump of butter, pepper and salt; pour over it half a pint of boiled milk and bake in the dish.

ANOTHER NICE DISH OF EGGS.

Take six raw eggs. Beat the whites and yolks separately very light; then mix them together. Add a teacup of rich milk (cream is better), a lump of butter, pepper and salt and a little parsley cut fine. Put them in a baking dish. Now place a spider on top of the stove. Put sufficient hot water in it to cook the eggs. Stir it all the time. As soon as they are thick send at once to the table, as they are not good if allowed to stand.

FRIED EGGS.

Melt some butter in a frying-pan, and when it hisses drop in the eggs carefully. Fry three minutes. Dust them with pepper and salt, and put them on a hot dish.

BREADED EGGS.

Boil them hard and cut them in round thick slices. Sprinkle with pepper and salt; dip each in beaten egg, then in fine bread-crumbs or powdered cracker, and fry in nice dripping or butter hissing hot. Drain off every drop of grease, and serve on a hot dish with sauce like that for fricasseed eggs, poured over them.

OMELET WITH CHIPPED BEEF. (Very nice.)

Beat the yolks and whites of eight eggs separately. Put two and a half tablespoonsful of smoked beef chipped fine in a frying pan, with two tablespoonsful of butter. Let them cook a few moments; season the eggs with pepper and salt; mix together. Pour in the beef; turn them as plain omelet. When brown, serve hot, garnished with parsley.

PLAIN OMELET.

Beat six eggs very light, the whites to a stiff froth, and the yolks to a smooth batter. To the latter, add a small cup of milk, pepper and salt, and lastly the whites, lightly stirred in. Have ready in a hot frying-pan a good lump of butter. When it hisses, pour in the mixture gently and set over a clear fire. Cook not more than ten minutes. Do not stir it, but as the eggs "set" slip a broad blade knife under the omelet, to keep it from burning. The instant hiss of the butter as it flows to the hottest part of the pan, will prove the wisdom of this precaution. If the oven is hot, set the frying-pan in it when the middle of the omelet is set. When done, turn it over on a dish. Eat immediately. I know by experience that these directions are worthy of note.

CHEESE OMELET, NO. 1.

One cup of bread-crumbs, one cup of grated cheese, two cups of milk, pinch of salt, little red pepper, two eggs beaten light, and added last. Bake five or six minutes in a quick oven.

PLAIN OMELET. (Very fine.)

Six eggs, whites and yolks beaten very light separately, half pint sweet milk, six teaspoonsful of corn starch, dissolved in milk very smoothly, one teaspoon of baking powder, salt and pepper, add the whites last, cook in butter. When nicely browned, roll over on a hot dish. Serve at once.

RUM OMELET.

Prepare a nice plain omelet, adding a little sugar; take half teacup of good rum, light it, and pour it while burning over the omelet. Serve at once.

EGG TIMBALES.

Six eggs, one gill of milk, salt and pepper to taste, two tablespoonsful of grated cheese; beat the eggs well. Add the milk and seasoning. Stir in the cheese. Pour into a well greased tin pan. Set them in a pan of hot water and bake. When the eggs look firm, turn them out on a flat dish, and pour white sauce over them.

OMELET SOUFFLÉE.

Whites of six eggs, yolks of three, juice of half lemon, three tablespoonsful powdered sugar. Grease the dish about one quarter size with butter; have the oven hot. Beat the whites to a stiff froth; beat the yolks separately. Add them to the whites, then the sugar and lemon. Stir carefully, and heap into the baking dish; dredge with powdered sugar and put in the oven. Bake about fifteen minutes until light brown. Serve at once. It may be baked in paper cases.

POACHED EGGS.

Break as many eggs as you wish to use, one at a time, and drop carefully into a spider filled with boiling water. When the whites of the eggs are well set, slip a spoon carefully under and take out, laying each egg on a piece of buttered toast. Put small piece of butter on each egg, and little salt and pepper.

EGG CUTLETS FOR SUMMER.

Egg cutlets are a new and delicious dainty for summer luncheons, and are as palatable as, while much less expensive than, sweetbreads or other delicate meat dishes. To make from four to six cutlets, requires three hard-boiled eggs, one cupful of milk, one tablespoonful of chopped parsley, one tablespoonful of butter and two tablespoonsful of flour. Cover the eggs with boiling water, and simmer them half an hour in a covered saucepan. Heat the milk in a double boiler, rub together the butter and flour, add to the milk, and stir until you have a thick, smooth mixture; season with one-half teaspoonful of onion juice and the parsley. Shell the eggs, cut them or chop them fine, and mix well with the sauce. Turn on a buttered platter and set in the ice-box until very cold. Then flour your hands and your molding-board, take a small quantity of the mixture in your hands, and mold it into the shape of a small cutlet about an inch thick. When ready to fry, the cutlets are to be coated with egg, and then with fine dry bread-crumbs, laid a few at a time in the frying basket and browned in boiling fat. The cutlets are served with a white sauce, garnished with green peas. To make the sauce, blend a tablespoonful of butter, the same quantity of flour, and a cupful of milk or cream, and when smooth season with a half teaspoonful of salt, a dash of white pepper and a half cupful of cooked green peas. Pour the sauce around, not over, the cutlets.

SAUCES AND DRESSINGS FOR SALADS.

BROWN CELERY SAUCE.

Stew the celery in a little water, then add mace, nutmeg, pepper, salt, a piece of butter rolled in flour, a glass of red wine, one spoonful of catsup or of Worcestershire sauce, half a pint good gravy. Boil all these together and pour them into the dish.

FOR ROASTED OR BOILED FOWL.

Take a large bunch of celery, wash it very clean, cut it in thin bits, and boil slowly in a little water until it is tender. Then add some beaten mace, nutmeg, pepper and salt, a good piece of butter rolled in flour. Boil all and pour in the dish. If preferred, add half pint cream, one glass white wine, and a spoonful of Worcestershire sauce.

ONION SAUCE FOR MUTTON.

Boil onions in milk and water, changing the water once or twice. Afterwards chop them fine; add pepper and salt and stew until done.

CHICKEN SAUCE.

Put a piece of butter the size of an egg into a bright saucepan, and when it bubbles add a teaspoonful of flour. Cook it and then add a little less than a pint of boiling water. When smooth take it from the fire; add the beaten yolks of two or three eggs, a few drops of lemon juice, pepper and salt.

SAUCE FOR ROAST VENISON.

Currant jelly made hot and a little lemon juice squeezed in it.

MAITRE D'HOTEL BUTTER.

This may be used for beefsteak, broiled meat or fish. Mix butter the size of an egg, the juice of half a lemon, and two or three sprigs of sparsley chopped very fine, pepper and salt all together. Spread this over any broiled meat or fish when hot. Then put the dish into the oven a few moments, to allow the butter to penetrate the meat.

MINT SAUCE.

Put four tablespoonsful of chopped mint, two tablespoonsful of sugar, and one quarter pint of vinegar into the sauce-boat. Let it remain an hour or two before dinner that the vinegar may be impregnated with the mint. Used for roast lamb.

TOMATO SAUCE.

Stew six tomatoes half an hour, with two cloves, a sprig of parsley, pepper and salt. Press this through a sieve. Put a little butter into a saucepan over the fire, and when it bubbles, add a heaping teaspoonful of flour. Mix and cook it well, then add the tomato pulp, stirring until it is smooth. Three or four tablespoonsful of stock will make a great improvement, and some add a few slices of onion at first.

SAUCE HOLLANDAISE.

Pour four tablespoonsful of good vinegar into a small stew-pan, and add some peppercorns and salt. Let this boil till reduced one-half; let it cool, then add to it the well-beaten yolks of four or five eggs, also four ounces of butter, more salt if necessary, and a very little nutmeg. Set the stew-pan on a very slow fire, and stir the liquid till about as thick as cream, then remove it immediately. Now put this stew-pan into another pan containing a little warm water kept at the side of the fire. Work the sauce briskly with a spoon, or with a little whisk, so as to get it frothy, adding little bits of butter (about as much as half the size of an egg). When the sauce has become light and smooth it is ready for use. It is used for boiled fish, cauliflower or asparagus.

ANOTHER HOLLANDAISE RECIPE.

Put a piece of butter the size of a pigeon's egg into a saucepan, and when it bubbles stir in with an egg whisk, an even tablespoonful of flour; let it continue to bubble until the flour is thoroughly cooked, when stir in half a pint of boiling water, or better still, of veal stock. When it boils take it from the fire, and stir into it gradually the beaten yolks of four eggs. Return the sauce to the fire for a minute to set the eggs without allowing it to boil. Again remove the sauce, stir in the juice of half a small lemon and fresh butter the size of a walnut, cut small to facilitate its melting. Stir all well with a whisk.

ESPAGNOLE SAUCE.

Melt butter the size of an egg. When hot add to it two or three tablespoonsful of flour. Stir this carefully over a slow fire until it is of a light brown. Mix in this half a pint of stock, broth or gravy. Then put it beside the fire to simmer until wanted, skimming it carefully and not allowing it to stick to the pan. Strain it just before serving, add one or two teaspoonsful of Madeira wine. This is to be eaten with quail.

MUSHROOM SAUCE.

Cut off the stalks of the mushrooms, and if they are large cut them in halves or quarters and throw them into a little boiling water, or, what is much better, stock, if you have it. Do not use more than is necessary to cover them. This must be seasoned with pepper, salt and a little butter. Boil the mushrooms till they are tender, then thicken the gravy slightly with a roux of butter and flour. Add a few drops of lemon juice, and then pour over the meat. To be served with beefsteaks, fillets of beef.

ROUX.

Roux is a mixture of butter and flour cooked. It is generally added uncooked to thicken a sauce or a soup, but the flavor is much better if it is first cooked, and the sauce or soup added to *it*. When the butter first comes to a boil in a small stew-pan the sifted flour is sprinkled in, and both are mixed well together over the fire with an egg whisk until the flour is well cooked. A part of the sauce or soup is then stirred in until it becomes smooth and thin enough to add to the main sauce or soup. If the roux is intended for a white sauce it is not allowed to color; if for a brown sauce it may be colored, or brown flour may be used.

DRAWN BUTTER.

Rub two teaspoonsful of flour into a quarter pound of butter and five teaspoonsful of cold water, set it in boiling water till it melts, and when it begins to simmer it is done. Do not set it on the stove as it fries the butter and spoils it. Work the flour in the butter so thoroughly as not to be lumpy. If it is to be used with fish, add hard-boiled eggs chopped fine. If with boiled fowl, put in oysters while it is simmering and let them become thoroughly heated.

HORSE-RADISH SAUCE.

Four tablespoonsful of grated horse-radish, one teaspoonful sugar, one of salt, half a teaspoon of pepper, two of mixed mustard and vinegar, and three or four tablespoonsful of cream. When served with hot beef put in a jar, which place in a saucepan of boiling water. Do not allow it to boil or it will curdle.

ONION SAUCE.

Peel the onions and boil until tender; then drain the water well from them. Chop and pour on them drawn butter together with a little rich milk; boil all up once. A turnip boiled with the onions makes them more mild.

EGG SAUCE.

This sauce is made like drawn butter with the addition of three eggs boiled hard and chopped fine. To be eaten with boiled fowl or fish. Caper sauce is also made like drawn butter, adding two tablespoonsful of capers with a little vinegar or the juice of a lemon.

APPLE SAUCE.

Pare and core tart apples, cut them in slices, rinse and put them in an earthen stew-pan and set them on the fire. Do not stir them till they burst and are done. Mash them with a spoon, and when perfectly cool sweeten with white sugar to taste. This is always an accompaniment to roast goose.

SAUCE FOR ROAST VENISON.

A little currant jelly heated, with lemon juice squeezed into it, is an excellent sauce for roast venison.

FISH SAUCE.

One ounce butter, one of flour; melt in a pan until it bubbles; then gradually add one gill of boiling water; take from fire and add the yolks of three beaten eggs, a little at a time, a saltspoonful of made mustard, one tablespoonful of Tarragon vinegar, three of good salad oil; gradually stir until smooth. Serve hot.

ANOTHER CELERY SAUCE.

Wash and pare a large bunch of celery very clean, cut it into little bits and boil it softly until it is tender. Add half a pint of cream, some mace, nutmeg and a little butter rolled in flour, then boil it gently. This is nice with fowls or any kind of game.

COMMON SAUCE.

Plain butter melted thick with a spoonful of walnut catsup or pickle is a very good sauce. But other things can be added to sauces.

OLIVE SAUCE.

Quarter pound French olives, half a pint stock, one teaspoonful lemon juice, salt and a little cayenne pepper. Carefully stone the olives by paring them round in ribbons so that they may recover their shape when stoned. Blanch them in boiling water, then throw them in cold water for five minutes. Stew slowly for half an hour in the gravy; add the lemon and serve hot.

WINE SAUCE FOR MEAT.

One pint currant jelly, half a pound butter, three tablespoonsful brown sugar, one of allspice, one pint port wine. Stew until thick. Good with venison, wild ducks and mutton.

PARSLEY SAUCE.

To a pint of hot drawn butter, add four tablespoonsful of chopped parsley. Season with pepper and salt and serve hot.

PUDDING SAUCE.

One cup white sugar, a piece of butter the size of an egg, one wineglass of wine. Cream the butter and sugar, add one egg well beaten, and half a wineglass of boiling water the last thing before serving.

WINE SAUCE.

One pound sugar, half a pound butter, well mixed and stewed a little. Then beat up two eggs and stir them in. Put it on the fire and stew it a little more, then take it off and let it get cool. Put wine or rum, and nutmeg into it. Just before dinner heat it well, so as to have it hot for use.

WINE SAUCE.

One cup sugar, one of butter, the yolk of one egg. Cream all together and season with wine. Before sending it to the table add four tablespoonsful of boiling water; beat the white of the eggs very light and stir in.

COLD SAUCE.

Half a teacup cream, one pound sugar, five ounces butter, nutmeg, vanilla, or grated lemon. Mix and beat thoroughly.

WINE SAUCE.

Three cups sugar, one of butter, one of wine. Set the cup in boiling water for one hour.

BUTTER SAUCE.

Three-quarters of a cup of butter, one and a half cups of powdered sugar, four tablespoonsful of boiling hot starch, made of flour or corn starch, with either brandy, maraschino, wine, lemon juice and best vanilla, or any other flavoring preferred. Stir the butter with a fork to a light cream; add the sugar, and continue to beat it for one or two minutes. Just before serving stir in with an egg whisk the boiling starch and the flavoring.

DELICIOUS SAUCE FOR BOILED FISH AND CAULIFLOWER.

Put one pint of cream in double boiler; when thoroughly heated, add one tablespoonful of butter and one of flour, which has been rubbed to a smooth paste. Let boil until it thickens; then add salt, cayenne pepper and lemon juice to taste.

MAYONNAISE DRESSING.

Put the uncooked yolks of two eggs into a *cold* soup dish; beat well with silver or wooden fork one minute; then add half teaspoonful of salt, dash of cayenne pepper, and if you like, half teaspoonful of mustard. Work these well together, then add drop by drop half pint or more of olive oil. Stir rapidly and steadily while adding oil. Do not reverse the motion or it may curdle. After adding one gill of oil, alternate occasionally with a few drops of lemon juice or vinegar, until a proper consistency. More or less oil may be added according to the quantity of dressing wanted. With care a quart bottle of oil may be stirred into the yolks of two eggs, alternating with a few drops of lemon juice or vinegar, after adding the first gill of oil.

In case the dressing should curdle, *i. e.*, the egg and oil separate, which makes the dressing liquid; begin anew at once with the yolks of two eggs in another plate, and after stirring them well, add by teaspoonsful the curdled mayonnaise, stirring all the while, and then finish by adding more oil as directed. In warm weather put the dish in which you make the mayonnaise on a piece of ice or in a pan of cold water; the oil and eggs should also be very cold. This dressing, if closely covered, will keep in the ice for a week. Tarragon vinegar may be used if desired.

WHITE SAUCE.

Melt one tablespoonful of butter; add to it one of flour, and one-half pint of white stock. Stir until it boils; season with pepper and salt. This is the foundation for many other sauces.

CHESTNUT SAUCE.

Boil one pint of chestnuts, when done peel and mash them fine. Rub one tablespoonful of butter and one of *brown* flour to a smooth paste, add one-half pint stock and one-half pint of cream or, one pint of stock and the chestnuts, stir continually until it boils. Season with salt, pepper, a little grated nutmeg and two wineglasses of Sherry wine. This quantity is enough for one dozen birds, or a large turkey.

SHAD ROE SAUCE.

Wash two shad roes in cold water. Put them in a saucepan, add a teaspoonful of salt, cover with boiling water, and cover, simmer gently for fifteen minutes. Drain, remove the outer skin and mash fine. Make a white sauce, add roe gradually, boil up once and it is ready for use. Season with Sherry wine and grated nutmeg. Serve with baked shad.

TARTARE SAUCE.

To one-half pint of Mayonnaise dressing, add three olives, one gherkin, one tablespoonful of capers chopped fine and one tablespoonful of Tarragon vinegar. Serve with any fried fish or soft-crabs.

A RICH SAUCE.

One pint water, three tablespoonsful flour or corn starch, half a cupful of butter, two cupsful of sugar, two eggs, half a nutmeg, and half a pint of Madeira or Sherry. Beat the butter and sugar to a cream; add the eggs well beaten, then the nutmeg. Heat the wine as hot as possible without boiling, bring the water to a boil in another vessel, and stir in the corn starch or flour (rubbed smooth with a little cold water), and cook it well for about two minutes. Mix well the ingredients off the fire.

STRAWBERRY SAUCE.

Half a cup of butter, one cupful of sugar, the beaten white of an egg, and one cupful of mashed strawberries. Rub the butter and sugar to a cream, add the beaten white of the egg and then the strawberries, thoroughly mashed. For baked puddings.

FOR A BURNING PLUM PUDDING.

After the pudding is placed on the dish, pour over it two wineglasses of alcohol, or brandy if you have no alcohol. Set it on fire just at the dining-room door. As soon as it is on the table pour quickly over it another glass of spirits. This is a beautiful dish.

COLD SLAW DRESSING.

Take half a pint vinegar (if very strong, add water) and one teaspoonful celery seed in a tin cup, and place it on the stove to boil. Have ready three well-beaten eggs, a good-sized lump of butter, with pepper, salt and mustard to the taste. When the vinegar comes to a boil pour it slowly on the mixture, stirring quickly all the time. Then return the whole to the fire for a few minutes, stirring to prevent its curdling, and set it aside to cool. When perfectly cold add two tablespoonsful of Lautier's olive oil, or two-thirds of a cup of thick cream, whichever you may prefer. This is enough for one good-sized hard head of cabbage, which should be cut very fine with a slaw-cutter.

ENGLISH CREAM SALAD DRESSING.

Half a teacup of vinegar put on to boil. Pour it boiling over an egg well beaten, then put it back on the fire, and stir it until it thickens, being careful not to curdle it. Then take it off and stir in one teaspoonful mustard, salt and pepper, and lastly three-quarters teacup of thick cream.

LETTUCE DRESSING.

To one salad bowl of lettuce the following is sufficient: One salt spoon of salt and a little pepper mixed in a large tablespoon. Then fill the spoon with vinegar, heaping, and, stirring quickly, pour it slowly all through the lettuce. Then pour three tablespoonsful of Lautier's olive oil over, and work it thoroughly with a fork and spoon, turning it over and over, so that the lettuce may be thoroughly impregnated with the dressing. Never cut but always break lettuce. It must never be left in water, as that destroys its crispness; but after washing put it on or near the ice.

FISH MAYONNAISE.

Take the yolks of four hard-boiled eggs rubbed to a paste with Lautier's salad oil. Add salt, pepper, mustard, two teaspoons white sugar, and lastly six tablespoonsful of vinegar. Beat the mixture until light. Have a pound or so of cold boiled fish cut in pieces an inch long. Just before pouring the dressing on add lightly white of one egg beaten stiff. Serve the fish in a glass dish, with six tablespoons of vinegar, and half the dressing stirred in. Spread the rest over the top, and garnish with lettuce.

DRESSING FOR LOBSTER SALAD.

Boil the lóbster, and when cold pick out the meat and mince it, reserving the coral for the dressing. Then take four hard-boiled eggs, one teaspoon made mustard, one of salt, two of white sugar, a dash of cayenne pepper, and of Worcestershire, Anchovy or Harvey's sauce. Vinegar to taste. Rub the yolks with a silver or wooden spoon till smooth. Add gradually all the ingredients, the coral last. Mix carefully, moistening with vinegar as they stiffen, adding more as the mixture grows smooth, until thin enough to pour on the lobster. Mix dressing and lobster well, and garnish the dish with the inner leaves of several heads, piling the lobster in the centre of the dish, with some dressing poured over it.

WHITE WINE SAUCE. (Good).

One cup of butter, two pounds of powdered sugar, three wineglasses of sherry or Madeira wine, one-half teacup boiling water, one teaspoonful grated nutmeg. Cream the butter with the sugar, adding a little of the boiling water at a time; beat very hard until creamy; then add the wine and nutmeg. Put into a saucepan and set this in pan of boiling water. Stir constantly; let it get very hot, but not boil. Take it from the fire, but leave the saucepan in hot water, until ready to serve. This sauce should be as white as milk, and is very nice. Enough for a large pudding.

HARD SAUCE.

Beat to a cream one-quarter cup of butter; add gradually one cup of powdered sugar, and beat until very light; add whites of two egg, one at a time, and beat all until light and frothy; then add one teaspoonful of vanilla or one tablespoonful of brandy. Heap it on a small dish, sprinkle lightly with grated nutmeg, and stand away on the ice to harden.

MONTROSE SAUCE.

Cover one heaping tablespoonful of gelatine with two of cold water, and soak half an hour. Put one pint of cream on to boil in farina boiler. Beat the yolks of three eggs and one-quarter cup of powdered sugar together until light; then stir into boiling cream. Stir about one minute, then add gelatine and stir until dissolved. Take from the fire; add one teaspoonful of vanilla, two tablespoonsful of brandy and four of sherry. Mix well and stand away to cool. This is a nice filling for cream puffs, or to use as a sauce for cake.

VANILLA SAUCE.

Put one pint of milk on to boil in farina boiler. Beat the yolks of four eggs and two tablespoonsful of sugar together until light; then add them to the boiling milk; stir over fire for two minutes; add vanilla and put away to cool.

"The Lautier Fils Company," of New York, importers of French salad oil, have the finest grade of oil I have ever tasted; it is so pure and sweet that it can be eaten on bread.

DISHES AND SALADS

SIDE DISHES AND SALADS.

CROQUETTES.

Take any kind of cold meat or fowl, with slices of ham, lean and fat. Chop them together, very fine, with one-third of stale bread grated, add salt, pepper, grated nutmeg, a little catsup, and a lump of butter. Mix all together, and make into small cakes or balls. Dip each cake into yolk of egg well beaten, cover quickly with grated bread and fry brown.

CROQUETTES.

Two ounces butter, two dessert-spoonsful flour. Stir them over the fire for a few moments, and add a teacupful cream. Stir it until it is thick as porridge. Have ready the white meat of fowl, minced very fine, and a little minced ham. Put it into the mixture, put it on the fire, stirring well but not long. When cold make into croquette shape, cover with egg and roll in bread-crumbs or cracker dust, and fry in boiling lard. Cold veal is quite as good as fowls.

POTATO CROQUETTES.

Peel one dozen potatoes, boil them in salt and water. When cooked place them in a cullender over the pot of boiling water from which they were taken. Steam them until they are dry and mealy. Beat up well some pepper, salt, and milk or cream, adding four eggs, which must be mixed with the potatoes while hot. When nearly cold form the croquettes. Beat up three eggs. Roll the croquettes first in the eggs, and then in stale bread-crumbs. Fry them in boiling lard for about five minutes.

VEAL CROQUETTES.

Melt a good-sized piece of butter in a stew-pan; add mushrooms (if you have them), a little parsley chopped fine, two tablespoonsful flour, salt, pepper, a little nutmeg. Let it boil until it thickens, then moisten with a little cream, two spoonsful of broth or gravy, the fat being taken off. Let this sauce be as thick as pap. Then take some cold veal chopped fine, both the fat and the lean; put it in the sauce, let it stand until cold, then make into balls. Roll them in cracker dust or bread-crumbs. Fry them a light brown and serve it with fried parsley.

TONGUE TOAST.

Take cold boiled tongue, mince it fine, mix it with cream, and to every half pint of the mixture, allow the well-beaten yolks of two eggs. Place it over the fire, and let it simmer a minute or two. Have ready some nicely toasted bread; butter it, place it on a hot dish, and pour the mixture over it. Send it to table hot.

POTATO SALAD.

Boil one egg hard. When cold, take out the yolk and rub it to a pulp with a wooden spoon; add a raw yolk, one teaspoon of vinegar, one of flour, one of salad oil, a little salt and pepper, a saltspoonful of mixed mustard, and a tablespoonful of sweet butter. Cut some cold boiled potatoes into thin slices and over these pour the mixture.

CHICKEN TERRAPIN.

Boil until perfectly tender a young chicken, pick into small pieces and put it in a porcelain stew-pan with a teacup of boiling water. Cream well together until perfectly smooth quarter pound of butter, and one teaspoonful of flour; when light beat in the yolks of two eggs. When the chicken is boiling hot add this, a little at a time, to prevent lumps. Boil a minute or two, stirring constantly. Add salt and pepper to taste. Take it off the fire and stir in half a gill of Madeira or Sherry wine.

CHICKEN SALAD.

Take three chickens and an equal quantity of celery, cut fine, and sprinkle both with salt. The yolks of four eggs, quarter box of mustard, one large bottle of Lautier's olive oil, half a teacup vinegar and a very little pepper. Beat well together, and just before going to table pour some of the dressing over the chopped chicken and celery. This is a sufficient quantity for fifteen persons.

WELSH RAREBITS.

To a dinner plate full of cheese put two tablespoonsful of vinegar, one of water, two of wine, half a teaspoonful of cayenne pepper, one large spoonful of butter. Mix all together, put it on to stew; after it has stewed well beat the yolks of two eggs and stir them in. Let it stand a few minutes; toast some bread, and butter it on both sides. Pour the mixture over it, and set it in an oven to bake. This is a very nice dish for luncheon or breakfast.

TERRAPIN, PHILADELPHIA STYLE.

Terrapins should be boiled, or rather thrown alive into boiling water for twenty minutes, and then taken out, carefully skinned, and the toe-nails taken off. This first water in all cases should be thrown away, as all the solvents of the body are contained in it, otherwise the terrapin will have a strong taste. Boil it for two hours in fresh water, or, if the terrapins are large, until the legs can be taken off easily, or the shells become detached. Take off first the two hind legs, and then carefully take out the sand bag and the end of the alimentary canal, which generally contains the last digested food. Then break off the fore legs, clean the head, and break up the neck; cut up the entrails fine, and carefully detach the eggs. Have a bowl of cold water ready to wash off the liver in case the gall should be broken in boiling. If not broken, detach it with a sharp knife from the liver, and should it break in handling plunge the pieces stained by it in cold water.

The Dressing.—For a full count terrapin: The yolks of four hard-boiled eggs should be rubbed up with one quarter pound of butter, one-half teacupful browned flour, one tablespoonful mustard, salt, cayenne pepper, and black pepper to taste. When the dressing is boiling add the terrapin, stirring all the time to prevent scorching. Just before taking from the fire, add a tumblerful of Sherry wine and boil up once. Serve hot.

TERRAPIN, MARYLAND STYLE.

Terrapins should be well washed, then thrown in a pot of boiling water, keeping the top on very tightly, as they are really better cooked with as little water as possible; principally by steam, is the best mode. You can tell when they are done, by the skin coming off easily, and also the bones leaving the meat. We use all of the terrapin, except the sand bag, and the end of the alimentary canal, which generally contains the last digested food. Cut up the entrails fine, and be careful in taking the liver from the gall; if the gall should break before taking it out, a little of the gall is an improvement to the terrapin. Cut it all up, and put in a chafing dish, to three large terrapins, one pound of butter, a little cayenne pepper, and salt, and add Sherry wine at the table, if you like it.

SWEETBREADS.

Veal sweetbreads are the best. They spoil very soon. The moment they come from market they should be put into cold water to soak for about an hour. Lard them or rather draw a lardon of pork through the centre of each sweetbread, and put them into salted boiling water, or if you have it, stock, and let them boil about twenty minutes or until they are thoroughly done. Throw them then into cold water for only a few moments. They will now be firm and white. Remove carefully the skin and little pipes, and put them in the coolest place until ready to cook again. The simplest way to cook them is to fry them.

FRIED SWEETBREADS.

Parboil them as just explained. Just before serving cut them in even-sized pieces, sprinkle them with pepper and salt, egg and bread-crumb them, and fry them in hot lard. They are sometimes immersed in boiling lard, yet oftener fried in the sauté pan. If sauté, when done put them on a hot dish, and turn out part of the lard from the sauté pan, leaving about half a teaspoonful. Pour in a cupful of milk thickened with a little flour. Let it cook, stirring constantly and season with pepper and salt; strain it and pour it over the sweetbreads. With green peas, serve without sauce. Sometimes they are served whole with cauliflower or asparagus heads, when the cream sauce is poured over both. They are excellent with tomato sauce or with macaroni cooked with cheese.

CHICKEN CROQUETTES.

Two chickens and two sets of brains, both boiled, two sprigs of parsley chopped, one nutmeg grated, one even tablespoonful of finely chopped onion, the juice and grated rind of one lemon, salt, black and red pepper to taste. Chop the meat very fine; mix all well together and add cream until it is quite moist, or just right for moulding. This quantity will make two dozen croquettes. Mould them into the shape of pears; dip them into beaten egg, and roll them in cracker dust or bread-crumbs, then fry in boiling lard. Any kind of cold meat can be made into croquettes, only substituting rice for the brains.

POTATO SALAD.

Slice some cold potatoes. In a good size dish chop six small onions, also some parsley, salt and a little vinegar to the taste. Then before serving put some mayonaise dressing over it, and serve very cold just off the ice.

CHICKEN CROQUETTES.

One and a half pounds of chicken, and two sweetbreads cut very fine with a knife; put a little salt and pepper and a very little grated nutmeg in it. Make a gravy of nearly one pint of milk; beat up the yolk of one egg and cook it in the milk, then stir in a spoonful of butter, mixed with two-thirds of a spoonful of flour. Cook this in the milk till it is ropy, then stir the chicken into it, and set it away to cool. Take out some of the gravy, as it may make it too soft, then add if it is needed. When cool, roll them into shape, dip them in white of egg, then in cracker, and boil them in hot lard. This makes one dozen croquettes.

IMITATION TERRAPIN.

Cut cold chicken, mutton or veal fine; sprinkle it with cayenne pepper and salt. Mash the yolks of three hard-boiled eggs, and put it with a little wine, walnut catsup, mustard, and a lump of butter in a stew-pan five minutes. Have a fourth hard-boiled egg, from which take the yolk and roll into little eggs like those of a terrapin. Scatter them through the dish when ready for the table. Garnish the dish with a few slices of lemon and some parsley.

LOBSTER SALAD.

Open a can of lobster and drain it well through a cullender. This takes some time. After the liquid is all drained off, have ready six eggs boiled hard. Make the yolks into a paste with six raw yolks, twenty-four tablespoons of oil, twelve of vinegar, twelve even teaspoons of mustard, and the same of salt. Mix well until it is a smooth paste. Sprinkle cayenne pepper over it when about to mix, and squeeze the juice of one lemon to this quantity. Lettuce is a great addition to it. Sturgeon is very nice fixed this way. Fresh lobster is much better than the canned.

COTTAGE CHEESE.

Take one or more quarts of sour milk, put it in a warm place and let it remain till the whey separates from the curd, then pour it into a three-cornered bag, hang it up and let it drain till every particle of whey has dripped from it. Then turn it out and mash it with a spoon until very fine, after which add a little milk or cream, with salt to taste. If you like, before sending it to table dredge a little black pepper over the top.

OYSTER PATÉS.

Take as many fresh oysters as you will need. Drain them, then place them on the fire in a stew-pan with butter, a little chopped celery, pepper and salt. Stew them, thicken it a little with flour and butter rubbed together, and stirred in. Let them cook a few moments, then have your patés baked and fill them with the oysters. Put them in the oven again, and let them bake a few moments until the oysters look a little brown.

CRAB SALAD.

Prepare the crabs as for devilling, leaving out the fat. Then prepare a mayonnaise dressing. Have some nice white lettuce; place the leaves in the bottom and all around the sides of a flat dish. Heap the picked crab in the centre. Put the dressing in a separate dish. Garnish the dish with slices of lemon or small red radishes.

CRAB CROQUETTES.

Prepare the crabs as for devilling, mince them rather fine. Season with butter, cayenne pepper and salt. Make it into shapes like croquettes by moulding in a wine-glass. Roll them in cracker dust, and fry in boiling lard. Add a little flour when moulding them to make them hold in shape.

BROILED PIGEONS.

Young pigeons, or squabs, are a great delicacy. Clean, wash and dry them carefully with a clean cloth, then split them down the back and broil them like spring chickens. Season with pepper and salt, and add plenty of butter when serving them.

CREAM SALAD DRESSING.

Mash the hard-boiled yolks of three eggs and the raw yolk of one to a perfectly smooth paste, add one-half teaspoonful of salt, one-quarter teaspoonful of black pepper, one tablespoonful of melted butter, then by degrees, one gill of thick cream, working and stirring all the time. Now add two tablespoonsful of vinegar, mix well and it is finished.

POTATO SALAD.

Pare and boil three good sized potatoes; when cold, cut them into thin slices, and mix them carefully with one onion chopped *very* fine. Over them pour the following dressing. One teaspoonful of salt, one saltspoonful of black pepper, nine tablespoonsful of olive oil, and three of vinegar, stirred thoroughly until the salt has all been dissolved. Sprinkle the dish with parsley chopped fine and put in a cold place for an hour or two.

TOMATO SALAD.

Peel the tomatoes, scoop out the inside carefully so as not to break the tomatoes, fill in with chopped celery, dressed with mayonnaise dressing, or fill with chicken salad. Serve on plates with crisp lettuce.

FRUIT SALAD DRESSING.

Mix together four tablespoonsful of sugar, one of maraschino, two of Champagne if you have it, one gill of sherry; stir until sugar is dissolved, and pour over the fruit.

FRUIT SALAD.

Peel and cut in thin slices, bananas, oranges or any kind of fruit; pour over them the fruit-salad dressing, and stand on ice for an hour or two.

CHEESE STRAWS.

Rub one-quarter pound of butter and one-half pound of flour together; mix lightly six ounces grated cheese with cayenne pepper to taste. Make into a light dough with one-half teacup of milk, in which dissolve one teaspoonful of yeast-powder, and enough ice-water to roll out thin. Cut into narrow strips five inches long, and one-half inch wide. Bake a light brown in a quick oven.

LOBSTER A LA NEWBURGH.

Cut up some fresh lobster in large squares, put it in a saucepan on the fire, with two glasses of good Sherry. When hot, take the yolk of a raw egg, a piece of butter, and half gill of cream; mix slowly with the lobster. Be careful not to let it boil any more. Season well to taste, and serve in a deep covered dish. Must not stand, but used as soon as made. About ten minutes' cooking is sufficient. Chafing-dish is best to cook it in.

WELSH RAREBIT.

Beat one egg in a saucepan, add to it five tablespoonsful grated cheese, one of butter, one-third teaspoonful of salt, a little red pepper, one teaspoon of mustard, five tablespoonsful of rich milk; thicken with a little corn starch, which has been mixed in a little milk. Serve on toast.

LOBSTER PATTIES.

Make some puff paste, and spread it in deep patty pans. Bake them before they are filled. Take fresh or canned lobster (of course it is always boiled before using); mix with it some white stock. Chop the lobster fine, and to a can of lobster, or two fresh ones, add the yolks of four hard-boiled eggs. Season with cayenne pepper, Sherry wine, nutmeg, and a little lemon juice, gill of sweet cream, and a lump of butter size of an egg. Let it stew until it comes to a boil; then fill the patties. Serve *hot*.

BEEF SAUTÉ.

Heat some thick slices of tender boiled beef in melted butter; keep the dish covered. When very hot, pour over a tablespoonful each of mushroom catsup and Worcestershire sauce. Serve on hot plates.

CHEESE PUDDING. (Philadelphia style.)

Put in a sauce-pan half a pound of good grated cheese, with a pint of new milk, six ounces of grated bread-crumbs, and two eggs well beaten; stir well till the cheese is dissolved, then put in a Dutch oven if you have one, or brown with a salamander, or be careful in baking it in your range. Serve hot for breakfast or lunch. Very nice.

CHICKEN CROQUETTES. (Very fine.)

To one large pullet chicken, well boiled, cut fine, removing all skin and gristle, add one pint of rich sweet cream, yolks of four eggs, piece butter size of an egg, large spoonful of sifted flour; flavor with nutmeg, cayenne pepper and salt. Cook over slow fire until the consistency of paste; then put

SIDE DISHES AND SALADS.

in your refrigerator until it cools; mould into oval patties or any shape you like. Dip them into the yolks of three eggs seasoned well, and then roll in beaten crackers or bread-crumbs; then put them in boiling lard; it is very important that the lard should be boiling, before the croquettes are put in. Two sweetbreads added to this receipt will make two dozen croquettes.

STUFFED POTATOES.

Take nice size smooth Irish potatoes, and put in the oven; let them bake slowly until well done, then remove all the inside very carefully so as not to break the skin. Mash the potatoes through the potato strainer; beat up one egg, yellow and white separately, a cup of rich milk in a pan on the fire; stir potatoes in the milk, then the egg (yellow first, then the white), butter and salt. Put this mixture into their jackets, taking care not to have it too thin, and place in oven for a few moments until brown. This is for six or eight potatoes. Nice lunch or breakfast dish.

FILLING FOR PATTIES.

Breast of one chicken chopped fine, one pair of sweetbreads parboiled and then cooked a short time in soup stock, one can mushrooms cooked in soup stock. Chop mushrooms and sweetbreads, but not too fine; season with salt. Make a sauce of soup stock, drawn butter and cream, and mix thoroughly.

ICES.

ORANGE WATER ICE.

Eight oranges, three lemons, three pounds loaf sugar, one box gelatine dissolved in cold water, enough to make one and a half gallons. Extract the oil of both oranges and lemons by rubbing the rind with lumps of sugar. Freeze as usual. Pour boiling water over the gelatine after it has stood in cold water half an hour.

CARAMEL ICE CREAM.

One small half teacup of white sugar in a pan, and stir over the fire until the sugar turns liquid and begins to smoke. Turn it at once into one quart of custard; stir rapidly. When cool, add one quart rich cream, strain and freeze.

ORANGE ICE CREAM.

Boil two quarts of milk. Stir in it while boiling one tablespoonful of corn starch mixed with a little cold milk, and the yolks of three eggs beaten light. Stir it briskly to prevent its curdling. When perfectly cold add one and a half pints of cream and the juice of six oranges. Sweeten to taste. Beat very light the whites of three eggs and stir them in just before freezing.

PARKER'S ICE CREAM.

One quart new milk, one vanilla bean, one tablespoonful of corn starch or flour; boil all together. When cold add one quart cream, three-quarters pound of sugar, beat the whites of six eggs to a froth and stir them in.

CHOCOLATE CREAM.

Scrape quarter pound of chocolate very fine, put it in a quart of rich milk or cream. Boil it until it is dissolved, stirring occasionally. Thicken with one egg. A vanilla bean boiled with the milk improves the flavor. When cream is used the egg may be dispensed with. Freeze in the usual way.

GRAPE SHERBET.

Take half gallon grape juice, sweeten to taste, then add two teacups of sugar to three teacups of orange juice, half teacup of lemon juice; then add this to the grape juice, and when ready to remove the dasher from the freezer, add the whites of three eggs well beaten with two tablespoons of sugar. Beat and pack to stand in ice and salt until hard.

CHOCOLATE ICE CREAM.

Grate half a pound Baker's chocolate very fine. Mix it into a smooth paste with a little fresh milk. Take three pints of morning's milk, put it on the fire to boil, then stir in the chocolate paste. Have ready the yolks of six eggs well beaten with one pound of white sugar. Pour the chocolate over this, boiling hot from the kettle, and put it all back on the fire stirring all the time till it thickens. Great care is needful as it is very apt to burn. When the chocolate custard is cold whip up five pints of cream and stir it in. Season slightly with vanilla. Now beat the whites of five eggs to a stiff froth, adding gradually while beating two tablespoonsful of pulverized sugar, and as soon as they are well mixed and the cream about half frozen, put it into the freezer, and you will find this addition a great improvement.

FROZEN PUDDING.

To three pints of new milk put three or four sticks of fresh cinnamon, two blades of mace, one and a quarter pounds of the best raisins, stemmed and stoned. Cover these tightly in the stew-pan and simmer slowly for fifteen minutes. Meanwhile beat very light the yolks of five eggs, adding slowly when light half a pound of pulverized loaf sugar. Make it as light and creamy as possible. When ready strain the milk so as to leave out the spice and raisins, but save the latter as they are to be put in after a while. Stir in the eggs and sugar when the milk boils, beating it until it simmers once. Then remove it from the fire, and when cold stir in one quarter pound of almonds that have been blanched, and pounded in a mortar with a little rose-water, then the raisins that were boiled in the milk, half a pound of the best citron cut into small very thin slices, and if preferred, a small portion of preserved ginger cut thin. Mix all well together, add a quart of rich cream, stir till nicely mixed and freeze as ice cream. A "Turk's Head" makes a very pretty mould for it.

TUTTI FRUTTI.

When a rich vanilla cream is partly frozen add candied cherries, English currants, chopped raisins, chopped citron or any other candied fruit chopped rather fine in about the same quantity of fruit as of ice cream. Mould it, and imbed it in ice and salt.

ORANGE ICE.

To four quarts water take five oranges and three lemons. Grate the rind of the oranges clean on lumps of sugar, but only use the juice of the lemons. Squeeze the pulps of the oranges and lemons, and put boiling water to them, then let it stand until the water is cold. Strain the water off, put about two pounds of sugar to this quantity in addition to the lumps of sugar used. Freeze as usual.

STRAWBERRY ICE CREAM.

Take half a gallon of rich cream perfectly sweet. Sweeten to taste; then take half a gallon nice ripe strawberries, mash them well in a marble mortar, with half a pound fine white sugar, or more if the berries are sour. Then mix the mashed berries into the cream and freeze hard. Raspberry and peach cream is made in the same manner.

LEMON ICE CREAM.

Take lumps of sugar and rub off the rind of six lemons on it. To one gallon of cream add the juice of two large lemons and two pounds loaf sugar. Put as much sugar to the juice as it will take. Then put the juice with the sugar, and the lumps on which the rind has been grated, to one gallon cream, and freeze hard.

PINEAPPLE ICE.

Grate three large pineapples very fine, add three quarts water, two and a half pounds white sugar, whites of six eggs beaten stiff with the sugar. Add this last and freeze hard. This is exceedingly nice.

LEMON SHERBET.

Make a rich lemonade, using two lemons to one pint water. Rub some of the rind with loaf sugar, so as to extract the oil, say about four lemons to a gallon. Take the whites of eight eggs beat to an icing, adding pulverized sugar; about two pounds sugar to a gallon, including the icing, is about the quantity, but it depends upon the size of the lemons and the amount of juice they have. A quarter of an ounce of Cox's gelatine dissolved and added is a great improvement.

FROZEN CUSTARD.

One quart milk, four eggs, two even tablespoonsful corn starch, and one cup sugar. Beat the whites of the eggs to a stiff froth with half a cup powdered sugar, and stir them in when the custard is cold just before freezing. Flavor with vanilla.

ICE CREAM.

To three quarts rich milk put two ounces isinglass. Boil all together, and strain before flavoring it. Any kind of seasoning.

PLOMBIERE.

Make a rich custard. When cold flavor it with wine and lemon. When it is half frozen add blanched almonds, chopped citron, brandy peaches cut up, and any other brandied or crystallized fruit. Fill the freezer half full of custard, and the remaining half fill with the fruit. Raisins are an improvement.

PEACH ICE CREAM.

Take perfectly ripe free-stone peaches. Pare them and mash them fine. Make them very sweet. To each quart of peaches add one quart rich cream or new milk. Mix well and freeze. Take one ounce Cox's gelatine melted in a cup of water. Boil the milk and pour it on the gelatine, and when cold mix with the peaches.

ICED JELLY.

Make calf's foot jelly, not very stiff, and freeze it. It is delicious. Serve in glasses.

CARAMEL CREAM.

Make a rich custard with one pint of morning's milk and six eggs. Have ready one and a quarter pounds brown sugar toasted (be careful not to burn it). Stir the sugar into the custard while both are hot. This will flavor one gallon of ice cream.

ALMOND CREAM.

Blanch and pulverize one quart of almonds; this should be done in a mortar, and a little new milk added to reduce the nuts to a fine paste. Use this with one gallon of cream, mixing the almonds in when the cream is nearly frozen.

PLAIN ICE CREAM.

Two quarts thick cream, one pound sugar, one pint new milk into which cut a vanilla bean. Put it on the fire, allowing the milk and bean to boil slowly, strain it through a wire sieve, permitting the small seeds of the bean to fall into the cream. When it becomes cool whip all to a froth and freeze, cutting it down frequently as it freezes.

BISQUE GLACE.

Half a gallon of cream, one and a half dozen macaroons (these must be stale, or if not, dried in a stove), pounded fine. Pour a little cream over them and allow them to stand till they soften; beat until very fine, then add the rest of the cream and freeze. It is not well to have the macaroons too thick in the cream.

CHOCOLATE ICE CREAM.

One quart of cream, one pint of new milk, two cups sugar, two eggs beaten light, and five tablespoonsful of Baker's chocolate rubbed to a paste with a little milk. Heat the milk almost to boiling, and pour by degrees in with the beaten egg and sugar. Stir in the chocolate, beat well three minutes, and return it to the inner kettle. (Always boil milk and custard in a vessel set within another of boiling water.) Heat until it thickens well, stirring constantly, then take from the fire and set aside to cool. Many like to flavor with vanilla. When the custard is cold beat in the cream. Freeze as usual.

COFFEE ICE CREAM.

Three pints cream, one cup black coffee very strong and clear, two cups sugar, and two tablespoonsful of arrowroot wet with cold milk. Heat a pint and a half of the cream nearly to boiling, stir in the sugar, and, when this is melted, the coffee, then the arrowroot. Boil all together for five minutes, stirring constantly. When cold beat it up very light, whipping in the rest of the cream by degrees. Then freeze.

STRAWBERRY ACID.

Dissolve four ounces of citric acid, in one-half gallon of water, pour it over two gallons of ripe strawberries, let it stand twenty-four hours and then drain. To every pint of juice add a pound of white sugar. Let it boil well for five minutes then let it stand three days before bottling. When ready to serve, add two tablespoonsful to a glass of ice water.

STRAWBERRY WATER ICE.

To one quart of strawberries, add one pound of sugar and juice of two lemons, mash them and stand aside one hour, then strain through a fine sieve; add one quart of water and freeze. This is enough for eight persons.

ROMAN PUNCH.

To one quart of lemon water ice frozen hard, add slowly one-half pint of champagne, one-half pint Jamaica rum, one gill maraschino, one teaspoonful of vanilla; beat well. Put in freezer, pack and cover well, and stand away for four or five hours. Serve in glasses.

FROZEN PUNCH.

The juice of six lemons and two oranges, one-half pint of champagne, one gill of rum, one-half gill of brandy, one pound of pulverized sugar; stir until sugar is dissolved; add one pint of water. Put in freezer and turn slowly until mixture is partly frozen. Remove the dasher, cover and stand away for two hours. It will require a long time to freeze. This will fill twelve glasses.

APPLE ICE CREAM.

To half a gallon of coddled apples, add one pound of white sugar and half gallon of sweet cream; stir well and have it frozen hard. This is a delicious dish.

DESSERTS.

PIG'S FEET JELLY.

One gallon of the jelly free from all grease, half a gallon of Lisbon wine, two pounds white sugar, six lemons, some sticks of cinnamon, a little mace, the whites of eighteen eggs beaten light, shells also put in. Mix all well. Boil a short
.. .. Strain it through a flannel bag

Wherever Cox's Gelatine is mentioned, in my book, I would suggest the use of Chalmers', as I consider it the *best* and cheapest on the market.

.. ..
in a saucepan, and let it boil a few minutes; pour it into a flannel bag to strain. Repeat this till it is clear, cut lemon peel very small, and pour the jelly on hot.

CALF'S FOOT JELLY.

One quart hard jelly, one pint wine, half a pound loaf sugar, though brown sugar will do as well, the juice of four lemons, whites of six or eight eggs beaten light. Stir all together until it boils. Strain through a bag; drop in lemon peel cut fine.

DESSERTS.

PIG'S FEET JELLY.

One gallon of the jelly free from all grease, half a gallon of Lisbon wine, two pounds white sugar, six lemons, some sticks of cinnamon, a little mace, the whites of eighteen eggs beaten light, shells also put in. Mix all well. Boil a short time until it looks clear. Strain it through a flannel bag inside a muslin one. If not clear, pass it through a second time. This will keep in cold weather for weeks.

CALF'S FOOT JELLY.

Take two feet and boil them in a gallon of water till it comes to a quart. When it is cold skim off the fat, take up the jelly clean, and put it in a saucepan with a pint of white wine, half a pound of loaf sugar, the juice of four lemons, and the whites of eight eggs well beaten. Stir all together in a saucepan, and let it boil a few minutes; pour it into a flannel bag to strain. Repeat this till it is clear, cut lemon peel very small, and pour the jelly on hot.

CALF'S FOOT JELLY.

One quart hard jelly, one pint wine, half a pound loaf sugar, though brown sugar will do as well, the juice of four lemons, whites of six or eight eggs beaten light. Stir all together until it boils. Strain through a bag; drop in lemon peel cut fine.

CALF'S OR PIG'S FEET JELLY.

Thoroughly cleanse and scrape the feet, and covering them well with pure water, boil until thoroughly done. Set the stock aside in a cold place to solidify. The next day carefully skim off the grease from the surface and measure the stock. To one gallon of stock put three pounds of sugar, half a gallon good bright-colored wine, the juice, and thinly sliced rind of six lemons, and the beaten whites of sixteen eggs. Stir all together over the fire until well mixed, and boil twenty minutes. Strain through a flannel bag as usual. This jelly will keep for many weeks. Add stick cinnamon, one ounce mace, one dozen cloves, one dozen allspice.

CREAM JELLY.

To one quart of the stock made from pigs' feet put one pint of sweet cream, one pint of fresh milk, and ten ounces of pulverized sugar. Flavor with extract of rose or vanilla. Melt together in a pan over the fire, strain and impart a pale pink tint, by the use of a little cochineal or pokeberry jelly. Mould it precisely as you do blanc mange. When firm, turn out the jelly into the centre of a shallow dessert dish of glass or china. Surround it with syllabub whipped to a light froth, and you have a very pretty and palatable dish.

LEMON JELLY.

One and three-quarter ounces of Russian isinglass, three and three quarter pounds of loaf sugar, and three lemons. Cut the isinglass into small pieces, turn over it one quart of cold water, and let it stand half an hour, then pour off the water. Put the isinglass into a pitcher with the juice of two lemons, and one cut in slices. Put in the sugar and a dessertspoonful of rose water. Over all pour three pints of boiling water, cover it and let it stand an hour or so until the isinglass is dissolved. Strain through a jelly bag into moulds, and set it in a cool place.

STRAWBERRY JELLY.

Soak a box of gelatine in one pint of cold water. When thoroughly soft add five ounces of white sugar, two quarts of strawberry syrup, and put it over the fire until the gelatine is perfectly dissolved. Pour it from the kettle into moulds or small jars, and you have a beautiful and nice flavored jelly. This recipe is meant for cool weather. In summer reduce the quantity of syrup by one-half.

SYLLABUB.

Syllabub gives a very nice finish to many desserts, and when called for it should be made in this manner: To half a pint of rich cream add half a gill of sweet wine, and two tablespoonsful of finely powdered white sugar, and flavor it with lemon juice. Whip it to a froth, removing lightly with a spoon all the foam as it forms, and putting it to the dish requiring to be ornamented.

TO MAKE JELLY WITHOUT BOILING.

To one package of Cox's sparkling gelatine add one pint cold water, the juice of three lemons, and the rind pared thin. Let it stand one hour, then add three pints of boiling water, half a pint of wine, one and a half pounds of crushed sugar. When the sugar is dissolved strain the lemon rind out and set it away to cool.

ORANGE JELLY.

Take the juice of about ten oranges. Strain it, and add three teacups of sifted white sugar. Pour one pint of cold water on one box of Cox's gelatine, and let it stand twenty minutes. Pour one quart boiling water on the gelatine, add the orange juice, then strain through a flannel bag, and set it away to cool.

QUINCE JELLY.

Select the finest quinces, lay them on shelves so as not to touch each other; keep them until they look yellow and have a fragrant smell. When about to use them take off the stems and blossoms, wash them clean, and cut them in pieces without paring. Put them into the preserving kettle, and just cover them with water. Stir them gently, putting in a little more water occasionally, until they are soft, then pour them into a jelly bag, and let all the liquid run through without pressing it. To each pint put one pound of loaf sugar, and boil it to a jelly. The bag *may* be squeezed for an inferior but very nice jelly. Cranberry jelly may be made in the same way.

JELLY MADE OF COOPER'S ISINGLASS.

Quarter of a pound of gelatine, three quarts hot water, one quart wine, four lemons, six eggs, yolks, whites and shells. Add a little cinnamon, a few cloves, sweeten with nice brown sugar. Boil all together until the particles are separated. Run through a jelly strainer.

BLANC MANGE, No 1.

Whip a quart of seasoned cream to a stiff froth. Take one ounce isinglass, and one pint of water, and set it on the fire till it is dissolved. Let it cool before the cream is mixed with it. Then stir the cream with the dissolved isinglass, until it is stiff enough to drop from the spoon. Wet the moulds, pour the mixture in, and set it in a cool place.

CHOCOLATE BLANC MANGE.

Boil two quarts of milk with half a pound of white sugar. Stir in quarter of a pound of grated Baker's chocolate mixed in boiling water. Let it boil twenty minutes. Then add four tablespoonsful of corn starch mixed with three-quarters of a pint cold milk. Boil it ten minutes longer, and pour into moulds.

IRISH MOSS BLANC MANGE.

Soak for several hours half a teacupful of Irish moss, changing the water frequently. Drain well, shaking the water from it. Put it into a kettle with half a gallon of new milk flavored with vanilla, and sweetened to taste. Let it boil five minutes, then strain and pour it into moulds.

ISINGLASS BLANC MANGE.

Boil two ounces of isinglass in one and a half pints of new milk, then strain it and pour in one pint of cream sweetened to taste, add one cup of rose water. Let it boil to the top of the kettle once and let it settle, then strain and pour into moulds.

BLANC MANGE. (Very fine.)

Blanch one ounce sweet almonds, and one ounce of peach kernels. When perfectly dry grate them. Then mix with one quart of cream or rich milk; put it into a pan with one ounce of isinglass, add the juice, set on the stove and stir constantly till the isinglass is dissolved; add eight ounces of sugar, remove the scum as it rises. Strain it through a sieve into a mould, and set it on the ice till it is ready for use.

SNOW PUDDING.

Dissolve one ounce of gelatine in one pint of cold water. Beat up the whites of six eggs, and after the gelatine has thoroughly dissolved pour on it one pint of boiling water, then stir in one pound of sugar, and the juice of four lemons. Beat all together and continue beating until it begins to thicken, then pour into a bowl. Serve with sweetened cream flavored with wine and nutmeg.

TRIFLE.

Cover the bottom of the dish with Naples biscuit cut in slices, soak them with wine; have a good boiled custard and pour it over. When cold put whipped cream on top.

RICE FLUMMERY.

Pick the rice but do not wash it, and grind it in a coffee or spice mill. To a large teacup of this add three pints of new milk, let it boil gently, stirring all the time. When done and quite thick pour it into moulds. Sweeten it with loaf sugar, and flavor with rose water, peach water or peach leaves. If made soon after breakfast and put into moulds it makes a very pretty dessert for dinner. To be eaten with cream.

BLANC MANGE.

Dissolve two ounces of isinglass in one pint of water, boiling, then put it on to boil. When done strain it, add the juice of two lemons and the rind. Beat light the yolks of twelve eggs, pour in the isinglass and lemon, put in half a pound blanched almonds well beaten. Sweeten with loaf sugar. Set it on the fire a few minutes but do not let it burn.

BLANC MANGE.

One and a half ounces isinglass, beaten, and boiled slowly over the fire for quarter of an hour in a quart of cream. Stir it all the time. When done take it off, sweeten to taste, strain it, add orange flower water and rose water, pour it into moulds. When cold, turn it out and garnish it with sweetmeats.

BLANC MANGE.

Dissolve two ounces isinglass in one and a half gills boiling water, then season one quart of new milk with sugar and rose water to the taste. Stir the isinglass in the milk, set it on the fire, and gently stew it till it jellies. While it is hot strain it through a sifter, then pour it in the moulds and set it to cool. To make it yellow add the yolks of two eggs.

DANISH BLANC MANGE.

Dissolve four ounces isinglass in a pint of water with a little cinnamon, and the juice of six lemons, the rind of two, and half a pint of wine. Set all to boil. Have ready the whites of eight eggs, well beaten, and the yolks of two; add to these one pint white wine. When well beaten together, strain the isinglass and pour the eggs and wine to it, straining them also; sweeten to taste; boil it as you do custard, about five minutes, and put it in moulds.

RICE BLANC MANGE.

Wash and pick a teacupful of rice, boil it in a pint of water till soft, and reduce to one-third; do not let it burn. Take it off and beat in about half a pint of cream or rich milk, boil a little more, then season to taste with powdered sugar and rose water, orange flower or peach water. Set it to cool and eat with cream; add wine if preferred. Put salt in the rice when boiling.

BIRD'S NEST BLANC MANGE.

Take half a package of gelatine, using a little more than half the quantity of water as in making jelly. When ready to strain put it into a large oval dish, fill it nearly to the edge, then set it away to harden. Take some egg-shells that you have broken just the end off in getting out the egg. Make a blanc mange of gelatine, flavor with vanilla and sweeten. Put this into the shells before it cools or hardens at all; then set the eggs on end in a vegetable dish, being careful not to let the blanc mange run out. Cut some very thin parings off the lemon rind, stew them in a little sugar and water. When cold lay each piece separately in a circle on the jelly, making two or three nests. Then break open the eggshells, take out the blanc mange, being careful not to destroy the shape, and lay it in groups like eggs inside the nests. This is a very pretty dish.

VELVET CREAM.

One coffee-cupful of wine, two-thirds of a cup of Cox's gelatine dissolved in one pint of water, one coffee-cupful of sugar. Set the mixture over the fire, and let it come to a boil, then strain it through a flannel bag. When it is nearly cold add one pint of good rich cream. Beat all well together, and put it into a mould.

APPLE FLOAT.

One pint stewed apples; when cold sweeten and flavor to taste. When ready to send to table, add the beaten whites of four eggs lightly stirred into it. To be eaten with cream.

APPLE MERINGUE.

Pare, core and stew ten apples in as little water as possible; season as you would sauce, putting in a very little butter. Put it into a pudding dish in a cool oven. Add the whites of four eggs well beaten, spreading them over the tops as you would icing. Sprinkle sugar on the top, and let it brown. To be eaten cold with cream.

APPLE SOUFFLÉE.

Stew the apples as if for sauce, adding a little lemon peel and juice. Lay them pretty high around the inside of a baking dish. Make a custard of the yolks of two eggs with one pint of milk. Add a little cinnamon and sugar. Let it cool, and then pour it into a dish; beat the whites, and spread them over the top, browning a little in the oven. If you sprinkle a little sugar over it, it will brown sooner. The apples should be about half an inch thick at the bottom and sides of the dish. This is very nice.

FLOATING ISLAND.

Two spoonsful of currant jelly, two of raspberry jam strained through a sieve, and the whites of four eggs. Beat the eggs well, then put in the sweetmeats, and continue beating until it is a fine froth. Lay thin slices of sponge cake or Naples biscuit in the bottom of your dessert-dish, cover them with sweetmeats and cream, or rich milk, and heap the froth high in the middle.

DESSERTS.

MOCK GOOSEBERRY FOOL.

Cut up and scrape as much rhubarb as will be enough to fill a glass bowl of the size you wish. Stew it in enough water to cover it well. When tender rub it through a cullender to a smooth pulp. To one quart of the fruit well sweetened and flavored with lemon peel, add a quart of sweet cream stirred smoothly in all well mixed. Heap the bowl up high with whipped syllabub. If you have no cream, substitute a quart of rich custard made with the yolks of six eggs. In place of the syllabub use the whisked whites of the six eggs, sweetened with six tablespoonsful of fine white sugar, and brown the top slightly with a hot salamander or clean shovel.

TRIFLE.

In the bottom of a deep glass bowl place bits of sponge cake, it matters not how stale, cut into squares or strips. A small piece of preserved citron, also cut into very thin slices and interspersed with the cake. Soak these in a gill of any kind of pleasant sweet wine. Then fill the bowl up to within an inch of the top with boiled custard, rich and cold. Lastly, heap the bowl up high with whipped syllabub.

IRISH MOSS BLANC MANGE.

Take a handful of the moss, wash it carefully, put it in in three pints of new milk; let it simmer on the fire until the moss dissolves, then strain it through a fine sieve; sweeten to taste. Season with vanilla, then pour in moulds, as soon as cool. Put on ice in Summer. To be eaten with whipped cream, seasoned with Sherry wine or vanilla. Very good for invalids and children.

TAPIOCA JELLY.

Soak a cupful of tapioca in four cupsful of water. Sweeten it, and set it in a pan of boiling water; let it cook an hour, or until it is thoroughly done and quite clear, stirring frequently.

When nearly cooked stir in the juice and grated rind of one lemon, and when done pour it into moulds. Serve with cream sweetened and flavored.

TAPIOCA JELLY.

Wash the tapioca two or three times. Soak it for five or six hours. Let it simmer in the same water, with some pieces of fresh lemon peel, until it becomes quite clear. Then put the juice of a lemon, a little wine and sugar, according to taste. Allow three tablespoonsful of tapioca to one quart of water.

TIPSY PUDDING.

Soak a sponge cake in Sherry wine, but dry pieces of cake of any kind can be used. When it is saturated enough, so that it will not fall to pieces, pour over it a boiled custard flavored with anything you like. If placed in a glass dish, decorate it with the beaten whites of the eggs poached, and with dots of jelly. If served in a common platter, squeeze the beaten whites, sweetened and flavored, through a funnel in any fancy shapes over the pudding, and put it into the oven till it is a delicate brown.

CHOCOLATE CUSTARD.

Three ounces Walter Baker's chocolate, three pints milk, four tablespoons white sugar, two of brown sugar. Prepare a soft custard of the milk and the yolks of five eggs (white of one). Dissolve the chocolate in a cup of warm milk and heat it to boiling. When cool, sweeten with brown sugar and flavor with vanilla. Pour the whole into a dish, and cover with the whites of the eggs beaten stiff with a little sugar. Brown slightly and serve it cold.

COLD CUSTARD.

One quart new milk and half a pint cream mixed, quarter of a pound powdered white sugar, one large glass white wine in which an inch of washed rennet has been soaked, and one nutmeg. Mix the cream, milk and sugar. Stir the wine into it and pour the mixture into custard cups. Set them in a warm place near the fire till they become a firm curd. Then set them on ice or in a cold place, and grate nutmeg over them.

AMBROSIA.

Slice oranges or pineapples in a glass bowl, sweeten well. Put a layer of fruit and a layer of cocoanut, grated, and so on till the bowl is full. Cover with grated cocoanut.

ORANGES WITH TRANSPARENT JELLY.

Half a dozen perfect oranges. Make a hole at the stalk with a circular tin cutter half an inch in diameter. Remove all the pulp and loose pith with a small spoon. Soak the oranges in cold water one hour, rinse again in cold water and drain on a cloth; put them in a deep pan and surround them with ice. Fill three with bright pink jelly and the rest with white. When the jelly is firm wipe the oranges and cut into quarters. Serve them on a glass stand.

IRISH CREAM.

Grate the rind and squeeze the juice of one orange into enough sugar to sweeten three pints of cream; whip it to a froth. Dissolve one ounce of isinglass, in one pint of water, and just before it congeals stir it into the whipped cream.

BAVARIAN CREAM.

Pour one pint of cold water over one box of Cox's gelatine and let it stand one hour. Then add one and a half pints of boiling water and two teacupsful of sugar. When nearly cold flavor it with vanilla. Churn up one quart of rich cream and beat the froth into the jelly when almost cold.

CHOCOLATE CREAM.

Scrape three ounces of Walter Baker's chocolate, and dissolve in boiling water. Boil one quart of new milk, one pint cream, flavor with vanilla. Then pour in the dissolved chocolate, and boil it twenty minutes while stirring. Beat the yolks of three eggs with half a pound of sugar, then put the whole in a kettle and let it boil fifteen minutes longer, stirring all the time to prevent its burning.

ALMOND CUSTARD.

One pint of cream. Blanch one and a quarter pounds of almonds with two spoonsful of rose water. Sweeten to your taste. Beat the yolks of four eggs very light. Stir it over the fire all the time till it is thick.

ALMOND SNOWBALLS.

One quart of milk made quite sweet, six tablespoonsful of rice ground in a mill. Sprinkle it in the milk while boiling, stirring it all the time till it is like small hominy, and drops from the spoon as clear as starch. When nearly cool stir in a teaspoonful of bitter almonds and one of vanilla. When cool wash the moulds with cold water, fill them, and set them on ice. Turn them out in dishes and dress with whipped cream seasoned with wine.

LEMON CREAM.

To the whites of eight eggs beaten very light put twenty-four spoonsful of water, the juice of two lemons. Sweeten to taste. Add one yolk of egg to color it. Stir it gently on the fire till it is very hot, but do not let it boil. Strain it through a thin napkin and serve it in glasses.

LEMON CREAM.

Five eggs, leaving out the whites of two. Four large lemons peeled, the juice of two. Half a pound sugar, one pint cold water. Mix all well together. Put it on the fire and stir until thick, but do not let it boil. When cool serve in jelly glasses.

DESSERTS.

BOILED CUSTARD.

One quart milk, eight eggs, one teacup sugar. Season with vanilla. Custard should be put into a custard boiler, or a tin pail. This should be placed in a kettle of boiling water, stirring the mixture constantly till it is a little thickened. If it is well stirred the custard will be a smooth cream, but if allowed to remain too long in the boiling water after it has begun to thicken it will curdle, and be spoiled. If any other flavor than vanilla is used, it should not be put in until the custard is cooked. It is best to boil the milk before adding the other ingredients, then it will not curdle.

SWISS CREAM.

Put two pints of cream into two bowls. With one bowl mix six ounces loaf sugar, the juice of two large lemons, two glasses white wine; then add the other pint of cream and stir the whole very hard. Boil two ounces isinglass in four small cupsful of water till it is reduced to half, stir the isinglass when lukewarm to the other ingredients, and put the whole into moulds.

VELVET CREAM.

One ounce gelatine, one quart cream, one teacupful wine. It must be scalded, but not allowed to boil. Sweeten to taste. Vanilla can be used as a flavoring. This is very nice.

SPANISH CREAM.

To one quart milk add half a box gelatine. Let it dissolve in the milk while it is heating before it comes to a boil, stir all the time. Beat the yolks of four eggs well, into five tablespoonsful of white sugar. Flavor with vanilla or lemon. As soon as the milk boils pour it on the yolks, and return it to the fire, stirring all the time. As soon as it comes to the consistency of custard pour it into a pan. Have ready the whites of eggs beaten to a stiff froth. Mix them well into the custard, and pour off into moulds.

STONE CREAM.

One quart milk, half a box of gelatine, sugar to taste. Let it stand ten minutes, then put on to boil. When boiled pour it on the yolks of three eggs previously beaten, and set it away to cool. When nearly cold flavor with vanilla and put in moulds.

LEMON CREAM.

Take the whites of seven eggs and the yolk of one, the juice of four lemons and the rind of one. Half a pint spring water, half a pound loaf sugar. Stir it on the fire till it thickens.

ITALIAN CREAM.

Half a box of gelatine dissolved in boiling water, add one quart boiling milk, in which dissolve a dessert-spoonful of corn starch. The whites of six eggs whipped to a froth, adding sugar by degrees. Strain the boiling milk upon this, then stir until cool and pour into moulds. Serve with a rich custard made with the yolks.

SPANISH CREAM.

Take half a box of gelatine, cover it with water, and let it stand about half an hour. Take one quart of milk, and let it boil up once or twice. Beat *very light* five eggs separately, and add sufficient sugar to sweeten them. Mix the eggs and sugar well together, pour the melted gelatine into the boiling milk. When perfectly dissolved pour it upon the sugar and eggs. Return it to the fire for a few moments, stirring all the time. Season with vanilla and pour into moulds. Eat it with cream.

SNOW RICE CREAM.

Put in a stew-pan four ounces of ground rice, two ounces sugar, a few drops of the essence of almonds (or any other essence), and two ounces fresh butter. Add a quart of milk; boil fifteen or twenty minutes, until it forms a smooth substance, but not too thick; then pour it into moulds that have been buttered, and serve when cold. It will turn out of the moulds like jelly. The rice must be well cooked.

SNOW.

Pour a teacupful of cold water over one ounce gelatine, let it stand twenty minutes, then add two pints boiling water. When dissolved set it to cool, but not to congeal. Beat the whites of six eggs very light, mix in two teacups of pounded sugar. Pour in the gelatine, season to taste, and beat all together three-quarters of an hour. Then put it in moulds. To be eaten with slip or custard.

SPANISH CREAM.

One quart of new milk, half an ounce isinglass, boil them together. Then pour it over the yolks of eight eggs well beaten. Sweeten and flavor to taste. After this is cold beat the whites of three eggs, and stir them in hard until it is well mixed, then pour it in a bowl or dish. Vanilla is the best seasoning.

SPANISH CREAM.

Three and a half pints milk poured on one ounce gelatine to soak, six eggs. Beat the sugar and yolks together, pour them into boiling milk, and let it cool, then mix the whites in after having beaten them well. Flavor with vanilla, and pour into moulds. Whipped cream is an improvement to be eaten with it. Only soak the gelatine in *one* pint of the milk.

ITALIAN CREAM.

Take one quart of cream and divide it into two parts. To one pint add half a tumbler full of wine, and the juice of two lemons and six ounces of sugar. Then take one ounce of isinglass and dissolve it in a cup of water. Then add it to the other pint of cream, stir all together and put into moulds.

CHOCOLATE CUSTARD.

To one pint of milk put the yolks of three eggs. Make the custard just as you would plain boiled custard. Have one bar of the sweetened Walter Baker's chocolate dissolved in a little water. After putting the custard on the fire the second time stir in the chocolate. Stir it very fast, just let it come to a hard boil, then take it off and sweeten it. When cold flavor with vanilla. When you put it in the dish or bowl have the whites of eggs and a little sugar beaten up on the top. Then hold the lid of an oven over it and bake it brown.

CREAM CUSTARD.

Mix one pint of cream with one of milk, five beaten eggs, one tablespoonful flour, and three of sugar. Add nutmeg or vanilla to taste. Bake the custard in cups in a quick oven.

BAKED CUSTARD.

Beat the yolks of four fresh eggs for at least half an hour; add five ounces pulverized sugar, then stir into the sugar and eggs one quart of rich new milk, cold. Add a teaspoonful of distilled rose water or any flavoring extract you like. Fill the custard cups and set them in a stone pan half filled with water which may be warm at first, not hot. Put the pan in a rather cool oven, and gradually increase to a moderate heat. In about twenty minutes dip a teaspoon into one of the custards to ascertain if it is firm. Judgment and great care are needed to attain skill in baking custard, for if left in the oven a minute too long, or if the fire is too hot, the milk will certainly whey.

BURNED CUSTARD.

Fill a glass bowl nearly full of nice boiled custard. Beat until perfectly light the whites of six eggs. To each egg allow one tablespoonful of pulverized sugar, which add gradually, beating all the time. Heap the bowl with this meringue, and with an iron plate or clean shovel heated red hot, brown it well all over until the delicate, much admired flavor is imparted that gives this the name of burned custard.

CHOCOLATE CUSTARD.

One division of a cake of chocolate dissolved in a little water. To this put one pint of new milk and the yolks of three eggs. Put the chocolate into the milk and boil a few minutes. Sweeten with quarter of a pound of sugar, and then pour it, boiling hot, over the eggs which have been previously beaten till light. Return all to the kettle and stir well until it thickens or is upon the point of boiling, when it must instantly be poured off and set to cool.

CHARLOTTE RUSSE.

One quart cream, half a box of gelatine, one cup of milk, half a pound fine sugar. Pour on the gelatine half a pint of cold water, let it soak, then dissolve it over the fire, mixing it with sugar. When all are dissolved let it cool, but not enough to congeal the gelatine. Whip the cream, beat the whole well together, and fill the moulds, which must be lined with sponge cake.

CHARLOTTE RUSSE.

One and a half ounces of gelatine dissolved in one pint of water, let it simmer to half a pint. Make a custard of four eggs to one pint of milk, let it cool. Boil one vanilla bean in milk also. Whip one quart of cream to a froth, lay it on a sieve after it is whipped. Stir the custard into the gelatine, then add the whipped cream. Beat all together, line a glass dish with lady-fingers or sponge cake, and serve.

CUSTARD WITHOUT EGGS.

One quart new milk, four tablespoonsful corn starch, and two of sugar. Season with nutmeg, or cinnamon if preferred, and salt to taste. The milk should be put in a skillet over a brisk fire; the corn starch, mixed with cold milk to prevent its lumping, stirred in while boiling. As soon as it is thoroughly scalded stir in the sugar, salt and spice. It may be baked in crust or cups. This is an excellent recipe. Vanilla is better than spice.

CHARLOTTE RUSSE.

Dissolve as much gelatine as one of Cox's packets contains —the size marked one shilling—in half a pint new milk. The milk should be poured cold over the gelatine, left to stand about half an hour, and then set over the fire in a stew-pan. Stir it steadily until the gelatine is thoroughly melted. Then set it aside. Beat up the yolks of four eggs, to which add ten ounces pulverized sugar. Add these to the dissolved gelatine and milk, which then return to fire, and stir rapidly till it thickens. Then pour into a china bowl, and having provided two quarts of rich cream, whip up and add to the custard all the foam that rises till the whole quantity is used. Pour the congealing cream into moulds lined with sponge cake, or ladyfingers, and the charlotte russe is made. To have this dish in perfection the mould should be set in a tub, and finely pounded ice or snow, and salt packed closely around, so that the cream may freeze. Only use fresh cream, and serve in twenty-four hours.

MANIOCA CREAM.

Six tablespoonsful of manioca, six well beaten eggs, one quart milk, one cup sugar; flavor to taste. Soak manioca in a little cold water till quite soft; boil the milk and while boiling stir in the manioca, and the yolks of the eggs beaten with the sugar. When sufficiently cooked, pour into a dish to cool, then add flavoring. Beat the whites of the eggs light, with half a cup of powdered sugar, and some vanilla and stir in the manioca. Whipped cream on top is a great improvement.

FRUIT JELLY.

One-half box of gelatine dissolved by pouring cold water over it, letting it stand until swollen; then pour one pint of boiling water over it, stirring it until it is all dissolved. Then add one pound of granulated sugar, the juice and grated rind of three lemons, juice of three oranges; strain it. Take four oranges, six bananas, one-half pound Malaga grapes; divide the oranges into small divisions, slice the bananas, put them into the bowl, you intend to serve them in, and when the jelly begins to congeal pour it over the fruit. Put on ice until the jelly is congealed. You can add other fruits, such as chopped pineapple, ripe strawberries, raspberries; any fruits that are in season.

1 cup hot maple syrup beaten into the yolks of 3 eggs — when cold stir into a pint of whipped cream. Put in a mold in ice.

Crème sambaglione or Mousse italienne
Take yolks of 12 fresh eggs & 4 glasses of madeira or other good white wine — sweeten to taste & add a pinch of cinnamon.
Put the whole in a saucepan over a slow fire & stir in turning it very fast with a whisk or the egg-beater (not turned by the handle) until the mousse thickens & fills the saucepan. Don't let it boil. Serve instantly.
(Instead of measuring wine in wine-glass — use ½ of an egg shell to each person estimating 1½ egg-yolks per person.)

Chocolate Sauce
1 cup powdered sugar
1 pt. milk
2 eggs
1 tablespoonful of cornstarch
1 teaspoonful of vanilla
2 oz chocolate

Reserve 3 tablespoonfuls of the milk & put the remainder on the stove in a double boiler. Mix the cornstarch with the cold milk & stir it in the boiling milk.
Scrape the chocolate & put it into a small frying pan with 4 tablespoonfuls of sugar & 2 of hot water. Stir over the fire until smooth and glossy — then stir it into the boiling mixture.

nally beat the sugar into this and then add the unbeaten yolks and stir this mixture into that which is boiling. Cook for a minute longer, stirring all the time.

On taking it from the fire add the vanilla extract.

Serve hot or cold.

PUDDINGS AND PIES.

BATTER PUDDING.

Sixteen tablespoonsful of flour, one quart of milk, six eggs, and a little salt; the eggs must be beaten to a stiff froth. After all are mixed beat it fifteen minutes till very light. This pudding may be either baked or boiled. Serve it hot, and eat it with sauce.

SWEET POTATO PUDDING.

Six eggs, two pounds potatoes, one pound sugar, one pound butter, one nutmeg, two large lemons. Crust in the bottom of the dish.

IRISH POTATO PUDDING.

Two and a half pounds potatoes, one and a half pounds sugar, one and a quarter pounds butter, six eggs, one nutmeg, three lemons, grated rind and juice.

COCOANUT PUDDING.

One quart boiled milk, thickened with four tablespoonsful of corn starch. While hot stir in one cup of butter. Beat four eggs with two cups of sugar. Grate two cocoanuts in the mixture. Bake in a crust, and season with vanilla.

BUTTERMILK PUDDING.

One pint of buttermilk, two eggs, one cup of white sugar, one-half cup of butter, three tablespoons of corn starch, one-half teaspoon of soda in the milk. Beat the eggs very light; mix all together, flavor with vanilla; bake in a nice pie crust. This will make two puddings.

JEFF DAVIS PUDDING.

One cup of butter or suet, one cup sour milk, one cup of molasses, teaspoon of soda in it, one cup of raisins, flour enough to make a stiff batter, one teaspoonful of ground cloves, one of allspice. Grease your pan; put it in and steam it from three to five hours.

DELMONICO'S PUDDING.

Five eggs, three tablespoonsful of pulverized sugar, two and one-half tablespoons of corn starch, two and one-half pints of sweet milk. Beat the eggs and sugar very light, leaving *out* three whites for the meringue. Stir in the corn starch; have the milk on boiling, and while it is boiling stir in the mixture very rapidly. By the time it is all in it will be done; pour into your pudding dish, and put in the stove a minute. Add six tablespoons of pulverized sugar to the three whites, one-half teaspoon of vanilla, and beat to a stiff icing. Beat it in a *bowl*, and put it on the pudding, and brown it lightly. Add one teaspoonful of vanilla to the pudding before baking it. Let it get very cold and serve it with cold cream.

PLUM PUDDING.

One pound of chopped suet, one pound of grated bread, one pound of raisins, one pound of grated or chopped apples, quarter pound of citron, ten eggs, one teacupful of cream seasoned with mace or nutmeg. Let it boil three hours. This makes a large pudding, and is very nice.

CHOCOLATE PUDDING.

Boil one quart of milk, adding three ounces of Walter Baker's chocolate. Stir it until it is dissolved. Then remove it from the fire. Six eggs (leaving out three of the whites) beaten light, adding sugar to taste; one pint of bread-crumbs. Pour on them the milk and chocolate. Season with vanilla, and bake like custard. When cool beat the three whites with white sugar and vanilla, and spread it on the top. Then put it back in the oven just long enough to harden.

LEMON PUDDING.

Three cups of water, thicken with corn starch till stiff. While boiling stir in nearly a cupful of butter, three cups of sugar, three well beaten eggs, and the juice and grated rind of three lemons. Bake in a crust.

POTATO PUDDING.

Boil one pound of potatoes, mash and rub them through a cullender. Stir to a cream three-quarters of a pound of butter and the same amount of sugar. Add to this gradually a wine-glassful of rose water, one glass of wine and one of brandy. The juice and grated peel of two lemons. If you have no lemons use powdered mace. Beat six eggs very light and add them by degrees to the mixture, alternately with the potatoes, and bake in a buttered dish.

BAKED WHORTLEBERRIES.

Eight eggs, seven cups flour, five cups sugar, one cup butter, one cup milk, two quarts berries, one nutmeg, one glass of wine, one teaspoon soda. Flour the berries; beat the eggs very light.

CURRANT PIE.

One teacup of red currants, one cup of sugar, yolks of two eggs, one tablespoonful of flour, one-half tablespoon of water. Mix and bake in lower pie crust. Beat the whites of the eggs, with one-half teacup of pulverized sugar, spread over top and brown slightly.

COTTAGE PUDDING.

One cup sugar, one tablespoonful butter, two eggs, one cup sweet milk, three cups flour, half a teaspoonful soda. Eat with liquid sauce.

CREAM CAKE PUDDING.

One teacupful of fine white sugar, three eggs, one teacup of flour, one teaspoonful of Royal Baking Powder. Bake in shallow tins.

Mixture for filling.—One quart milk, four tablespoonsful corn starch, two eggs, two cups sugar. Season with lemon or vanilla.

APPLE PUDDING.

Ten eggs, leaving out five of the whites, one pint of stewed apples put through a strainer, half a pound of butter, the grated rind and juice of two large lemons. Sugar to taste. Paste at bottom of dish. Very fine.

INDIAN MEAL PUDDING.

Four eggs, the weight of three eggs in meal, half a pound white sugar, quarter pound butter. Beat the sugar and butter together. Then add the eggs, lastly the meal. Beat quickly and bake in a quick oven. Flavor with the juice and grated rind of one lemon. When it is sufficiently cool spread currant jelly over the top. A sauce is an improvement.

COTTAGE PUDDING.

One pint flour, one cup sugar, one cup milk, one egg, one tablespoonful butter, one teaspoonful of soda, one teaspoonful cream of tartar or one teaspoonful of Royal Baking Powder. Mix all well together; beat it hard and bake in a dish. To be eaten with wine sauce.

TYLER PUDDING.

To six eggs add three cups of sugar, one and a half cups of butter, one cup of cream and one grated nutmeg. Beat it well and bake in pie crust.

SWEETMEAT PUDDING.

Five eggs, the yolks and whites beaten separately, one teacupful of preserves, one cup of sugar and one cup of melted butter. Bake quickly and serve up hot.

SPONGE PUDDING.

Half a cup butter, half a cup sugar, two and three-quarter cups of flour, one cup of milk, four eggs, two spoonsful of cream of tartar, one teaspoonful of soda, the juice and rind of one lemon. Bake moderately for one hour.

Sauce for the above.—Half a cupful butter, one cup sugar, the yolks of two eggs, one teacup of flour, one glass of wine or lemon juice. Cream the butter and sugar. Mix all together and pour on a teacupful of boiling water. Stir it all the time until it begins to boil.

BOILED RICE PUDDING.

Quarter pound rice, half a pound of stoned raisins, half a teaspoonful of salt. Tie in a pudding bag, allowing room to swell. Boil it two hours and serve with hard sauce.

PRUNE PUDDING.

One pound stewed prunes mashed through a cullender. Whites of six eggs beaten stiff, three tablespoons white sugar. Bake fifteen minutes.

PRUNE PUDDING, No. 1.

Take one pound prunes, boil till tender enough to take seed out, two cloves and juice and rind of one lemon; take not quite half box gelatine, dissolve in cold water, then add the hot prunes and pour in a mould. Serve with seasoned cream, whipped, and sherry wine.

CARROT PUDDING.

One pound of carrots boiled and mashed fine, one pound raisins, half a pound currants, half a pound of suet chopped fine, eight tablespoonsful of flour, four of brown sugar, one of mixed spices, one nutmeg, one egg. Mix all well. Boil for four hours, then put it in a dish and bake twenty minutes.

BLACKBERRY PUDDING.

Half a pound butter, one pound brown sugar, half a pound flour, four eggs beaten light. Cream the butter and sugar till light; add the eggs and flour alternately. After pouring in the baking dish put on the top one quart of blackberries (raw). To be eaten with wine sauce.

APPLE PUDDING.

One and a half pints of coddled apples, the peel of three lemons, the juice of two, one and a quarter pounds sugar, half a pound butter, one teacupful of cream, eight eggs, leaving out three of the whites. Melt the butter, add the cream, stir in the eggs, sugar, butter and lemon peel. Put it on the fire, let it get quite hot, then put it in puff paste crust and bake. The whites must be beaten to a stiff froth with sugar; add the juice of the lemons and put it over the pudding. Let it brown a few moments. To be eaten cold.

TAPIOCA PUDDING.

*Half a pint tapioca soaked for six hours in a quart of milk, five eggs, sugar to taste, nutmeg, one tablespoonful of wine or brandy, grease the dish and put pieces of butter on the top. Bake it for one hour.

POTATO PUDDING.

Take ten eggs, one pound sugar, three-quarters of a pound of butter creamed, one pound potatoes boiled and run through a cullender while hot, a small cup of cream. Part of the sugar to be added to the butter and the rest to the eggs, which add to the potatoes. Flavor with orange peel or mace; a small portion of French brandy is an improvement.

CUSTARD PUDDING.

One pint milk, six eggs, three large spoonsful of corn starch and two of sugar. To be eaten with a sauce of wine, butter, sugar and nutmeg.

RICE MERINGUE.

One cup rice, ten tablespoonsful sugar, three eggs, one quart of milk. Soak the rice in cold water for two hours. Then put it on the fire with the milk and boil until done. Beat the yolks of the eggs with three spoonsful of sugar and milk while boiling. Beat the whites with the rest of the sugar, add lemon juice to your taste. Put in a dish, lay the whites on top and bake till brown.

ORANGE PUDDING.

One pound butter and one pound sugar, beat to a cream. One glass brandy, one glass wine, ten eggs beaten light. Pare two oranges and boil the rind until it is tender, then beat it in a mortar and squeeze in the juice, also the rind and juice of one lemon. Bake in a pie-crust.

VELVET PUDDING.

Five eggs beaten light, one teacup of sugar, four tablespoonsful of corn starch mixed in a little cold milk and added to the eggs and sugar. Boil three pints of milk, pour it over the eggs, and stir while boiling until it becomes thick. Flavor with vanilla, and pour into a baking dish. Beat the whites of the eggs with a teacupful of sugar. Pour it over the top, and return it to the oven to brown.

The sauce is as follows: Take the yolks of two eggs, one cup of sugar, one tablespoonful of butter. Beat all together, and add a cup of boiling milk. Put it on the fire, let it come to a boil, and flavor with vanilla.

BAKED APPLE DUMPLINGS.

Roll out some dough thicker than piecrust, and enclose a handful of sliced ripe apples, well covered with butter and sugar. Bring the edges together as in any other dumpling. When as many are made as desired, place them side by side in a pudding dish, spread butter and sugar over them, and pour boiling water enough to half cover the dumplings. Put them in the stove, and cook moderately fast until they are nicely browned. The butter and sugar make a nice sauce flavored with nutmeg.

APPLE SAGO.

One cup of sago, one quart of boiling water poured on it. Season with milk, lemon and sugar. Pare and core as many apples as will stand in the dish. Pour over them the sago, and bake one hour. Serve them with sugar and cream.

FLORENTINE PUDDING.

Boil one quart of rice in one quart of milk until very soft. When sufficiently cold add the yolks of three eggs, a little salt, one cup of white sugar, one grated lemon, and a little of the juice. Beat all light, then put in a dish, and pour over the top the whites of the eggs well beaten. Add a little sugar. Put it in the oven long enough to brown nicely.

BOILED PUDDING.

One teacupful of milk, one of molasses, one of chopped suet or butter, one of raisins stoned and chopped fine, three and a half teacups of sifted flour, one teaspoonful of soda, one of cream of tartar, or one teaspoonful of Royal Baking Powder, and one of salt. Mix all together, beat it well, pour it in a cloth, tie it up tight, and boil it four hours.

MERINGUE PUDDING.

Pour one quart of warm milk over a pint of grated bread, add the yolks of four eggs well beaten, one cup of sugar, a small piece of butter, the rind of one lemon. Then put it to bake. Beat the whites of the eggs quite light, and add to them one and a half cups of sugar and the juice of the lemon. Spread this on the pudding when it is cool, then put it in the oven and let it brown a little. This pudding will be improved by a layer of stewed apples nicely seasoned or some preserves put between the pudding and the whites of the eggs before replacing in the oven.

MERINGUES.

The whites of nine eggs beaten very stiff. One pound of granulated sugar beaten into the eggs. Have ready some boards which will fit in the oven. Cover them with paper, which must be thoroughly wet, never greased. Put the egg and sugar into little forms about the size and shape of a goose egg. Place them on the boards, and put them into a moderately warm oven, and let them cook until they are a delicate brown. If you have a tin oven put them into that, if not, open the oven doors for an hour or two till the outside is quite hard. Remove them from the paper, and scrape out gently all the soft inside, which can be used again, and put the shells to dry in the oven. When the inside is thoroughly dry take them out, fit them together, two and two, and put them in a stone jar. They will keep some time if air-tight. When ready to be eaten fill them with whipped cream, sweetened and flavored, or with ice cream.

WHORTLEBERRY PUDDING.

Four eggs, three and a half cups flour, two and a half cups sugar, half cup of butter, half cup of milk, one quart berries, half glass wine, half nutmeg, half teaspoonful soda. Blackberries may be used if preferred.

1, 2, 3, 4 PUDDING.

Four eggs, three teacups of flour, two cups sugar, one cup butter. A teacupful of buttermilk, with a small teaspoonful of soda. Season to taste and bake like cake.

APPLE CHARLOTTE.

One dozen juicy apples, chopped in the same proportion of stewed apples, quarter loaf bread grated; butter a baking dish well; cover the bottom with apples, spices, sugar and small lumps of butter. Then put in a layer of bread, and so on till the dish is full, bread being the last layer, well buttered.

DANDY JACK PUDDING.

Four eggs, two tablespoonsful of corn starch, one quart milk, one cup sugar. Beat the sugar, corn starch and yolks of the eggs together with one cup of the milk. Scald the rest of the milk and put the above with it. Flavor with lemon or vanilla. Beat the whites of the eggs with a little sugar to a stiff froth, and spread it on top of the pudding after it is cold, and set it in the oven to brown.

COTTAGE PUDDING.

One quart flour, two teacupsful of milk, two teacupsful of sugar, quarter pound butter, one pound currants, two teaspoonsful of Royal Baking Powder. Bake one hour and serve hot with wine sauce. Half this quantity is sufficient for a small family.

POTATO PUDDING.

One pound potatoes, one pound loaf sugar, half pound fresh butter, the yolks of eight eggs, and the whites of four. One teaspoonful of beaten mace, or the rind of one lemon and half the juice. Add citron if you like it. Boil the potatoes dry; squeeze them in a coarse cloth and put them in a marble mortar. When milk-warm add the butter well washed, beat them until perfectly light, then add them to the eggs and sugar beaten very light, then strain them through a hair sieve.

BREAD PUDDING (Boiled).

Boil one quart of milk and put in it half pound of grated bread. Stir it over the fire till it is thick, then take it off and when pretty cool add six eggs, a small quantity of salt, and two and a half pounds of currants. Put in a mould, boil one hour. Eat with sauce.

BREAD PUDDING (Boiled).

One quart grated bread, one pound currants or raisins, one pound suet, half pound sugar, eight eggs, two spoonsful of brandy, nutmeg, four spoonsful of cream. Boil it in a cloth three hours.

BAKED BREAD PUDDING.

To one quart cream or new milk boiled, add a penny loaf of bread grated very fine, five eggs, one nutmeg, one-quarter pound butter, quarter pound sugar. Stir all together and bake one hour.

BAKED BREAD PUDDING.

One pint of stale baker's bread grated. Pour over it one quart of cold milk, one teacup of white sugar, a piece of butter the size of an egg, the grated rind of one lemon, the yolks of four eggs well beaten. Put it in a greased dish and bake. After the pudding cools spread over it some preserved pineapple. Then beat the four whites to a stiff froth, adding a teacupful of white sugar and the juice of a lemon. Spread this over the pudding, and set it in the oven a few minutes, but do not let it brown.

SWEET APPLE PUDDING.

One pint scalded milk, half pint of Indian meal, a teaspoonful of salt and six sweet apples cut in small pieces. This makes excellent jelly.

CARDINAL RICHELIEU'S PUDDING. (Very fine).

Take a thick round sponge cake baked in a scalloped pan. Split it in three slices and spread each slice with currant jelly and put them nicely together, then pour over it half a pint of white wine, and let it stand over night. The next morning stick small pieces of citron, and blanched almonds all over the cake, then pour over it a rich custard flavored with vanilla.

GROUND RICE PUDDING.

Boil one pint of milk with a small piece of lemon peel. Mix quarter pound of ground rice with half pint of milk, two ounces of sugar, and one of butter. Add this to the boiling milk. Keep stirring constantly. Take it off the fire, break in two eggs and continue stirring. Then butter a pie dish, pour in the mixture, and bake until done.

DRIED PEACH PUDDING.

One pound suet, one pound bread, one pound peaches, one cup of milk to soften the bread, one cup flour, one cup sugar, one teaspoonful cloves, and nine eggs. The peaches must be parboiled, cut in fine pieces, and flavored before mixing. The ingredients are mixed and boiled like plum pudding, served hot with wine sauce. A very nice dessert.

APPLE FLOAT.

To one quart of apples stewed and well mashed, put the whites of three eggs well beaten, four heaping tablespoonsful of pounded loaf sugar. Beat them together for fifteen minutes, and eat with cream.

APPLE TRIFLE.

Take four pippins, boil them till they are soft, strain them, then take an equal quantity of loaf sugar, beat them together with the whites of three eggs, until it is perfectly light, then place some slices of sponge cake in a dish, strew bright jellies over the cake, and wet it with sweet wine, then put the apples over this and ornament it as you please.

FLOAT.

Take the whites of six eggs, five tablespoonsful of acid jelly, and three tablespoonsful of sugar. Beat all together until very light. Have a bowl three-fourths full of frothed cream, which has been flavored with wine and sweetened to taste. Place this lightly on top of the first preparation.

PEACH COBBLER.

Prepare some plain pastry from three pints flour and three-quarters pound of mixed butter and lard. Line a good sized baking dish with the pastry, and pour in two quarts of freshly stewed peaches, closing the dish with a cover of pastry. Let it bake till brown. This should be accompanied by tumblers of rich milk when brought to the table.

PEACH PUDDING.

Fill a baking dish about three-fourths full of ripe juicy peaches pared, stoned, and cut into medium sized pieces. Beat light the yolks of three eggs. Add four tablespoonsful of white sugar, three of milk or cream, and three of sifted flour. Add the beaten whites, and after sifting three tablespoonsful of sugar over the fruit, pour on the batter. Mix all well together, and bake three-quarters of an hour. Eat hot with sauce.

BAKED PLUM PUDDING.

Chop one pound of suet very fine, removing all the skins and strings. Mix with it two pounds of sifted flour, one pound each of dried currants and stoned raisins, and one ounce of preserved citron cut fine. Moisten with four eggs beaten till smooth, stirring hard all the time till a white batter is made (a pint of milk should be sufficient). Sprinkle in half a pound of sifted sugar, and beat all well together. Pour into well buttered tin pans, and bake for three hours in a slow oven.

PLAIN PLUM PUDDING.

Break into small pieces a stale loaf of baker's bread, letting it soak in milk until it has absorbed all it will, then drain it off thoroughly, and work out all the milk you can with a spoon. If you have any beef suet add a little, but it will do without. Then stir in half a teacupful of molasses, half pound brown sugar, half pound stoned rasins, quarter pound of currants rolled in flour, and a few pieces of citron. Boil in either a mould or a pudding bag. Eat with wine sauce. This is very nice for ordinary occasions.

RICE MERINGUE.

One cupful of carefully sorted rice boiled in water until soft. When done drain it so as to remove all the water. Cool it, add one quart new milk, and the well beaten yolks of three eggs, three tablespoonsful of white sugar, and a little nutmeg. Pour it into a baking dish, and bake about half an hour. Let it get cold. Beat the whites of two eggs, add two tablespoonsful of white sugar, flavor with lemon or vanilla. Drop or spread it over the pudding and slightly brown it in the oven.

PLAIN RICE PUDDING.

Two quarts milk, half pint of rice, and sugar to taste. Put it into a tin pan and bake slowly one hour. Currants and raisins may be added before cooking. To be eaten cold.

BIRD'S NEST.

Pare six or eight apples (Spitzenbergs or Greenings are best), remove the core, leaving the apples whole. Place them in a baking dish, then make a thin batter, using one quart of milk, three eggs, with sufficient corn starch to thicken it. Pour it in the apples and around them, sprinkle with sugar and bake. Eat hot with cream and sugar.

STRAWBERRY TAPIOCA.

Soak over night a large teacupful of tapioca in cold water. In the morning put half of it in your pudding dish. Sprinkle sugar over the tapioca, then on top of this put one quart of berries, sugar, and the rest of the tapioca. Fill the dish with water so as to cover the tapioca about a quarter of an inch. Bake in a moderately hot oven till it looks clear. Eat cold with cream or custard. If not sweet enough add more sugar at the table, and in baking if it seems too dry, a little more water is needed. This is delightful. A similar dish may be made with either peaches, or pineapples, pared and sliced, instead of strawberries.

TAPIOCA PUDDING.

Quarter pound of tapioca soaked over night. In the morning pour off and put in one and a quarter quarts of boiling water; sweeten and flavor to taste. Take six or eight tart apples, pare, core and stand them in a baking dish. Fill the middle with sugar and a little cinnamon, pour the tapioca over, and bake until the apples are done. Eat cold with cream. If preferred the apples can be sliced.

BAKED BATTER PUDDING.

One quart sifted flour, butter size of an egg, one pint milk, half teaspoon salt and four eggs. Scald the milk and melt the butter in it. When partly cooled stir in the well beaten yolks, then salt and flour. When cold stir in lightly, the whites beaten stiff. Bake in rather large patty-pans, and serve at once with sauce. They should be light puffs. Strawberry sauce is very nice with them.

GERMAN TARTS.

The yolks of half a dozen hard-boiled eggs, two raw eggs, half a pound butter, half a pound sugar, and flour enough to make a stiff dough. Cream the butter and sugar together, then rub the yolks in until perfectly fine, then the raw eggs, then the flour. Roll and put in pie plates. Place pieces of tart, jelly, or preserves through it, and cover with strips of the dough. This is a very nice recipe.

QUEEN'S PUDDING.

One pint of fine bread-crumbs, one cup sugar, one quart milk, the yolks of four eggs, the rind of one lemon, and a piece of butter the size of an egg. Bake it until *just done*. Have the whites of the eggs and the juice of the lemon well beaten. Spread jelly or preserves on the top of the pudding, then the froth. Bake very little, just to brown on the top. To be eaten cold with cream. A delicious dessert.

MOLASSES PUDDING.

Three eggs, one cup sugar, one cup molasses, one cup cream, one teaspoonful soda, three cups flour, one and a half of butter. To be eaten with wine sauce. Very good.

BROWN BETTY.

One cup bread-crumbs, two cups chopped tart apples, half a cup brown sugar, one teaspoonful cinnamon, two tablespoonsful butter. Butter a deep dish and put in a layer of apples at the bottom; sprinkle with sugar, a few bits of butter, and some cinnamon; then put a layer of bread-crumbs. Proceed in the same manner till the dish is full, having bread for the top layer. Cover it closely and steam it three-quarters of an hour in a moderate oven, then uncover and brown quickly. Eat hot with sugar and cream or with a sauce.

GERMAN PUFFS.

To one pint milk add six eggs well beaten, four tablespoonsful flour, one spoonful melted butter, and a grated nutmeg. Mix these ingredients well, leaving out the whites of three eggs for sauce. Pour the mixture into cups well buttered, filling them half full. Bake in a quick oven. Turn them on a dish and pour the sauce over them.

The Sauce.—The whites of the three eggs made into a thin icing with crushed sugar, to which add lemon juice or rose water.

LEMON PUDDING.

Beat eight eggs very light, whites and yolks separately, half a pound of butter, half a pound sugar. Cream butter and sugar together. Stir this gradually into the eggs. Add the juice of two lemons, and the grated rind if desired.

LEMON PUDDING.

Juice and rind of three large lemons, one pound loaf sugar, half a pound butter, one pint cream, nine eggs beaten light. Mix well and bake in crust.

BLACK PLUM PUDDING.

One pound of chopped raisins, one pound currants, quarter pound citron cut fine, half a pound suet free from strings, half a pound of butter, half a pound white sugar, one and three quarter pounds of flour, six eggs, whites and yolks beaten separately, half a pint milk, half a cup brandy, one grated nutmeg, one tablespoonful mace, one tablespoonful of cloves. Boil five hours. This is sufficient quantity for eight or ten people.

ENGLISH PLUM PUDDING.

To make what is termed a pound pudding take one pound of raisins well stoned, and one pound of currants thoroughly washed. Chop a pound of suet very fine, and mix all together. Add quarter pound of flour or bread finely crumbled, three ounces of sugar, one and a half ounces of grated lemon peel, a blade of mace, half a small nutmeg, one teaspoonful of ginger, half a dozen well beaten eggs. Work all well together, put it in a cloth, tie it firmly, allowing room for it to swell, and boil it not less than two hours.

PLUM OR SUET PUDDING.

Seven eggs, one pint new milk, half a pound of grated bread, half a pound flour, one and a half pounds of suet, one and a half pounds of raisins, one glass of brandy, two ounces sugar, half a nutmeg, one teaspoonful of ginger, one ounce of salt. Leave out the raisins if you wish. Boil it four hours.

APPLE PUDDING.

Take twelve apples pared and cored, boil them in a saucepan with a small piece of butter till they are soft, twelve eggs, the crumbs of a penny loaf of bread grated, half a nutmeg, a little rose water, sugar to your taste, quarter pound of butter melted, citron or orange peel. Paste in the bottom of the dish.

ANOTHER IRISH POTATO PUDDING.

Take two pounds peeled potatoes, boil and strain them through a cullender, half a pound butter, eight eggs, half a pint of cream, one pound white sugar beaten with the eggs. Spice and wine to taste. Cream the butter well.

ANOTHER SWEET POTATO PUDDING.

One pound sweet potatoes, half a pound sugar, half a pound butter, three eggs, one nutmeg, a little mace or cinnamon. Make like Irish potato pudding.

PLAIN BAKED PUDDING.

One quart new milk, six eggs, leaving out three whites, four tablespoonsful flour. Beat all well together, and bake in a deep dish. One teaspoonful of salt. To be eaten with sauce.

CRACKER PUDDING.

Six soda crackers, three teacups of water, three of loaf sugar, the pulp and grated rind of two lemons. Bake in a slow oven. Let the crackers dissolve in cold water. Bake with or without paste.

SPONGE PUDDING.

Half a cup butter, one and a half pounds sugar, three cups of flour, one cup milk, four eggs, two spoonsful cream of tartar sifted in the flour, one spoonful of soda, the juice and rind of one lemon. Bake in a moderate oven. In place of cream of tartar and soda, you can use two teaspoonsful of Royal Baking Powder.

PUMPKIN PIES.

Boil a pumpkin soft and dry. While hot add to enough for four pies one pint cream, half pound of butter, one and a half pounds sugar, six eggs. When it has cooled add cinnamon, nutmeg and a little orange peel. Brandy is an improvement.

FRITTERS.

Thicken one and a half pints of milk. When cold add four eggs beaten light, then add flour sufficient to make a batter. Set it away to rise. When light fry in boiling lard and serve up hot.

PANCAKE.

One pint cream, three tablespoonsful of wine, half pound flour, six eggs, leaving out half of the whites, quarter pound butter. Mix all well together and fry thin.

BELL FRITTERS, No 1.

Put a piece of butter the size of an egg into a pint of water, let it boil a few minutes, thicken it very smoothly with a pint of flour. Let it remain a short time on the fire, stirring constantly that it may not stick to the pan. Then pour it into a bowl, and let it get cold. Add six eggs, breaking one at a time, and beating it in till all are broken, and the dough is quite light. Put a pint of lard in a pan, and let it boil, and then drop the batter in. When the fritters are brown and crisp serve them up hot, and sprinkle with sugar.

THICKENED MILK FRITTERS.

Take one pint of thickened milk, and stir in it while it is hot, a large spoonful of butter, and when cool add the yolks of four eggs well beaten. Fry in boiling lard.

PANCAKES FRIED WITHOUT BUTTER OR LARD.

Six eggs well beaten, one pint cream, four ounces sugar, a glass of wine, half a nutmeg, and as much flour as will make it almost as thick as ordinary batter. Heat the frying-pan tolerably hot and pour in the batter thin.

ANOTHER RECIPE FOR PANCAKES.

Four yolks and two whites of eggs, one pint milk, half pint flour, a little salt, one teaspoonful ginger and a wineglass of brandy.

PANCAKES.

Put into a basin quarter pound sifted flour, one egg, quarter gill milk. Stir to a smooth paste; then add one and three-quarter gills of milk, two ounces fresh butter melted, and a small pinch of salt. Mix all well and if lumpy strain it. Put a small piece of butter into a cake pan; when melted pour in two tablespoonsful of the batter, spread it so that it covers the pan entirely. Fry till brown on one side, then toss it over till the other side is cooked and turn it out on a dish. When all the batter is cooked sprinkle the pancakes with sugar, and serve on a very hot dish with a cut lemon.

FRENCH FRITTERS.

One quart milk, boil half of it, mix the other half cold with one quart of flour. With this last thicken the boiling milk, and let all cook together till well done. While cooling beat ten eggs light. Add one teaspoonful of salt. Beat the eggs into the batter, adding a spoonful at a time until all is in. Have a small kettle half full of boiling lard. Allow not quite a spoonful of the batter to a fritter. Take them out before they turn dark and put them in a drainer.

APPLE FRITTERS.

Make a smooth batter of half a pound of flour, three eggs and half a pint of sweet milk; salt to taste. Cut a dozen large juicy apples into slices, after peeling and coring them. Throw the slices into the batter. Have ready a pan of equal parts of lard and butter boiling hot. Take the batter up in a ladle, allowing a slice of apple to each fritter, and drop into the hot lard. Fry brown, drain a moment, and serve with powdered sugar and nutmeg.

CORN FRITTERS.

To six ears of grated corn, add four tablespoonsful of sweet rich cream, half a coffee-cup of flour, and the yolks of three eggs. Beat the whites separately, and then stir them in. Salt and fry them as other fritters in hot butter. Milk can be used in the place of cream, but it is not so nice. This is a delicious dish for breakfast or for dessert with wine sauce.

GERMAN FRITTERS.

Cut slices of bread half an inch thick, remove the crust and soak them in milk, beat up two eggs, pour them over the bread and fry it in butter. Sprinkle powdered sugar over the fritters.

PANCAKES.

One and a quarter pounds of flour, nine eggs, one quart of milk, a little salt, beat the eggs well, add the milk, then stir in the flour. If still too thick, thin it with water or milk. The batter should be very thin, and very well beaten. Drop a piece of lard in the pan, and fry the cakes very thin.

CITY PUDDING.

A layer of grated bread covered with sugar, to which add a little cinnamon, and nutmeg. Put on it some lumps of butter, and a layer of sliced apples a quarter inch thick. Then add another layer of bread, sugar, spices, and butter, and so on in layers till the pan is full. Then pour on a wineglass of water. Bake for three-quarters of an hour. Serve with hard sauce.

ANOTHER WHORTLEBERRY PUDDING, No. 1.

Take half a pound of butter, half a pound sugar, three-quarters pound of flour, and five eggs to one quart of berries. Rub the berries in the flour and bake in a dish. Serve it with sauce.

A GOOD PUDDING FOR WINTER.

Grate a loaf of stale bread. Peel and chop fine half dozen apples. Add to the grated bread a little sugar and nutmeg, and put in a deep dish alternate layers of bread and apples, having the lower and upper layer of bread. Pour over this a teacup of water, and a few pieces of butter. Bake as you would other puddings.

PEACH PUDDING.

Take large open-stone peaches, peel and stone them, halve them, and place them in a dish with the bowls up. Make a very sweet custard and pour over the peaches. Then bake them.

PLUM PUDDING.

Take slices of light bread spread thin with butter, and put them in a pudding dish in alternate layers of bread and raisins till within an inch of the top. Add five eggs well beaten and stir in one quart milk. Pour it over the pudding, after adding sugar and spice to taste. Bake twenty-five minutes. Eat with liquid sauce if preferred. Before using the raisins boil them in a little water, and put all in.

LEMON PIE.

Beat the yolks of two eggs, with four tablespoonsful of sugar, one of melted butter, and the juice and grated peel of one lemon, half a teaspoonful of water. When cool beat the whites to a froth with two tablespoonsful of white sugar, and spread it over the pie. Put it in the oven and just let it brown.

OMELET SOUFFLÉE.

Break the yolks of six eggs into a basin, beat them until light, and flavor with lemon juice and grated lemon. Add six tablespoonsful of sugar. Beat well together, and mix in lightly five tablespoonsful of cream. Place the omelet pan, with a small piece of butter, in a quick oven. Pour in the eggs, and stir in lightly with a fork the well beaten whites. Let it cool five or six minutes. Dust the omelet well with pulverized sugar, and serve as quickly as possible, for it begins to fall when exposed to the air. It must be served in the dish in which it is baked.

OMELET AU RHUM.

Add a sherry-glassful of sugar to six eggs, and make the omelet as a plain omelet. When turned on to the dish sprinkle a little sugar on top, and pour over it five or six tablespoonsful of rum. Set it on fire, and send it to table burning..

PUMPKIN PIE.

Cut the pumpkin into thin slices, and boil until tender in as little water as possible. Watch carefully that it does not scorch. Drain off all the water. Mash and rub it through a sieve, adding while warm a small piece of butter. To every quart of the pumpkin, after mashing, add one pint new milk or cream and four eggs, the yolks and whites beaten separately. Add white sugar to taste, also cinnamon and nutmeg. A very little brandy is a great improvement. The oven in which they are baked must be hot, or they will not be brown. It is as well to heat the batter scalding hot before pouring into the pie dishes.

BOILED ROLY-BOLY PUDDING.

Make a puff paste, and roll it out into a square about a quarter of an inch thick. Spread over it, leaving an inch uncovered at the edges, almost any kind of fruit or berries, such as strawberries, raspberries, etc., sweetened, or preserves. Roll it tight. Sew it in a cloth, allowing room to swell. Boil or steam it an hour. Serve with almost any kind of pudding sauce.

APPLE PUDDING.

Two teacups of apples stewed and strained, two of sugar, one of butter, seven yolks of eggs. Take five whites, and half a cup of sugar, beat very light and spread over the puddings. Brown slightly.

QUINCE PUDDING.

Take six large ripe quinces stewed and strained, half a pint sweet cream, half a pint sugar, seven eggs; leave out all the whites but two. Add lemon juice to taste.

THICKENED MILK PUDDING.

One quart milk. When it boils stir in enough flour to thicken it like mush; add a piece of butter the size of an egg. When cold add five eggs well beaten. Bake in a moderate oven. Season to taste, and serve with sauce.

COCOANUT PUDDING.

One large nut grated, half pound butter, half pound sugar, whites of six eggs, and season with lemon or wine. This is sufficient for four large puddings.

SWEET POTATO PUDDING.

One and a quarter pounds potatoes, half pound butter, three-quarters of sugar, half cup of milk, half cup wine, one teaspoonful cinnamon, half a nutmeg, and three eggs. This will make six puddings.

CREAM PUDDING.

Five eggs, three quarters pound butter, one pound sugar, one pint cream, a little nutmeg. Bake quickly.

PUMPKIN PIE.

One quart steamed pumpkin, six eggs, six ounces butter, a pound and one-quarter of white sugar, one and a half pints of milk, cinnamon and nutmeg to taste; lemon if preferred.

PLUM PUDDING.

Five eggs, one pint milk, half a loaf of bread soaked in the milk, half pound butter, same of raisins, same of currants, one ounce citron, salt, sugar, and spice to taste. Let it steam four hours.

CREAM PUDDING.

Six eggs beaten well, one quart cream, six tablespoonsful of flour. Mix well together; add a little rose water, half a nutmeg, one teaspoonful ginger, half a teaspoonful salt. Put in a well floured cloth, and let it boil for three quarters of an hour. Cold sauce or wine sauce, as you prefer.

BOILED APPLE DUMPLINGS.

Pare and core large tart apples. An apple corer is better than a knife to cut out the seeds as it does not divide the apple. Make a paste with one pound of flour and half a pound butter. Cover the apples with the paste; tie them in cloths, but allow room to swell. Tender apples will boil in three-quarters of an hour. Serve hot. Eat with sauce. Quince and cherry dumplings are made in a like manner.

BAKED PEARS.

Take quarter peck of pears, wash and put them in a pan, with one pound brown sugar, and half pint of water. Bake in a moderate oven until the fruit is tender. When cool, and before sending to table sift white sugar over them.

BALLOONS.

One pint milk, three eggs, one pint flour. Separate the eggs, beat the yolks until light, and mix them with the milk, stirring all into the flour gradually. Beat it well with one saltspoonful of salt, then whisk the whites until stiff and dry, and stir through lightly, half at a time. Butter small cups, fill them half full of the mixture, and bake in a quick oven. When done turn them out of the cups, place them on a heated dish, and send them to table hot. Eat with wine sauce.

POTATO PUDDING.

One pound sugar, and one-half pound of butter creamed, one pound boiled potatoes, mashed through a cullender, one wineglass of brandy, one of wine, and some grated nutmeg.

MERINGUE PUDDING.

Yolks of five eggs, one pint cream, quarter pound sugar. Boil it in a tin placed inside of one of boiling water. Stir all the time till it thickens. Ice it with the whites of four eggs, and brown it in the oven a little. Flavor as you like.

BAKED CUSTARD.

Take three eggs and one pint milk. Beat the whites very light; then add the yolks and beat them together. Warm the milk and sugar, then stir in the eggs. Flavor as you like. Fill the custard cups, and set them in a pan of cold water inside the stove. Leave it until the water boils; the custard should then be solid. Grate nutmeg over it.

MINCE MEAT.

Three pounds suet chopped fine, three pounds chopped tart apples, three pounds stoned raisins, two pounds currants, washed and dried, one pound citron, cut fine, preserved orange or lemon peel. Then two ounces ginger, one of cinnamon, two dozen cloves, two nutmegs, one dozen allspice, all pulverized, half pound brown sugar, one pint rum or brandy. Cover all with cider, and put it in a tightly closed jar. Keep it always covered with cider. Add a little brandy or rum after putting it in the paste. Always have a top crust to mince pies, and serve them hot.

MINCE MEAT.

Two pounds of fresh beef tongue, two and a half pounds suet, two pounds raisins, two pounds currants, two and a half pounds sugar, two and a half pounds apples, one and a half nutmegs, half ounce mace, cloves, allspice, and cinnamon, one pint wine, one quart brandy, quarter pound citron. Each time the pastry is made add a little cider to moisten it.

PLAIN FAMILY PASTE.

Two pounds flour, half pound butter, half pound fresh lard. Mix as for puff paste.

PUFF PASTE.

One pound two ounces flour, one pound butter, one tumbler full of ice water. Take half of the flour, and mix it with a quarter pound of the butter, and the ice water, working it

with a knife and not touching it with the hand. Flour the
board, turn out the paste, dredge it thickly with flour, and
roll it quite thin. Then take another quarter pound of butter
and spread it over the paste, dredging it again with flour, and
folding in the sides and ends. In this manner roll and spread
the butter and flour until all is used. Always roll paste *from*
you, and do not touch it with the hand except when obliged.
Put it in a cold place until ready for use. Very fine.

NICE PASTE FOR DUMPLINGS.

To one pound flour add a little salt, and as much boiling
water as will make it into a stiff dough. Flour the pie
board, turn it out and work it lightly, then take a piece,
roll it thin, and cover the fruit with it.

ORANGE ROLY-BOLY.

Make a light paste as for apple dumplings, roll it in an
oblong sheet, and lay sweet oranges, peeled, sliced, and seeded,
thickly, all over it. Sprinkle with white sugar. Grate a few
teaspoonsful of the rind over all, and roll it up closely, folding
down the end to secure the syrup. Boil it in a pudding bag
for one hour and a half. Eat with lemon sauce.

RICE MERINGUE.

Take four eggs, one pint of milk, make in custard just like
boiled custard, only you use whites and yolks of eggs, but
season with vanilla and sweeten to taste. Boil a teacup of
rice; beat up four eggs, yolks and whites very light; add
two teacups of sugar, to this add your rice whilst hot to the
eggs, and a pint of hot milk and two teacups of stoned raisins,
and two teacups of sugar and some vanilla. Put in to bake;
when done, take out and pour the custard you have made
over the dish and put back in the oven to brown. Let it get
very cold in the ice, then serve. A very fine pudding.

Old English Plum Pudding (Mother's recipe)
1 lb raisins stoned
1 " currants washed & dried
1 " suet chopped very fine
1 cup grated crumbs of stale bread
¼ lb candied citron chopped very fine
The thin rind of a fresh lemon chopped very fine
2 teaspoonful of salt
4 nutmegs grated
½ teaspoonful cloves
½   "   allspice
½   "   mace
1 cup sugar
1 lb sifted flour
Mix altogether (dry) in a good sized pan
Then beat 8 eggs & add a little milk & wine
& mix very thoroughly
Boil it 8 hours.
See that the water is boiling when it is put in
& does not stop boiling
Be particular to have a kettle of boiling
water to fill it up as it boils away
It is good without the wine & brandy
It should be stiff enough when put in
the cloth to hold a spoon upright.
It is better to mix overnight & then one can
add more milk if necessary next morning.
Leave room for it to swell & put a tin
plate at the bottom to prevent it from
sticking.

Prune Pudding (Fay R Brown)
  1 cup pitted chopped, stewed prunes
  whites of 6 eggs
  ½ teaspoonful gelatine
  ½ cup sugar
  Cream of tartar
  Serve hot with whipped cream.

Basis of Soufflé or sponge (Miss Tillmann)
Allow for each person.
1 white of egg beaten stiff
1 yolk " " "
{ 1 level tablespoonful butter }
{ 1 "   "   "   flour   }
1/3 cup of " milk
make into a thick cream sauce — add yolk of egg & last the stiff white!
This can be made into a cheese or vegetable Soufflé or a sweet one.

CAKES.

"In all receipts where a baking powder is to be used, I recommend the Royal as the very best on the market, and I have been forced to this conclusion after having tried all others."

MEASURES FOR CAKE.

One heaping quart of sifted flour—one pound.
Three coffeecups of sifted flour even full—one pound.
One quart of unsifted flour—one pound.
One pint of soft butter—one pound.
Two teacups of soft butter—one pound.
One and one-third pints of powdered sugar—one pound.
Two coffeecups even full of sugar—one pound.
One heaping pint of granulated sugar—one pound.
Two teacups of granulated sugar—one pound.
One and three-quarter teacups of brown sugar—one pound.
Three and one-half teacups of meal—one quart.

COCOANUT POUND CAKE.

One pound sugar, three-quarters pound butter, one pound flour, ten eggs, one pound grated cocoanut, half a wineglass rose water, one grated nutmeg. Beat butter and sugar very light, stir in the rose water, beat in one-fourth of the flour. Beat the eggs well and stir them in by degrees, add the remaining flour, half at a time, and lastly the cocoanut. Butter and paper the pan, put in the batter, smooth it over evenly with a knife, bake in a moderate oven.

COCOANUT CAKES.

One pound cocoanut, half pound white sugar, one tablespoonful flour. Grate the nut, mix the sugar and flour with it, work all well together. Make it out in little balls, place them on tins, bake in a quick oven. To prevent the cakes getting too brown on the under side place several thicknesses of paper under them.

KISSES.

Half pound powdered white sugar, add whites of five eggs. Beat the eggs to a stiff froth, add sugar by degrees, then drop on white paper with a small spoon at least an inch apart; put this paper on a board or on many thicknesses of paper; put them in a quick oven. Pass a knife under them, slip them off the paper, and put two together.

WHITE CAKE.

Two cups of sifted flour, three-quarters of a cup of butter, whites of six eggs, one and one-quarter cups powdered sugar, one teaspoonful of Royal Baking Powder sifted in the flour. Cream butter and flour, and sugar and eggs, and mix together. Season with vanilla or bitter almond. Bake in flat bread pans, and ice.

MOUNTAIN ASH CAKE.

Two large cups of pulverized sugar, two large cups of sifted flour, one large cup of milk, one large cup of butter, two teaspoonsful of Royal Baking Powder, sifted in the flour. Whites of seven eggs, cream, butter, adding by degrees corn starch, milk, flour, lastly eggs into which the sugar has been beaten. Flavor with anything you like and bake in moderate oven.

ICING.

Whites of four eggs; four tablespoonsful of sugar to each egg.

SUGAR CAKE.

Two quarts of flour, three teacups of sugar, one of butter, one of lard, one of cream, three eggs, two teaspoonsful of soda dissolved in the sour cream. Cream, butter and sugar, add eggs beaten separately, then the cream, lastly sift the flour in slowly. Season with nutmeg and cinnamon.

SUNSHINE CAKE.

Whites of ten eggs, beaten stiff. Sift three-quarters pound of granulated sugar three times and add to the eggs gradually. To the whites and sugar, add the beaten yolks of five eggs, the grated rind of one-half an orange and three teaspoonsful of the juice. Put one teaspoonful of cream tartar in six ounces of flour and sift three times; add this to the eggs. Bake without greasing the pan.

ICING FOR CAKE.

One-half pound of sugar, one-half gill of water; let it boil three minutes and pour while boiling on the white of one egg; beat until stiff. Season with orange juice.

WHITE FRUIT CAKE.

Three cups of sugar, one of butter, five of sifted flour, two cups of seeded raisins, whites of twelve eggs, three teaspoonsful of Royal Baking Powder, tablespoonful of brandy, one cup of milk. Cream, butter and sugar, add milk, then flour (into which baking powder has been sifted), and eggs alternately, lastly raisins, which have been dredged in flour. Bake in one loaf.

GINGER BREAD. (Very nice.)

To two full quarts flour, one pint molasses, two pounds brown sugar, three-quarters pound butter and lard, four eggs, four teaspoonsful of Royal Baking Powder, one small teacup of sweet milk. These proportions make a stiff batter; add currants or raisins if you like. Butter your tins, let it bake slowly. Take a clean feather, dip it in a little molasses, rub it over the top. Let it set in the pans until cool. Season with two tablespoonsful ginger, one cinnamon, one nutmeg.

CHOCOLATE CAKE.

One-half cake Walter Baker's chocolate, one cup of brown sugar, one-half cup of milk, yolk of egg. Mix all together and cook until thick, and let cool. A scant one-half cup of butter, one cup of brown sugar, one-half cup of milk, two cups of flour, two eggs, two teaspoonsful Royal Baking Powder. Flavor with vanilla; add the caramel before the flour and white of eggs.

LEMON BUTTER.

Six eggs, one-quarter pound butter, one pound sugar, rind and juice of three lemons. Mix together and set in a pan of hot water to cook, let it be of consistency of apple butter.

"BLACK CAKE," No. 1.

Four pounds raisins, four pounds currants, one pound citron, fifteen eggs, one and one-half pounds flour, one and one-half pounds butter, two pounds of dark brown sugar, one-half pint black molasses, two pounds almonds, blanched and sliced, one ounce cinnamon, one ounce mace, one ounce allspice, one ounce nutmegs. Bake very slowly; keeps a year good.

SPICE CAKE.

Four eggs, whites of two left out for icing, one cup butter, two cups of brown sugar, one cup of sour milk, two cups of flour, two tablespoonsful of cinnamon, one tablespoonful of cloves, one grated nutmeg, one and one-half teaspoonsful of soda (in the cream), and a pinch of salt. Bake slowly.

GINGER CRACKERS.

One-half pound butter, one-half pound brown sugar, one and one-half pounds flour, one pint black molasses, one tablespoonful ginger, one teaspoonful cloves, one of cinnamon, one of soda dissolved in warm water. Make soft and roll out as thin as possible. Bake quickly.

WHITE MOUNTAIN CAKE. (Best.)

Six cups white sugar, six cups flour, one and one-half cups of butter, three cups of milk, three cups corn starch, whites of twenty-one eggs, six teaspoons of Royal Baking Powder, three of vanilla.

Frosting for it.—Whites of eight eggs; five tablespoon-ful pulverized sugar to each egg. Beat frosting well.

FIG CAKE.

Two cups sugar, three of flour, three eggs, one-half cup butter, one cup milk, two teaspoons of Royal Baking Powder. Bake in three layers.

Filling for Fig Cake.—One-half pound figs, one cup raisins (both chopped fine), juice of one lemon, one cup water, one-half cup sugar. Boil all together until it jellies. Spread between the layers when cold.

GINGER BREAD.

One cup sugar, one cup sour milk, one cup butter, four of flour, two well beaten eggs, ginger, cinnamon, allspice and cloves. One-half pound stoned raisins and chopped citron, greatly improves it.

TEA CAKES.

Two pounds flour, one pound butter, one and one half pounds brown sugar, four eggs, one teaspoonful Royal Baking Powder.

CUSTARD FOR CAKE.

One ounce flour, one quarter pound sugar, yolks of three eggs. Mix well together, then add one-half pint milk. When well mixed, boil until stiff. Flavor with vanilla or orange.

CHOCOLATE CAKE.

Three teacups of sifted flour, two cups of granulated sugar, one cup of butter, five eggs, beaten separately, one cup of sweet milk, two small teaspoonsful of Royal Baking Powder. After the cake is mixed, melt over steam one-quarter pound of Walter Baker's chocolate; stir it in. Bake in layer tins, with the chocolate icing between each layer. Very nice.

LADY-FINGERS.

Ten eggs, one pound sugar, three-quarters pound butter. Beat the eggs with the sugar until very light, then stir in the flour with a teaspoon, put them on white paper in the usual form, sift over them white sugar, bake in a quick oven. When done take them off with a knife, put two together, and put to cool.

POUND CAKE.

One pound butter, one pound sugar, one pound flour, one pound eggs, one large spoonful rose water or a wineglass of brandy, one nutmeg grated, and a little mace. Butter and line the pan with paper, put in the batter, and bake in a moderate oven.

CHOCOLATE CAKE.

One cup of butter, two cups of sugar, three and a half cups of flour, one scant cup of sweet milk, five eggs, leaving out the whites of two. Add two teaspoonsful of Royal Baking Powder in the flour. When hot frost with the whites of two eggs, one and a half cups powdered sugar, two teaspoonsful vanilla, six tablespoons of grated Walter Baker's chocolate.

SUGAR GINGER BREAD.

One pound flour, quarter pound butter, half pound brown sugar, half teaspoonful soda dissolved in milk. Mix with milk or warm water. Have the dough stiff enough to roll *very thin*. Bake in a quick oven.

GINGERSNAPS.

One cup *dark* molasses, one cup *dark* brown sugar, one cup lard, and two tablespoonsful of ginger. Boil all these together just five minutes. Let it get perfectly cold, and work in as much flour as it will require to work it on the board. Also put one *small* teaspoonful soda dissolved in hot water. Roll thin and bake in a quick oven.

COCOANUT CAKES.

The whites of four eggs, one pound cocoanut grated, one pound white sugar. Mixed without beating; flour enough to keep them from sticking.

CUP CAKE.

Four teacups of flour, three of sugar, one of butter, one of cream, two wineglasses of wine or brandy. Nutmeg and mace to your taste. Five eggs. You can add fruit if you like. Mix it as black cake. One teaspoon of soda.

CUP CAKE.

One cup butter, two of sugar, three of flour, four eggs, put mace or nutmeg or any seasoning you like. A teaspoon of Royal Baking Powder. A pound of currants or raisins is an improvement.

ORANGE CAKE.

Six eggs, their weight in sugar, the weight of four eggs in flour. Beat eggs and sugar together, then add whites beaten very light; stir in flour last. Season with grated rind and juice of a large orange.

DOUGHNUTS.

Two pounds flour, rub four ounces butter, one and a quarter pounds white sugar, three eggs, mace and nutmeg. Make into a rising with a cup of yeast and milk sufficient. Let them rise well. Fry in lard. Cover with pulverized sugar whilst hot. Cinnamon and sugar is an improvement.

TUCKER'S CAKE.

One and three-quarter pounds of flour, one and a quarter best brown sugar, three-quarters pound of butter, four eggs, one pint of milk, one teaspoonful of soda. Beat these together, add nutmeg and a little wine. Bake in a shell or large mould and eat with sauce.

LADY CAKE.

The whites of sixteen eggs, half pound fresh butter, three-quarters pound sifted flour, one pound fine sugar, two ounces of thin shelled almonds or rich peach kernels, three wine-glasses of rose water. Bake it in a pan like pound cake, ice it over with plain icing.

ORMSKIRK GINGERBREAD.

Two eggs beaten light, two pounds flour, one pound brown sugar, three-quarters pound butter or lard, one pint of molasses, one ounce of ginger, one ounce cinnamon, mixed; beat well together. To make very rich add candied lemon or orange peel. It must be dropped with a spoon in the pan.

JUMBLES.

One pound of flour, one pound brown sugar, three-quarters pound butter, whites of six eggs, one glass of wine, half a glass of brandy, one nutmeg, one teaspoonful of mace, half pound blanched almonds rolled in loaf sugar. Half pound of butter is sufficient when almonds are used.

SOFT GINGERBREAD.

Four cups of flour, two cups brown sugar, two cups molasses, one cup butter, one cup cream, two cups of milk, four eggs, one teaspoon of soda, one teacup of ginger.

SCOTCH CAKE.

Rub three-quarters pound of butter, into one pound of flour. Mix one pound powdered sugar, large spoonful of cinnamon. Mix into the dough with three well beaten eggs. Roll thin and bake in a quick oven. Grate sugar over them while hot. Generally you will have to drop it from a spoon, as it is almost impossible to roll it.

SPONGE CAKE.

Balance ten eggs with sugar, six eggs with flour, break twelve eggs, leaving out the yolks of two. Beat the yolks and whites separately, until very light, then mix; add the sugar, few spoonsful at a time, stir in the flour in small quantities, beat the mixture very little. Add the peel and juice of one large lemon. To be baked with a slow heat.

SUGAR CAKES.

One and a half pounds flour, one pound butter, half pound sugar, either brown or white. Work these all together; add any seasoning you like.

POUND CAKE GINGERBREAD.

Three cups flour, two of brown sugar, one of butter, three eggs, one teaspoonful soda, dissolved in a cup of milk. Ginger and other spices to taste.

GINGER CAKE.

Three pounds flour, one pound sugar, one pound butter, quarter pound ginger, one quart molasses.

JUMBLES.

Two pounds flour, one pound butter, one pound sugar, two eggs, half a teacup of cream, four spoonsful of rose water, lemon juice, orange peel; roll them in sugar, and bake in a moderate oven.

SOFT GINGERBREAD.

One cup butter, one and a half molasses, one and a half sugar, one of cream, four eggs, four cups flour, one teaspoonful soda, two teaspoonsful cream tartar or two teaspoonsful of Royal Baking Powder. Ginger and a little cinnamon.

RAISIN CAKE.

Two cups brown sugar, one of butter, one of molasses, one of milk, three eggs, one teaspoonful soda, two teaspoonsful cream tartar, or two teaspoonsful of Royal Baking Powder, one pound raisins, or currants if you choose, five cups flour.

CHEAP PLAIN CAKE.

Two cups sugar, half cup butter, one of milk, two eggs, three cups flour, two teaspoonsful of Royal Baking Powder.

COFFEE CAKE.

Two pounds flour, one pound sugar, half pound butter, half pound raisins, one cup of cream, one of yeast, four eggs. Spice to your taste.

CHEAP BLACK CAKE.

One teacup molasses, one of sugar, one of butter or lard, five eggs, two tablespoonsful of ginger, half a nutmeg, one teaspoonful of soda dissolved in half a teacupful of sour milk, or two teaspoonsful of Royal Baking Powder. Add sufficient flour to make it stiff, so that it will drop from a spoon.

SUPERIOR GINGER LOAF.

Five teacupsful of flour, one teacupful of brown sugar, two of molasses, two of sour cream, one of butter, six eggs, two tablespoonsful of ginger, two of cinnamon, two teaspoonsful of mace, one of cloves, two of soda, dissolved in the cream, one pound of currants, one pound of raisins.

BRIDE'S CAKE.

One pound flour, one pound sugar, three-quarters pound butter, the whites of eighteen eggs; flavor with bitter almonds; beat very light.

GINGERSNAPS.

Half pint molasses, one teacupful of brown sugar, half teaspoonful of soda, a little salt, two tablespoonsful of ginger, one cupful of lard. Warm the molasses, stir soda in it, then the sugar; mix all together and roll out thin.

HARD GINGER CAKE.

Six pints flour, one pound of sugar, one pint molasses, one pound butter, five tablespoonsful of ground ginger, one teaspoonful of soda in six tablespoonsful of buttermilk. Mix well together; roll out thin and bake quickly.

STARCH CAKE.

Three coffee-cupsful of butter, three of new milk, nine of flour, three of corn starch, four teaspoonsful of cream of tartar, two of soda, or four teaspoonsful of Royal Baking Powder, and the whites of eighteen eggs. Weight, three pounds.

COLD WATER CAKE.

Three cups flour, two of sugar, four eggs, half cup butter, two spoonsful Royal Baking Powder, one goblet cold water.

COCOANUT JUMBLES.

Two pounds flour, one pound sugar, one pound butter, two eggs, half teacup of cream, four tablespoonsful rose water, and two grated cocoanuts. Beat the yolks and whites together, then cream the butter and put the eggs in. Mix all well together; roll them in sugar, and bake over a slow fire.

RICE SPONGE CAKE.

Nine eggs, the weight of them in sugar, the weight of six eggs in ground rice. Mix the sugar and rice together, have the whites and yolks of the eggs beat separately, pour the eggs all in at a time into the rice and sugar, beat them well together for about a quarter of an hour, add the juice of one lemon or teaspoonful of rose water.

JUMBLES.

Three pounds flour, one and a half pounds butter, one and a half pounds sugar, mix them well together, and make it up with six eggs well beaten, three spoonsful of rose water, one stick cinnamon.

KISSES.

Three eggs, one pound sugar, beat light, half a glass rose water.

DOUGHNUTS.

Three pounds flour, one and a half pounds sugar, one pound of butter, all cut up together, six eggs beat very light, two cups yeast, spice as you please; wet it with milk into a light dough, and set it to rise.

CRISP GINGERBREAD.

One pound butter, one pound sugar, one quart molasses, quarter pound ginger if good, flour sufficient to roll them out.

MACAROONS.

One pound almonds, let them be scalded, blanched, and thrown into cold water, then dry them in a cloth and pound them in a mortar, moisten them with orange flower water and the white of an egg to prevent their oiling; one pound sugar, four eggs; beat all well together, and drop them on sheets of paper buttered, sift sugar over and bake them quickly. Be careful not to let them get discolored.

COCOANUT DROPS.

Grate your cocoanut, and set it before the fire or in the sun to dry, then mix with it an equal quantity of loaf sugar powdered, and as much white of an egg as will make the whole into a light paste. Flour some thick white paper and drop on it, bake it in a very slow oven. They take some time in doing.

QUEEN OF CAKES.

One and a quarter pints flour, quarter pint butter, three-quarters pint sugar, whites of six eggs, one tablespoonful whiskey. This is enough for three layers. While baking prepare your icing as follows: one pound sugar, boil until it ropes, then pour it over the whites of four eggs which have been beaten to a stiff froth. Beat hard, and add gradually quarter pound citron cut in shreds, quarter pound figs, cut in small pieces, half pound raisins seeded and cut, one pound almonds, blanched. Beat all thoroughly, and as it cools spread between the layers of cake on the top and sides. White filling for same cake: one pint very rich cream thoroughly chilled, one teacup icing sugar, whites of two eggs well whipped. Beat the cream till stiff and keep on ice, then add the sugar; three eggs, and flavor to taste.

BLACK CAKE.

Three pounds butter, three pounds dark brown sugar, twenty-eight eggs, three glasses brandy, two of rose water, three pounds flour, six pounds currants and raisins, two ounces mace, two ounces nutmeg, half ounce cloves, two teaspoons soda, dissolved in the brandy.

MINNIE'S PREMIUM CAKE.

One cup butter, two cups sugar, one and a half of flour, one and a half corn starch, one cup thick cream, one teaspoonful cream of tartar, half teaspoon soda, four eggs. Beat yolks and whites separately.

FLORENCE JUMBLES.

Beat one pound butter to cream, then add the whites of three eggs, one and a quarter pounds flour, beat them well together, powder and sift one pound loaf sugar, half of which beat in the cake, reserving the other half to roll it out with. Nutmeg to your taste. Bake on tins; they will not bear removing until they have become cool.

WHITE MOUNTAIN CAKE.

One pound flour, one pound white sugar, half pound butter, six eggs, one teacup sweet milk, one teaspoon soda, dissolved in milk, two teaspoons cream of tartar mixed with the flour. Bake in loaves or jelly tins, and flavor with extract bitter almond according to taste.

BLACK CAKE (Cheap).

One and three-quarter pounds flour, one and a quarter pounds brown sugar, one pound butter, one pound raisins, one pound currants, four eggs, one pint milk, one teaspoon soda, one nutmeg, with other spices, wine and brandy.

FRUIT CAKE.

One pound butter, one pound sugar, one and a quarter pounds flour, ten eggs, quarter pint brandy, one ounce cinnamon, same of nutmeg and allspice, one pound citron, three pounds currants, four pounds raisins.

GINGER POUND CAKE.

Six eggs, two cups butter, four cups sugar, two cups molasses, six to seven cups flour, two cups sour cream, one teaspoonful of soda. Ginger and spice to taste.

ICE CREAM CAKE.

Two cups sugar, three cups flour, the whites of eight eggs, one teaspoonful cream of tartar, half a teaspoonful soda, half a cup sweet milk or one teaspoonful of Royal Baking Powder. Bake in thin cakes.

ALBANY CAKE.

One and a half pounds flour, half a pound butter, one egg, one cup cream, one pound brown sugar, one teaspoonful soda dissolved in the cream, two ounces cinnamon. Mix sugar and flour together, then work in the butter, then add the cinnamon. Beat the egg and mix it with the cream. Roll out in sugar, not flour.

LEMON JELLY CAKE.

Make a sponge batter. The filling is as follows: One pound white sugar, half a pound butter, the juice and rind of five lemons, whites of five eggs beaten to a stiff froth. Stir all together, and put it on the fire till it comes to a boil, then set aside to cool. When cool bake the sponge cake in sheets, spread the mixture thickly on it, and make a roll, wrapping it so as to hold it together.

STRAWBERRY SHORT CAKE.

One quart flour, two heaping teaspoonsful of Royal Baking Powder, half a teaspoon of salt, butter the size of an egg, a little milk, and two quarts of strawberries. Mix the baking powder into the flour, then rub in the butter till it is a stiff smooth paste. Add enough milk to make a soft dough—rather softer than for biscuits. Spread this on two pie tins and bake quickly. When partly cool split them open, and spread them with butter and strawberries plentifully mixed with sugar. Serve with cream. This can be made with sour milk as follows: To two teacupsful of sour milk, add one teaspoonful of soda, then three-quarters of a teacup of butter or lard partly melted, and enough flour to make a soft dough. These cakes can be made in the same way with currants, blackberries, cut peaches, chopped pineapples, or raspberries.

DOUGHNUTS.

One cup sugar, not quite half a cup butter, half cup sour milk, with half a teaspoonful soda dissolved in it, four eggs, a little nutmeg, and flour enough to roll them out.

ORANGE CAKE.

Beat the whites of three and the yolks of five eggs separately, two cups sugar, half a cup butter, half a cup cold water, two and a half cups flour, two teaspoonsful Royal Baking Powder, and the rind and all the juice of one orange except one tablespoonful of juice. Cream the butter and sugar together, put in the grated rind and juice, and beat it light. Then add the cold water, part of the flour (sifted and with the powder in it), then the eggs, and the rest of the flour alternately. For the frosting beat up the whites of two eggs, add the tablespoonful of orange juice, and two small cups of sugar; beat all up light. Bake the cake in two square tins. When they are a little warm put frosting between and a layer on top.

DROP JUMBLES.

Two eggs, two cups sugar, one cup butter, one teaspoon soda, half a cup milk or cream, spice or any flavoring, to taste, and sufficient flour to make them drop from a spoon.

FRENCH BUNS.

One pound flour, one pound sugar, half a pound butter, eight eggs, one teaspoonful of soda, two teaspoonsful of cream of tartar or two teaspoonsful of Royal Baking Powder, one teacup of sour cream, and one large lemon. Cream the butter and sugar, beat the eggs very light and separately. After the butter is well creamed stir in the flour the last thing. Bake twenty minutes. Cut it, while hot, in small squares.

LEMON BUTTER (for filling Cake).

Twelve eggs, two pounds of sugar, half pound butter, six lemons, rind and juice. Mix all together, and stew on a slow fire till as thick as honey, stirring constantly. Bottled, this will keep for weeks.

COCOANUT CAKES OR BALLS.

The whites of four eggs, one pound of cocoanut, one pound of loaf sugar, mixed together without beating. Flour enough to keep it from sticking.

GOLD CAKE.

The yolks of fourteen eggs, three-quarters pound of butter, one pound flour, one pound of white sugar, juice and peel of two lemons. Cream the butter and grate the peel.

SILVER CAKE.

The whites of fourteen eggs, six ounces of butter, three-quarters pound of flour, one pound white sugar. Season to taste.

SOFT GINGERBREAD.

One pound butter, half pound brown sugar, two pounds flour, one quart molasses, eight eggs, two ounces ginger, half ounce cloves, one teaspoonful of soda. Mix as pound cake. Fruit may be added.

SODA CAKE.

One pound brown sugar, one pound flour, four eggs, quarter pound butter, one teacup of milk, two teaspoonsful of cream of tartar and one of soda, or two teaspoonsful of Royal Baking Powder, dissolved in the milk. Bake quickly.

JELLY TWIST.

One cup flour, one of sugar, four eggs, one teaspoonful of Royal Baking Powder.

Jelly for the above.—Half a pound of sugar, half pound butter, whites of three eggs, rind and juice of three lemons. Let this jelly boil a few minutes, and then set it aside to cool. Bake the cake in a long pan. When done lay it on a clean coarse cloth, then spread the jelly over it. Roll the cake up, wrapping it carefully in a cloth until cool.

MARBLE CAKE.

Light part.—One cup butter, three of white sugar, five cups of flour, half a cup of milk, half a teaspoonful soda, the whites of eight eggs; flavored with lemon.

Brown part.—One cup butter, two of brown sugar, one of molasses, one of milk, four of flour, one teaspoonful of soda, one egg, and the yolks of eight. All kinds of spices. When ready, mixed, and beaten well, put it into deep pans, first a layer of dark, then of white, and so on, finishing with the dark.

FRUIT CAKE.

Ten cups flour, four of brown sugar, five of butter, four of molasses, two of cream, ten eggs, two teaspoonsful of soda. Mix the butter, molasses, and cream, and melt them, then stir in the sugar. Beat the eggs very light, mix in the flour two pounds of stoned raisins, two pounds of currants, half pound citron, with spice to taste. Bake in a slow oven.

GINGER POUND CAKE.

Two pounds flour, one pound brown sugar, half pound butter, twelve eggs, two teacupsful of ginger, two nutmegs, one teaspoonful soda, two large spoonsful of mixed spices, one pint of molasses. Very nice.

GINGERBREAD.

One and a half pounds of flour, quarter pound butter, quarter pound sugar, one ounce ginger, one dessert-spoonful of allspice, one teaspoonful carraway seed, one pint molasses.

SOFT GINGERBREAD.

One pint molasses, three eggs, one cup sugar, one cup of lard or butter, or both mixed, one cup buttermilk, one teaspoonful soda, two teaspoonsful ginger. Make it just stiff enough to drop from the spoon.

GINGER CRACKERS.

One quart molasses, four pounds flour, one pound butter or lard, ginger to taste. Mix well, roll and bake.

GINGERBREAD.

One pint New Orleans molasses, one dessert-spoonful of soda, put into the molasses, and beaten hard, half cup lard or butter, one cup of hot water, melted and mixed, one tablespoonful of ginger, five even cups of sifted flour.

GINGERNUTS.

Three pounds flour, one pound butter, half pound lard, one pound brown sugar, one pint molasses, one gill cream, two ounces ginger, two ounces cinnamon, one nutmeg. Put the butter and lard into the flour, then the spices, then the sugar, molasses, and cream. Work it well, roll it out, cut it in small cakes and bake.

GINGERBREAD.

One heaping tablespoonful of butter. Pour over it a cup of molasses. Add a small teaspoonful of soda, dissolved in a little warm water. Stir in well a cupful of sour milk, and a large tablespoonful of ginger. Then add a pinch of salt and three teacups of flour. Beat one egg well into the batter, and bake in greased tins.

SUGAR CAKES.

One pound brown sugar, six ounces lard, half a pint sour cream, two small teaspoons of soda, one quart flour.

Season with mace, nutmeg, or cinnamon; one egg. Flour enough to roll them out.

ANGEL'S FOOD CAKE.

The whites of one dozen eggs, one and a half cups of pulverized sugar, one cup flour, one teaspoonful cream of tartar sifted in the flour, one dessert-spoonful of vanilla. Sift the sugar once, and then sift it into the cake. Sift the flour three times, and then sift it into the cake. Dip up a teacup of flour. Bake half an hour in a moderate oven, as you would sponge cake, without greasing the pan.

NICE CAKE FOR THE YOLKS.

Eight yolks, one cup sugar, two cups flour, half a teacup of butter, half a cup sweet milk, and one teaspoonful of Royal Baking Powder.

SILVER CAKE.

Two cups sugar, two and a half cups flour, whites of eight eggs, half a cup of butter, half a cup sour cream, half a teaspoonful of soda, one spoonful cream tartar. Vanilla seasoning.

SILVER CAKE.

Two cups sugar, three-quarters cup butter, one cup milk, four cups of flour, whites of four eggs, one teaspoonful soda, two teaspoonsful cream tartar, or two teaspoonsful of Royal Baking Powder. Cream the butter and sugar, and flavor with almonds.

SPICE CAKE.

Two teacups brown sugar, half a cup butter or lard, two teacups flour, half a cup sour milk, one teaspoonful soda, three teaspoonsful powdered cinnamon, three of cloves, two of allspice, three of nutmeg, four eggs. Put the soda in the milk and spices in the flour.

COFFEE CAKE.

Two cups brown sugar, three-quarters pound butter, one cup molasses, one of strong coffee, one teaspoonful soda, one of cloves, one of cinnamon, one nutmeg, four eggs, one pound five ounces flour, and one pound chopped raisins. Cream the butter and sugar, put soda in the molasses, then the coffee.

CRULLERS.

Four eggs beaten very light, three teacups of white sugar, one of milk, five tablespoonsful of melted butter, three and a half teaspoonsful Royal Baking Powder sifted in the flour, one nutmeg grated, flour enough to roll out. Cut in round cakes, take a piece out of the centre of each with pepper-box top. Boil in lard, and dip in sugar while hot.

STRAWS.

One egg, one teacup of thick cream, half a teacup sugar, one teaspoonful of Royal Baking Powder, flour sufficient to make a dough. Spices to taste. Boil it in hot lard.

DOUGHNUTS.

Two and a half pounds flour, one and a half pounds sugar, four ounces butter, three eggs, two nutmegs, a little mace, one teacupful yeast, half a pint milk made into rising. They can be risen with acid and soda, a large teaspoon and a half of each to this quantity; double of acid, or two teaspoonsful of Royal Baking Powder.

LEMON CAKE.

Two ounces of butter, four ounces white sugar, two eggs, the rind of two lemons and the juice of one. Beat the eggs separately. This mixture is sufficient for one jelly cake of ordinary size. It must all be stewed together, and allowed to cool before spreading it over the cake.

APPLE CAKE.

Three and a half cups dried apples, three cups molasses, three and a half cups flour, half a cup butter, two eggs, one teaspoonful soda, two teaspoonsful cream tartar or one teaspoonful of Royal Baking Powder, one teaspoonful cinnamon, half a teaspoonful cloves, one nutmeg. Wash the apples and lay them in water all night; in the morning chop them fine, and boil them in the molasses slowly for one hour. When partly cool stir in the butter, and other ingredients. Bake in deep pans and frost them.

HORSE CAKE.

Five pounds flour, two tablespoonsful butter or lard, four tablespoonsful ginger, one quart molasses, one tablespoonful soda in half a pint buttermilk, one teacup brown sugar.

CORN MEAL CAKE.

Four eggs, half a pound butter, one pound sugar, one pound corn meal. Take out one handful of meal and add one of flour. Flavor with mace and brandy. Bake in muffin rings.

COCOANUT BALLS.

Peel and grate four nuts by hand, and not on a patent grater. To each nut allow half a pound of sugar and one teacup of water. Boil this into a thick syrup, and pour it over the grated nuts. When it is cool enough to handle make them into balls the size of a walnut, and put them on plates or panes of glass to dry. Keep them in a warm place for several days, turning them occasionally. A dry cloth put under them makes them dry quicker.

CHOCOLATE CAKE.

Three cupsful of flour, two cupsful of sugar, one cupful of butter, one cupful sweet milk, one teaspoonful of cream of tartar, half a teaspoonful of bicarbonate of soda. Prepare the ingredients as usual in cake making. Bake in shallow tin plates. This quantity poured into six plates will make the cakes of the proper thickness; or, bake in one loaf, and when nearly cold cut it into slices horizontally, and then spread the prepared chocolate over each slice. (See Chocolate Icing.)

CHOCOLATE ECLAIRS.

Take the weight of four fresh eggs in sugar, and half the weight in flour, mixing with the latter half a teaspoonful of cream of tartar, and quarter teaspoonful of soda very thoroughly, or the éclairs will not be light. Beat the yolks of the eggs until light, add slowly the sugar, as you do for sponge cake, having it just as light. Alternate the beaten whites of the eggs with the flour, and bake in pans having compartments, dropping a spoonful of butter in each, or in a paperlined and well-buttered pan, making the cakes is nearly the size of lady-fingers as possible. The oven should be quick, and when done take out, place two together, allow them to cool, and cover with the chocolate.

STRAWBERRY SHORTCAKE.

Take one quart of sifted flour, stir thoroughly into it half a teaspoonful of carbonate of soda, also one teaspoonful of cream of tartar, a tablespoonful of butter, one tablespoonful of salt, and about a coffee-cupful of water. It is best mixed with a knife, and, if possible, do not put your hands into it except to roll it out. The dough should be as moist as you can well manage. Roll it smoothly out, making two round cakes of about half an inch in thickness. Bake in a quick oven. When done split the cakes open, put the slices in a large dish, butter them, cover each slice with berries and sugar, having the top layer of berries. Pour cream over all.

PINEAPPLE SHORTCAKE.

Take sufficient flour for one pie dish, a piece of butter the size of a small egg, a tablespoonful or two of sugar, the yolk of an egg, two teaspoons of Royal Baking Powder, a very little salt, and milk enough to make a soft dough. Do not kneed the dough, but just barely mix it, and press it into the pie plate. The baking powder, butter, sugar and salt should be rubbed well through the flour, and then the other ingredients quickly added. A couple of hours before bringing the cake on the table take a very ripe, finely flavored pineapple, peel it, cut it thin as wafers, and sprinkle it thickly with sugar. Then cover it close. When time to serve split the cake, spread the pineapple between the layers, and serve with sugar and cream. Do not butter the cake; it would destroy the delicate flavor.

FLORIDA CAKE.

The grated rind and juice of one lemon, one pound flour, one pound best brown sugar, half pound butter, one teacup of sour milk or cream, five eggs beaten light, two small nutmegs, and one teaspoonful pounded mace. Mix as you would pound cake, reserving half of the milk for the last, to which add one teaspoonful of soda. Grease the tins and pour the batter in. Use slow heat at first.

GINGERBREAD.

Three pounds flour, one pound sugar, one pound butter, one pint molasses, one egg, and half a teacupful of ginger.

FRUIT CAKE.

Two pounds currants, two pounds raisins, one pound citron, one pound flour, one pound sugar, one pound butter, twelve eggs, one tablespoonful of mace, the same of cinnamon, three nutmegs (the spice must be beaten and sifted together), and two glasses of wine. Cream the butter and sugar, add the eggs, which must be beaten very light, then add the other ingredients alternately.

GINGERBREAD.

Four cups flour, one cup sugar, one cup molasses, three-quarters cup of lard or butter, one cup boiling water, one egg, one tablespoonful of soda, ginger and cinnamon to taste. Drop in biscuit pans.

BUTTER SPONGE.

The weight of twelve eggs in sugar, six in flour, and six in butter, twelve eggs and one lemon.

GINGERBREAD.

One pint molasses, four eggs, half a pound brown sugar, one teacup of ginger, cloves and allspice, one teaspoonful of soda dissolved in a cup of cream, flour enough to make the batter as thick as pound cake. Then add half a pound of butter. To be baked in moulds.

POUND CAKE.

To one and a half pounds of butter creamed, add two pounds flour, two pounds sugar, and eighteen eggs well beaten. Put alternately into the butter the sugar, flour, and beaten eggs. Continue to beat them together until quite light, then add lemon peel, one nutmeg, and one gill of brandy.

SOFT GINGERBREAD.

Two cups of butter, two of sugar, two of molasses, and two of milk, six of flour, six eggs, two teaspoonsful of ginger, and one of soda.

FRENCH LOAF BREAD.

One pound flour, one pound sugar, half a pound of butter, one pound raisins, eight eggs, quarter gill of wine, one nutmeg. This makes two loaves. Bake it one hour and a half.

COCOANUT CAKES.

One pound cocoanut, one pound of sugar, half a pound of butter, half a pound of flour, one grated lemon, and six eggs.

ICING.

The whites of three eggs beaten to a stiff froth. To this add one tablespoonful of powdered sugar at a time till twelve have been added. Flavor with lemon or vanilla.

BOILED ICING.

One and a half pounds of sugar and one pint of water boiled together till it ropes. Have ready the whites of seven eggs beaten stiff. Pour the syrup into a bowl and stir it until it is only milk warm, then put in the eggs and beat it for an hour.

BOILED ICING.

Two and a half cups of sugar, water enough to moisten and boil. Beat the whites of three eggs to a stiff froth. When the sugar is clear from boiling pour it over the eggs, stirring very fast. Put in half a teaspoonful citric acid pulverized, and flavor with vanilla.

ICING.

Take one pound of powdered or flour sugar (not the common pulverized) and the whites of four eggs. Put the sugar to the eggs before you beat it at all. Then beat until it is stiff. Spread it on the cake with a wet knife, wetting it in cold water each time you use it. Set it in front of the stove to dry, or in an oven with the least particle of heat. The cake must be nearly cold. You can flavor the icing with rose, orange, or lemon; if the latter, add a very small portion of the grated rind. It is much nicer to add sugar to the eggs before beating than afterward.

BOILED. ICING.

To one pound of the finest pulverized sugar, add three wineglasses of clear water. Let it stand until it dissolves. Then boil it until perfectly clear. Beat well the whites of four eggs. Pour the sugar into the dish with the eggs, but do not mix them until the syrup is lukewarm, then beat all together for one hour. Season to your taste with vanilla, rose water, or lemon juice. The first coating may be put on the cake as soon as it is well mixed. Rub the cake with a little flour before you apply the icing. While the first coating is drying continue to beat the remainder. You will not have to wait long if the cake is set in a warm place near the fire. This is considered an excellent recipe for icing.

CHOCOLATE ICING.

Put two ounces of Walter Baker's chocolate into a shallow pan, and place it where it will melt gradually but not scorch. When melted stir in three tablespoons of milk or cream and one of water. Mix all well together, and add one scant teacupful of sugar. Boil about five minutes, and while hot, and when the cakes are nearly cold, spread some evenly over the surface of one of them. Put a second one on top, and so on alternating cake and icing. Then cover the top and sides, and set in a warm oven to harden. This icing does not stick to the fingers, and in making chocolate éclairs, those most palatable cakes, this recipe is very satisfactory.

ICING.

One teacup of pulverized sugar, moisten with water very slightly, and put it in the stove till dissolved; do not let it boil. Pour this while hot into the whites of two well-beaten eggs, and stir it till thoroughly mixed. Then flavor with vanilla or lemon.

CHOCOLATE ICING.

The whites of two eggs, four tablespoonsful of Walter Baker's chocolate, one and a quarter cups sugar. Flavor with vanilla.

COMMON GINGERBREAD.

Two and a half pounds flour, half pound butter, two tablespoonsful ginger and one teaspoonful soda, dissolved in water. This is excellent for children.

COOKIES.

Five cups flour, three of sugar, one of butter, one egg, half a teacup of milk, half a teaspoon of soda, one lemon.

DROP GINGER CAKES.

Four eggs, one quart flour, one cup lard, one cup sugar, one cup sour cream, one tablespoon soda, dissolved in a little vinegar, one tablespoonful ginger, one of cinnamon, one pint molasses. Drop a tablespoonful of the mixture at a time into a greased pan and bake.

SPONGE CAKE.

Thirteen eggs, one and a half pounds pulverized sugar, three-quarters pound flour, and the juice and rind of two lemons. In making sponge cake first beat the whites and yolks separately, very light, then to the yolks add the sugar, mixing thoroughly. To this add the whites. Beat all together, then cut in the flour with a knife. Last of all add the lemon. A great improvement to sponge cake is after greasing the pans to drop a piece of butter the size of a small nutmeg in each pan.

CRULLERS.

Four eggs beaten separately, one pound pulverized sugar, one teacup of sour cream, one teaspoonful soda, a lump of butter the size of an egg, and flour enough to roll them out. Fry in plenty of hot lard.

LIGHT GINGERBREAD.

Two pounds flour, one pound butter, one pound sugar, one pint molasses, six eggs, one teaspoonful of soda, one wineglass of rose water, and three tablespoonsful of ginger.

QUICK DOUGHNUTS.

One cup butter, two cups sugar, four eggs, one cup sour milk or cream, one teaspoonful soda, one of nutmeg, half a teaspoonful of cinnamon, and flour enough to roll in plenty soft dough. Fry in hot lard. Royal Baking Powder can be used instead of soda or cream of tartar.

ORANGE CAKE.

Six eggs, one pound flour, one pound sugar, half pound butter, one teacup of sweet or sour cream. Take six oranges, grate the peel, leaving out that of three. Then cut off all the white skin, and be careful not to let any seeds get in or the cake will be bitter. Use the peel with layers of oranges, alternately with icing, between the layers of cake, and bake in jelly cake tins.

SUGAR CAKE.

Three pints flour, nine eggs, one and a half pounds sugar, three-quarters pound butter, one teaspoon soda, half teacup sour cream. Leave out the yolks of four eggs.

NUT CAKE.

Eight eggs (whites only), one-half pound butter, one-half pint milk, one pound sugar, one pound flour, one teaspoon Royal Baking Powder, one teaspoon extract almond. Cream your butter and sugar, add milk and flour and seasoning. Beat eggs very light and add last. Bake in jelly pans. This will make two of three layers each. Icing: Make a boiled icing of three cups of sugar and one gill of water. Let it boil until it will harden in water. Beat the whites of two eggs very light and pour the syrup over them, beating all the time. Season with teaspoonful of extract of vanilla. Add one cup of stoned raisins and one of English walnuts. Put this between the layers and on top. This quantity is enough for about one. I generally break the nuts into about four.

A DELICIOUS CAKE.

Make a white cup cake as follows, and bake in tins as for jelly cake: Flour one and a quarter pints, granulated sugar three-quarters of a pint, whites of six eggs, butter one-quarter pint, whiskey one tablespoonful. This is enough for three layers. Now make an icing, as follows: Sugar one pound, boiled with one teacup of water till it flies off the spoon in strings. It takes from eight to ten minutes *boiling*, but the length of time can best be determined by experience, and it must not be stirred more than possible. If it shows a tendency to turn to sugar put in the white of an egg and beat it. When this is sufficiently boiled pour it over the whites of four eggs which have been beaten to a stiff froth, beat hard till it whitens, then add the following ingredients which have been previously prepared: One-quarter pound citron cut in shreds, one-quarter pound figs, cut in shreds, one-half pound raisins, one pound blanched almonds cut in half. Mix these all together and add gradually to the icing; beat very hard till it begins to stiffen, and spread between and on the sides of the cakes. Conserved fruits may be added to this icing and are very nice.

In all receipts in which chocolate is to be used I recommend Walter Baker & Co.'s as the purest and most reliable, and this I know from actual test.

Lizzie Borcher's Tea Cookies

1/2 cup Butter
1 " Sugar
3 eggs
Flour enough to roll
2 teaspoonfuls baking powder.

Hartmanns Cookies

1 1/2 cups of butter
1 2/3 " of brown sugar
2 " " rolled oats
2 " " flour
2 eggs
2 teaspoonfuls of baking powder
Roll very thin.

Agnes Bowman's Coffee Cake

3 Tablespoonfuls melted butter
creamed with 1 cup granulated
2 eggs dropped in one at a time
1 cup milk
3 cups of sifted flour
3 teaspoonfuls of yeast powder
Put in sifted butter, sugar, cinnamon
& chopped nuts on top
Bake from 15 to 20 minutes

Mrs Schmidt's Sour Cream Cookies
2 cupfuls sugar
2 eggs
1 cupful sour cream
½ " butter
1 teaspoonful soda, dissolved in hot water
vanilla
Enough flour to thicken
½ teaspoonful salt.
Add raisins, currants, cocoanut or nut

pan needs <u>no</u> grease.

PRESERVES.

QUINCE JELLY AND MARMALADE.

Take one peck of quinces and wash them. To this add three quarts of water, and boil it until the fruit is soft, then put them into a cullender and let the liquid drain through. Strain it through a flannel; add one pound sugar to one pint of liquid, and boil it until it jellies. Sift what is left in the cullender through it. Then to two quart bowls of quince put three pints of sugar; stir it well; put it over the fire and stir it twenty minutes. Then put it into bowls and cover with paper.

PRESERVED QUINCES.

Choose fine large quinces, pare, core and quarter them. Cut out carefully any defective parts; put them in a preserving kettle with as much water as will cover them, and let them scald till they become soft, but do not let them break. Then take them out, lay them on a dish, and allow one pound loaf sugar to each pound of fruit. To each pound of the sugar add half a pint of the water the quinces were boiled in. Then put it on the fire, and boil and skim it till perfectly clear. Then put in the fruit; let it cook until it appears clear and of an amber color, then take it out, put it in jars, and pour the syrup over while warm. When cold cover with paper soaked in brandy, and tie it or paste it tight over the jars.

ORANGE MARMALADE.

Peel the oranges, and cut the peel into thin slices, then throw them into cold water. Boil them until tender. Take all the rind and tough skin from the oranges. Make a syrup, allowing one pound of sugar to a pint of water, and a pound of oranges mixed with the peel. Boil all together for two hours, or until done. Put it into moulds. When cold it is ready for use.

GREEN TOMATO PRESERVE.

One peck of green tomatoes. After paring them slice them. Cut up six lemons, take out the seed, add six pounds of sugar, and boil until done. Green ginger is an improvement.

MELON MARMALADE.

Pare and weigh the watermelon rinds, and lay them in strong brine for a week; soak in water until fresh enough, and then boil in water till they are tender. Take half a pound white sugar to one pound of the rind; let it boil till it begins to thicken. Add one box of dissolved gelatine to twelve pounds of marmalade. Stir it frequently, and let it boil until you can slice it. When cold flavor with lemon.

BRANDY PEACHES.

Take fresh, ripe, clingstone peaches, pour boiling lye over them, and rub off the down with a coarse cloth. Make a syrup of half a pound of sugar to each pound of peaches. Boil and skim the syrup, put in the peaches, and let them boil fifteen minutes; take them out of the syrup and cool them on a dish. Boil the syrup again to one-half, and let it cool. When cool add an equal quantity of French, apple, or peach brandy, and stir it well. When the peaches have cooled put them in a jar and pour on the syrup. Close the jar tight.

GREEN CITRON PRESERVE.

Pare the citron, and cut it into small or fancy pieces; take out the seed and use the pulp and rind. To twelve pounds fruit add one pound green ginger, four lemons, sliced thin, and with the seeds taken out. To each pound of fruit use one and a quarter pounds sugar, and one pint water. Boil it three or four hours. Do not put the lemon in till the citron is nearly ready to take up. Put the ginger in the sugar and make the syrup. Let the rind lie in cold water all night.

WATERMELON RIND PRESERVE.

Cut the rind into various shapes, and put it into salt and water for one night. Boil it in clear water three times; in the second water throw a piece of alum. Keep the rind closely covered with leaves while boiling, and after each " boil " throw it immediately out of the boiling water into clear cold water, in which let it remain until it gets cool. When it can be pierced with a straw it is sufficiently done. Have a syrup prepared of one and a quarter pounds of sugar, to each pound of rind. After draining the water from the rind through a cullender, throw it into the syrup with lemon peel cut into strips, or, if preferred, green ginger. Let it boil slowly until quite transparent.

WATERMELON RIND JAM.

Pare the rind and lay it in cold water for an hour or two, then put it in fresh cold water, and let it come to a boil. Put it in cold ginger tea and let it remain all night. Then put it in fresh ginger tea, made with the same ginger, and boil it till you can pass a straw through it. Drain it through a cullender; weigh the rind and chop it fine. Allow three-quarters pound sugar to a pound of the rind, and boil it clear. One lemon will season two pounds of rind, half pound ginger will season six pounds rind. Divide the ginger and make fresh tea, instead of using the other.

PRESERVED APPLES.

Apples for winter use should be preserved in November, and they will keep until June. Take firm pippins, pare and core them carefully, leaving them whole. Drop them in cold water as fast as pared to prevent their turning dark. Make a syrup of one pound of white sugar, and half a pint water to each pound of apples; clarify and skim it well. Wipe the apples, and put as many in the skillet as will go without one being on top of another. Let them boil quickly till they look clear, then take them up carefully and lay them on dishes, and put others in the same syrup. When all are done if the syrup should seem too thin, boil it up after the apples are all taken out. Cut the peel of several lemons in thin rings, boil them till soft, then throw them in the syrup. If you only want the apples to keep a few weeks, they may be preserved with half pound sugar.

GRAPE JAM.

One peck fox grapes, quarter peck good apples (cooking apples), seven pounds sugar. Pour a little water to the grapes, then set them over the fire and let them come to a boil. Then strain them through a cullender. Stew the apples and add them with the sugar to the grape juice. Cook until stiff.

RASPBERRY PRESERVE.

To every pound of fruit allow one pound of white sugar pounded, and let it boil twenty minutes without stirring it. When done, put it into small glasses as directed for strawberries, and set it in the sun for some time.

PLUM JELLY.

Take sound ripe plums (if damsons, an incision must be made in them), put them in a stone jar, cover it with bladder, and place it in a deep pan of water over the fire. Let the water boil gently till all the juice has come from the fruit. Strain through a jelly bag, and boil with an equal weight of loaf sugar, stirring all the time. This should cook for about twenty minutes.

APPLE JELLY.

Select apples that are rather tart and highly flavored; cut and core them without paring. Place them in a porcelain preserving kettle, cover them with water, and let them cook slowly till the apples look red. Pour into a cullender, drain off the juice and let this run through a jelly bag, then return it to the kettle, which must be carefully washed, and boil it half an hour. Then measure it, and allow half a pound of sugar to every pint of juice, and boil quickly for fifteen minutes. The juice of apples boiled in shallow vessels, without a particle of sugar, makes the most sparkling, delicious jelly imaginable. Red apples will give a jelly the color and clearness of claret, while that from light fruit is like amber. Take the cider just as it is made, not allowing it to ferment at all, and, if possible, boil it in a very large flat and shallow pan.

HODGE-PODGE.

To each pound of fruit put three-quarters pound of Havana sugar, or half a pound loaf sugar. Do not pare any of the fruit except peaches. The fruit must be cut as thin as possible in slices. Peaches, pears, apples, or quinces, and half ripe cantaloupe can be used. Mix all well together, and let it stand twelve or fourteen hours, or till it floats in juice, then put it in the skillet and let it boil until it looks clear. It takes double the time to boil that any other preserve does. Add ginger and lemon peel.

PRESERVED FIGS.

Scrape out the insides and boil them in clear water till you can run a straw through them. The water must be changed two or three times. When they are sufficiently boiled lay them on a coarse cloth to dry. Make a syrup of an equal quantity of sugar with the fruit, and boil them in it, some time, putting in some ginger. In two weeks boil them again.

CANTALOUPE PRESERVE.

Cut a green cantaloupe into any shape you choose, pare off the outside rind, and take out the soft inside. Let the rind stand an hour in cold water. To the rind put a lump of alum the size of a nutmeg, and place grape leaves in the bottom of the skillet, and put in the rind and alum, with as much water as will cover them. Put on more leaves, and let them boil slowly till you can run a straw through them, then take them out and lay them on a dish. When cold put the rind in strong ginger tea, and let them stand one night. Make a syrup of ginger tea. To each pound of rind allow one pound of sugar, and boil all together as you do watermelon rind.

PRESERVED STRAWBERRIES.

Take one pound sugar, sprinkle it over one pound of strawberries, let it stand a short time to make a syrup. Add to each pound one gill of currant juice, or a few drops of lemon. Very little time will boil them. Let them cool in a dish before putting them in jars.

PRESERVED PINEAPPLE.

Cut the fruit in slices and lay it in a dish; strew fine sugar over it to make a syrup. When sufficient juice has been extracted let it boil till clear and tender. Allow one pound of sugar to each pound of fruit.

CURRANT JELLY.

Gather the currants when just ripe. Pick them carefully from the stem; press them thoroughly with the hands, and strain (without squeezing) through a flannel bag. One pound sugar to one pint juice. Put the juice into the kettle, and let it come almost to a boil; skim several times, and then put in the sugar. Boil rapidly a few minutes. This makes the fairest jelly, but the quantity is not so great as when the currants are heated before straining.

CRAB APPLE JELLY.

Put them in a kettle and cover them with water. Let them boil till they burst, then strain them through a flannel bag.

To every pint of juice put one pound sugar. Boil hard for fifteen minutes. Skim well. When done put into glasses before it cools.

CURRANT JELLY. No. 1.

Strip the currants from the stalk, then put them in a kettle and cook them until the juice is extracted, then boil the juice twenty minutes. Add one pound sugar (heat the sugar in a pan before adding it) to one pint of juice, and boil it five minutes longer. When done, if it is not perfectly clear, strain it while hot through a piece of muslin, and put it into glasses. It is just as well not to let it boil any more after the sugar has been added, but to let it stand and thoroughly dissolve.

CURRANT JELLY.

Ten pounds of currants make seven pounds of jelly. Put in a preserving kettle, add to that quantity one and one-half pints of water. Boil them well down. Strain through a flannel bag. To one pint of juice, add one pound of white sugar. Put the juice in the kettle. When it comes to a boil, stir in the sugar slowly, until it boils; then remove from the fire, pour into jars or glasses. Let it remain open a while, before sealing.

GOOSEBERRY JELLY.

Wash the berries, and put them into a kettle with some water to cook them. When they soften let them boil hard twenty minutes, and set them away in the kettle overnight. Then squeeze them through a cloth, and allow one pound sugar to one pint of juice. Let the juice heat up, add the sugar gradually, and let it stand until dissolved, but do not let it boil.

BLACKBERRY JAM.

Choose large, fully-ripe blackberries, weigh them, and allow three-quarters pound of sugar to a pound of fruit. Mash sugar and fruit together. Put the whole into a preserving kettle. Skim it while boiling, and stir it frequently. Let it boil until it thickens. When done put it in small pots or glasses, and when cold cover with brandy paper, and paste or tie them close. Any kind of fruit may be made into jam by following these directions. Peaches are nicer (small ones) with the skin on.

CHOPPED APPLE PRESERVE.

Take equal quantities of granulated sugar and apples. To every three pounds sugar put one pint water. Boil in a thick syrup with one ounce of race ginger. Chop the apples in pieces half an inch square. Boil them in the syrup until clear.

PRESERVED STRAWBERRIES.

To every pound of fruit put one pound of pulverized loaf sugar. When they are half done drop in a small piece of alum the size of a filbert to every five pounds.

GREEN TOMATO JAM.

Sixteen pounds of green tomatoes, ten large lemons, ten pounds of sugar. Pare the tomatoes, and add three-quarters of a pound of green ginger.

PEACH CAKES.

Take dry soft peaches and peel them. Then spread them on dishes, and mash them till they are reduced to a pulp, but do not mash until the juice comes out. Weigh them before mashing, and allow a quarter pound white sugar to one pound of fruit. Mix the sugar and peaches, and spread it out on plates or dishes to dry. When they are dry enough to handle make them into cakes about the size and thickness of water crackers. Put them back on the dishes, and turn them over every morning. When dry pack them in sugar.

HOME-MADE RAISINS.

Gather the grapes when ripe; after washing them on the bunches pick them off. Make a thick syrup of two pounds of sugar and one pint of water. Drop the grapes into the kettle, and keep them in the syrup until they split open, when most of the side will settle in the kettle. Skim them out, and after drying them on plates pack them down in sugar. The same syrup can be used several times. These are very good in puddings or cake.

CANDIED ORANGES.

Choose fine sweet oranges; peel and quarter them. Make a syrup of one pound of sugar to a pint of water, and let it boil till it comes to the candying point. Dip the oranges into this candied syrup, and place them on a sieve to drain. Put this sieve over a large flat dish that will catch the dripping syrup, and let the oranges remain so in a warm place until the candied syrup upon them is dry and crystallized.

PEACH LEATHER.

Take ripe peaches, cut them up, and cook them so they can be rubbed through a cullender. Then put them in a kettle with very little sugar, say about two pounds to a large kettle full. (I have made them best without any sugar at all as they dry better.) Cook them a little more, then spread them very thin on large tin waiters, such as are made with drying fruit. Place them in the hot sun. In four days they should be dry enough to take off. Cut them in thin strips, and roll up in shapes with white sugar. Apple, pear, or quince leather is made in the same way.

CONSERVED PEACHES OR PEARS.

Take nice ripe peaches or pears, and peel them. Have ready a syrup of one pound of sugar to four of fruit. Boil the fruit in the syrup about half an hour; spread it on dishes and dry it in the hot sun. When dry roll them in sugar, and pack in jars.

Scrape & prepare rind of watermelon, keeping only the white part.
Cut in pieces about one by two inches
Soak in salt & water for 24 hours
Freshen by pouring water through it in the
   collander & put to soak in ice water for 2 hrs
Put in the pot with fresh cold water & boil
until very tender (so that a straw passes
thro' easily)
Make a syrup in the proportion of about
1 1/2 cups of vinegar to 3 cups of sugar,
cinnamon, cloves & allspice.
Boil until quite thick & pour hot over
the fruit which has been placed in a
bowl.
Let stand over night
Drain the syrup off & add more sugar,
vinegar & spices - about 2 cups sugar &
2 cups vinegar.
Boil until quite a thick syrup & pour
hot over the fruit which should have
been put in the fruit jars.
Let stand a week before eating

Danish Strawberry Preserves.

Get firm, large berries & stem but do not wash them. Weigh 3/4 lb of sugar to every pound of fruit & arrange them in a deep porcelain kettle, sprinkling the sugar lightly between layers of the fruit. Cover & let this stand all night or, if the weather is very hot & damp prepare them early in the morning & let them stand 6 hrs.

Heat slowly to the boiling point, skimming very thoroughly & simmer 15 minutes.

Take the kettle from the fire at exactly this moment & cover with a thin cloth & stand it away all night without moving.

In the morning, heat again very slowly & skim. Let it simmer 10 minutes & take from the fire. Strain off the juice without breaking the berries & boil juice not more than 5 minutes. Add the fruit when you take the kettle from the fire & put into hot glass jars, with new rubbers & glass tops.

The cans must be sterilized by being boiled half an hour & the rubbers should be put in very hot water for 10 minutes.

If these preserves are kept in a cool, dark place, they will be as good after years as at first.

All strawberry preserves lose color unless kept in the dark, so unless the closet is dark cover with brown wrapping paper or bury in a box of sand.

Cherries can be preserved by the same rule but if very sweet use only 1/2 lb sugar to a lb of fruit.

GENERAL DIRECTIONS FOR MAKING PICKLES.

Pickles may be made at any time during the winter or summer provided that you have cucumbers, *mangoes*, or even peaches, which, having been gathered fresh during their season, were put in a strong brine, and kept entirely under by the pressure of weights, so as not to be exposed to the air. When you take the vegetables or fruit out of the brine, soak them for a day or two in cold water. Then put them over the fire in a kettle, covering well with weak vinegar. Let them gently simmer until parboiled, or rather tender, but by all means do not let them cook till they become soft. Cucumbers are ruined by long cooking, which destroys their crispness, and almost renders them inedible. Let them remain in this vinegar until you are ready to supply the final seasoning and the strong cider vinegar needed for the preparation of all kinds of pickles. A delay of a week will do no harm, although the process may be completed forthwith if you prefer. The horseradish used in pickles must be scraped and dried; the garlic must be soaked from three to ten days, changing the water once or twice a day; the mustard seed bruised; spices are put in without any preparation. When onions are used, they need only be sliced and scalded.

PICKLES AND CATSUPS.

RAGOUT PICKLE.

One gallon green tomatoes, sliced, one gallon chopped cabbage, one pint sliced onions, quarter pound mustard seed, one ounce celery seed, one ounce allspice, half ounce cloves, four tablespoonsful of whole black peppers, one and a half gills of salt, one pound brown sugar, three quarts vinegar. Boil all together one hour or until clear. It may be used in a week, and will keep a year.

CHOPPED TOMATO PICKLE.

Two gallons of tomatoes well chopped, five tablespoonsful of mustard, three gills mustard seed, two tablespoons of allspice, two of ground pepper and two of cloves, one gill of salt, one and a half pints of onions chopped fine, two pounds of sugar, three quarts strong vinegar. Put all on the fire together, and boil until well done. The tomatoes should be green, and the skins pared off. This recipe applies equally to cabbage.

DAMSON PICKLE.

Two pounds damsons, one pound sugar, one pint vinegar. Add mace, cloves, and cinnamon. Stew the fruit and spice in vinegar until done.

WALNUT PICKLE.

Put the walnuts in salt and water, let them stand a fortnight; then boil them. After taking them out of the brine put them in vinegar. Then put them in fresh vinegar, with any kind of spice you like.

GREEN TOMATO PICKLE.

One peck green tomatoes cut in thin slices; sprinkle them with salt, and let them stand two days. Twelve onions sliced, one-ounce bottle mustard, half pound white mustard seed, quarter ounce of turmeric, one dozen cloves, one ounce ground pepper, and one ounce allspice. Mix all together. Put in a kettle a layer of tomatoes, onions, and spices, alternately. Cover them with vinegar, and let them simmer an hour.

GREEN TOMATOES PICKLED WITHOUT BOILING.

One gallon of tomatoes sliced thin, six sliced onions. Sprinkle with salt, and let them remain overnight. Take them out and let them drain till evening. Add six moderate-sized green peppers, chopped fine, three tablespoonsful of ground mustard, half pint white mustard seed, one tablespoonful cloves, same of allspice and of black pepper, all mixed together. Pack in a jar, cover with vinegar, and in one month it is fit for use.

PICKLED DAMSONS.

To every two pounds of damsons put one pound sugar, half a pint of vinegar, add mace, cloves, allspice, and cinnamon to taste. Place the fruit in a jar, then scald the vinegar, spices and sugar together, and pour it over the fruit for six successive mornings, covering the jar each time very closely, to prevent the flavor from escaping. This pickle is fit for use in two weeks.

MARTYNIA PICKLE.

Put the young pods in strong brine for a week or ten days, then take them out and wash them clean in fresh water. After this put them in vinegar to soak out the salt and weedy taste they would otherwise have. They should remain in this vinegar two weeks; then take them out and drain them well, then put them in a jar with the following ingredients: One gallon vinegar, a large handful horseradish, one teacup allspice, half teacupful cloves, two pounds of brown sugar, four onions, and two pods of red pepper. The spice should be bruised in a mortar, and the onions and horseradish sliced. Boil all these in vinegar, and pour it over the prepared martynias.

PEACH MANGO.

Lay the peaches in salt and water for two days, then take them out and wipe them dry. Take out the stones, and fill with the following mixture: Minced garlic, horseradish, bruised mustard seed, and sliced ginger root, celery seed, and onion. Tie the peaches round with thread, and strew over them cloves, broken cinnamon, and turmeric. Season cold vinegar with made mustard, ginger, and nutmeg and sugar. Pour the vinegar over the peaches, and set the jar in a cool place for three months. Oil may be added to this filling if desired.

PICKLED ONIONS.

Peel the onions, and put them in salt and water not very strong for six days, changing the water every other day. Then boil some vinegar, putting in two handsful of salt. Let it stand until perfectly cold, and then pour over the onions. A tablespoonful of mustard to each quart is an improvement.

YELLOW PICKLE.

Gather firm, early York cabbages, cut them in half, cover them thickly with salt, and let them stand one night. Scald it next day, and spread it on a cloth to dry, turning it frequently. When well dried put it for one or two days in plain vinegar made very yellow with turmeric. When it is a good yellow, drain it, and put in spiced vinegar, cucumbers, and other vegetables, prepared as usual. To two gallons of vinegar, add three pounds of brown sugar, a handful of clove garlic, and a handful of horseradish cut in thin slices, one cup of white mustard seed, one cup of black pepper, two ounces of turmeric in a thin bag, half ounce of mace, a small quantity of celery seed, half a pound of white ginger soaked well, sliced, and dried; one tablespoonful of the oil of cloves. Keep the jar in the sun covered up very close, and stir the pickle frequently. This will be ready for use in four or five months.

YELLOW PICKLE.

Take cabbage, cucumbers, peaches, and any other fruit or vegetable desired, and put them in salt or vinegar for two or three weeks, one pound of rare vinegar, half pound of garlic, four ounces of allspice, two ounces of long pepper, two ounces of turmeric, one pint of white mustard, and a handful of sliced horseradish. Bruise all of these together, and put it into two gallons strong vinegar. Set it in the sun, and stir it every day. Leave it until the horseradish looks yellow, then wipe the pickle and put in the vinegar, and let it stand in the sun several days.

PICKLED CUCUMBERS.

Peel and slice the cucumbers half an inch thick, chop onions, and salt both. Let them lie six hours in salt, then strain, and put in a stone jar, sprinkling each layer with black and red pepper, and fill the jar with cold vinegar, covering with sweet oil. This pickle will be fit for use by the first of January.

GREEN CUCUMBER PICKLE.

Wipe the cucumbers well after taking them out of the brine. Let them soak a few days in vinegar. Wipe them dry again. If preferred cut the cucumbers in slices about a quarter inch thick. Divide the cucumbers into three or four parts, and between each part put the following: Allspice, cloves, mace, nutmegs, and peppers in the same quantities as you use in yellow pickle, about two ounces to seventy-five cucumbers, also celery seed—but fresh celery is better—and a little onion. Between each layer put this mixture, with plenty of brown sugar, allowing six or eight pounds to a large jar. Cover with strong vinegar. Tie the mouth of the jar securely, and place it in a large iron pot filled with water. Let it boil until you can run a straw through the pickles.

PEACH PICKLE.

To as much vinegar as will cover four dozen peaches add three dozen allspice, as much pepper, and two tablespoonsful of salt. Boil and pour over the peaches while it is hot.

FRENCH PICKLE.

Half peck green tomatoes, one head of white cabbage, sixteen green peppers, taking out the core and seeds, twenty small white onions, one and a half pounds white mustard seed, one ounce celery seed, one ounce green ginger, three dozen pods red pepper, one dessert-spoonful of cayenne pepper, four stocks horseradish, scraped, and one teacup of salt. Boil it four hours, covering well with cider vinegar, adding more as it boils away. When cool add a small bottle of olive oil. Chop all the ingredients very fine. Put it in jars and close them very tight until fit for use.

RIPE CANTALOUPE PICKLE.

To six pounds of fruit cut in slices two pounds of sugar; make a rich syrup with one gallon of vinegar. Boil and skim it, and add spices according to taste; ginger, mustard seed, cloves, allspice, horseradish, and whole grains of black pepper. First boil the cantaloupes in weak alum water for about fifteen minutes; cut and drain them well, then put them in the syrup, and boil until clear.

BOILED CABBAGE PICKLE.

Take one peck of cabbage after it is cut for pickle. Put a layer of cabbage, and sprinkle with salt, and so on until all is put in. Let it lie all night, then squeeze it from the pickle. Put in four chopped onions. Put the cabbage in a kettle, cover it well with vinegar, boil it one hour, and then add two pounds of sugar, two ounces turmeric, one ounce mace, half ounce cloves, half teacup black pepper, half teacup of ginger, half ounce allspice, two ounces celery seed, four tablespoonsful of mustard, and one quarter pound white mustard seed. Put it on the fire again and let it boil one hour longer.

CHOWCHOW PICKLE.

Half a peck green tomatoes, two large heads of cabbage, fifteen good-sized onions, twenty-five cucumbers, one pint horseradish, half a pound mustard seed (white), one ounce celery seed, one ounce turmeric, half a teacup ground black pepper. Cut the tomatoes, cucumbers, onions, and cabbage small, and pack them in salt for one night. In the morning drain the salt off, and lay them in vinegar and water for a day or two, then drain them again. Boil the spices in half a gallon of vinegar, with three pounds brown sugar, and pour it over while hot. Repeat this for three days, then mix five ounces mustard and half a pint of the best salad oil. Add two quarts more of vinegar when the pickle is cold. This is good to eat in two months.

No. 1 OIL MANGOES.

Put melons in strong brine for a week. Take out and simmer in weak vinegar until green; let them remain in this vinegar one day, then stuff them. For forty large melons take the following: One and a half pounds white mustard seed, one and a half pounds black mustard seed, two ounces pounded pepper, one ounce pounded ginger, one ounce whole allspice, three ounces whole cloves, a large handful of garlic chopped fine, six onions chopped, one ounce pounded mace, one tablespoonful salt, four ounces brown sugar, half a teaspoonful red pepper, one pint scraped horseradish, one teacup salad oil mixed with a little vinegar. Prepare two gallons of strong vinegar as follows: One cup of whole black peppers, half a cup whole allspice, half a cup whole cloves, one cup scraped horseradish, four onions sliced, one cup garlic, one ounce ground ginger, four ounces black mustard seed, one cup bruised celery seed, two pounds brown sugar. Boil these ingredients in vinegar, and when cold pour over the mangoes. If not sufficient to cover the mangoes add more.

OIL PICKLE.

Cut cucumbers in thin slices, add one third as many onions as cucumbers, sliced very small. Salt them well in layers, let them stand five hours, then pour them into a cullender to drain. To two gallons of cucumbers put two tablespoonsful of ground pepper, the same of allspice and of cloves, half a pint olive oil, quarter pound mustard, and as much cider vinegar as will well cover them. Mix all together, and put them in jars tightly covered. Keep them in a cool place. They will be fit for use in a few weeks.

SWEET CANTALOUPE PICKLE.

Cut one dozen cantaloupes into quarters; if large, into eight pieces each. Pare them and cut the soft part out, then lay them in a jar and cover them with vinegar all night. The next morning to each pint of vinegar add three-quarters pound sugar, one tablespoonful of cloves, half a tablespoon of mace, four large sticks of cinnamon. Boil and skim it, then put in the rind and let it boil until transparent. Take it out and put it on dishes, leaving the syrup to boil for half an hour longer, and pour it on the cantaloupes while hot. When cold put in a jar and tie up.

CHOWCHOW PICKLE.

Slice three dozen large cucumbers, four large green peppers, half a peck of onions, same of green tomatoes, add one pint of small red and green peppers. Sprinkle one pint of salt over them, and let them drain overnight. In the morning add the following: One ounce mace, one of white pepper, same of white mustard seed and of turmeric, half ounce of cloves, same of celery seed, two pounds sugar, three tablespoonsful of table mustard, and a handful of sliced horseradish. Cover with vinegar, and boil all together for half an hour.

PICKLED CHERRIES.

To every pound of cherries allow half pound of loaf sugar, half pint of cider vinegar, half ounce each of powdered cinnamon, mixed whole cloves, and allspice, and a few blades of mace. Put the cherries in a jar. Boil the other ingredients in the vinegar for five minutes, and when boiling pour the liquor over the fruit. Cover closely for a week.

PICKLED WALNUTS.

Take a peck of walnuts, tender enough to be easily punctured by a pin. Put them in a jar, and pour over them a very strong brine, boiling hot. In a fortnight they will have begun to brown considerably. They should then be taken out, drained, and laid in the sun until they turn black. Put them back in the clean jar, and having boiled two gallons of vinegar with two ounces each of allspice and cloves, and whole grains of black pepper, also a little mace, pour this spiced vinegar hot over them.

TO MANGO CUCUMBERS.

To two dozen cucumbers put a quarter ounce mace, the same of cloves and allspice, half ounce of ginger, three-quarters ounce of pepper, four ounces of horseradish, same of garlic, half ounce mustard seed. Boil two gallons of vinegar with the spices, and pour it on the cucumbers. The cucumbers, after lying eight days in salt and water, should be greened, by lining the kettle with green leaves, and sprinkling with alum.

YELLOW PICKLE.

Six quarts vinegar, four ounces mustard seed beaten fine, one spoonful of salt, one dozen coriander seeds beaten fine, one grated nutmeg, six ounces ginger soaked in salt and water, then sliced and dried, six of garlic peeled, and salted three days, two spoonsful of beaten turmeric. Have a wooden cover to the pot, and tie it up close with a bladder or sheep skin, set it away three weeks, putting it by the fire, or, if warm weather, in the sun, stirring it up once every three days. Prepare the vegetables by washing them in brine that will bear an egg, until they turn yellow. Put some of the brine they were washed in over the fire; let it boil briskly, then throw in the pickles. Let them remain a few minutes, then take them out and put them in the sun to bleach. Have ready the jar with equal quantities of vinegar and water, a handful of salt, and half ounce of turmeric. Let the vegetables remain twenty-four hours in this, and then drain them out. Stuff the mangoes, and put them in pickle-pots. Put cabbages in the oven until the leaves fall, then tie them in bundles and put them in the jar for three days. Asparagus must be salted and dried three days in the sun. Cabbage can also be dried in the sun.

PICKLED ONIONS.

In the month of September choose the small, white, round onions; take off the brown skin. Have ready a clean tin stewpan of boiling water; throw in as many onions as will cover the top. As soon as they look clear on the outside take them out as quickly as possible, and lay them on a clean cloth, covering them close with another. Then scald more, and so on till all are done. Let them remain till they are cold, then put them in a jar or wide-mouthed bottle, and pour over them the best white wine vinegar just hot. When cold cover them.

GREEN TOMATO PICKLE.

Cut one peck of green tomatoes into slices. Sprinkle them with salt, and let them stand twenty-four hours. Take six large onions, one bottle of mustard, quarter pound mustard seed, half ounce cloves, one ounce ground pepper, half ounce ground ginger, and one ounce allspice. Put them in a kettle in alternate layers of tomatoes and spice. Cover them with vinegar, and let them simmer until the tomatoes look quite clear. Add quarter pound celery seed. When done and cold add more vinegar, a handful of fresh spices, onion, and two pounds brown sugar.

WALNUT PICKLE.

Gather walnuts about the 10th of June, when you can stick a pin through them. Lay them in salt water for two weeks, then take them out, scrape them, and rub them with a coarse towel. Then lay them in fresh water for three days, changing the water daily. Put garlic, allspice, and black pepper into vinegar, and pour it boiling on the walnuts. If they are rather old and hard, scald them in an iron pot. Cloves are an improvement.

PEPPER MANGOES.

Put the peppers in strong brine for two weeks, then put them in fresh water till free from salt. Take a piece out, and fill with grated horseradish, white mustard seed, a little grated onion, and a few cloves of garlic, with ground cinnamon, mace, black and green pepper to taste.

MARTYNIA PICKLE.

Gather when young and tender; wipe them and put them in strong brine till you wish to pickle them, then let them soak in clear water for twenty-four hours. Put them in an iron pot, and cover them with vinegar and cold water, then let them simmer slowly until they blacken. Do not let them boil. Put them in a two gallon jar, chop four onions fine, add one pound brown sugar, one handful of sliced horseradish, and the same of cloves and allspice, one ounce race ginger, one ounce celery seed, two ounces mustard seed. Sprinkle these all in the jar. Boil strong vinegar, and pour it over the pickle. Set a plate over the jar to cover while hot.

ROUGH AND READY PICKLE.

Slice six dozen cucumbers, half a peck green tomatoes, one dozen bull-nose peppers, one dozen silverskin onions. Salt them separately and let them stand overnight. Next morning press them perfectly dry, and mix them together, having chopped the onions and peppers fine. Put half a teacup of black pepper, same of allspice, half a pound white mustard seed, one ounce celery seed, some horseradish, and a few cloves. Cover well with vinegar and let it come to a boil. To every gallon of the mixture put half a pound of brown sugar.

CHILLI SAUCE.

Twenty-four ripe tomatoes, eight onions, six peppers, eight coffee cups of vinegar, eight tablespoons of sugar, the same of salt, one tablespoonful of cinnamon, one of allspice, one of nutmeg, and one of cloves. Boil all well together and seal while hot. This is superior to tomato catsup.

CUCUMBER SWEET PICKLE.

Slice the cucumbers about one inch thick, and boil for an hour in weak alum water, then take them out and lay them in cold water, leaving them until perfectly cold, then boil again in fresh alum water half an hour. Drain the fruit well, and make a syrup of one pound of sugar to each pound of fruit. To four pounds of fruit one pound cider vinegar. Boil the syrup, then put in the fruit, and let it boil until it is transparent. Add mace, and if the syrup is not thick enough continue to boil it after the fruit is removed. When cold sprinkle in some white mustard seed.

RIPE CANTALOUPE MANGOES.

Use ripe cantaloupes, small ones of course; pare them, cut a slit in each, and remove the seed carefully. Then put them into brine strong enough to bear an egg, and let them remain for nine days, after which fill them with the following mixture: Three ounces crushed white ginger, three ounces of horseradish, scraped into shreds, six ounces black mustard seed, bruised, three quarters ounce mace, three quarters ounce cloves, one and a half ounces of whole black pepper, one and a half ounces turmeric, and three pounds of brown sugar, two and a quarter ounces cucumber out of brine, chopped small. Mix all together. When the mangoes have been filled put them into a jar and cover with boiling vinegar. The above quantity will fill about twenty-four small melons.

GREEN TOMATO PICKLE.

Puncture the tomatoes with a fork; place them on a dish and sprinkle them with salt. Let them remain two or three days, and then rinse off the salt in clear water. Put them in a preserving kettle, cover them with water, which keep scalding hot for an hour, then take them out and put them in jars. Boil the vinegar with some cloves, allspice, and stick cinnamon. When cold pour sufficient over to cover them.

HYDEN SALAD.

To one gallon chopped cabbage add half a gallon of green tomatoes chopped fine, also one quart green peppers, from which the seeds have been extracted, one quart chopped onions. Strain it and throw away all the juice. Add one tablespoonful of beaten mustard, two of cinnamon, one of cloves, three of celery seed, two pounds sugar, two tablespoons salt, and one gallon vinegar. Mix well and boil for twenty-five minutes. Add less pepper if you prefer.

TO PICKLE NASTURTIONS.

Gather the berries when full grown but young, put them in a pot; pour boiling salt and water over them, and let them stand for three or four days. Then drain off the water and cover them with cold vinegar, which is seasoned with mace, black pepper, allspice, and cloves. These will be fit to use in two months, and are delicious.

RECIPE FOR TOMATO CATSUP.

Four tablespoonsful of salt to one gallon of peeled tomatoes, four tablespoonsful of ground pepper, half a tablespoonful of allspice, four pods of red pepper, and three tablespoonsful of mustard. Add sliced onions according to taste. One pint vinegar.

BETTER RECIPE FOR TOMATO CATSUP.

Gather the tomatoes when quite ripe, cut them in thin slices, put a thick layer of tomatoes and a layer of salt alternately in a stone jar until full, then boil it gently half an hour. Rub it through a hair sieve, and to every gallon add four roots of horseradish scraped, a small onion stuck full of cloves, quarter ounce of mace, quarter ounce cloves, quarter ounce nutmeg, one ounce allspice, two pods red pepper, or one ounce black pepper. Boil all together, and when done add at the rate of half a pint of vinegar to every gallon of catsup, and one pint of wine to every three quarts. Bottle it as soon as sufficiently cool, and cork it immediately, keeping it tight.

CUCUMBER CATSUP.

Take thirty-six full-grown cucumbers, pare and slice them; two quarts onions also pared and sliced, and one pint of salt. Mix all together, and spread them out to drain for six or eight hours, then place them in a large bowl, and add the following: Quarter pound brown sugar, half a pint sweet oil, half a pound mustard seed, quarter pound ground black pepper, and two quarts of boiling vinegar. Mix all thoroughly, and put in small jars, filling up with cold vinegar, to cover the cucumbers; on the top of each jar put a little sweet oil, and seal up tight.

WALNUT CATSUP.

Pound the walnuts, and let them stand two or three days in hot sun, then pour enough vinegar over them to cover them, and boil it. Then strain out the pounded walnuts. Add pepper, cloves, salt, onions, and a little more vinegar; put it on again and boil it, adding whatever spice you prefer. After boiling strain out the spice, and bottle the catsup. Age improves it very much.

COLD TOMATO CATSUP.

Half a peck ripe tomatoes, half a gallon good vinegar, one teacup of salt, one cup of mustard seed ground fine, four red peppers, three tablespoonsful of black pepper, a handful of celery seed, and a cup of grated horseradish.

A No. 1 TOMATO CATSUP.

To half a bushel of ripe tomatoes peeled, add one quart of good vinegar, one pound salt, quarter pound black pepper, half pound allspice, one ounce cloves, six ounces mustard, twenty cloves of garlic and onions, two pounds brown sugar, and a handful of peach leaves. Boil three hours, stirring all the time. When cool strain through a coarse cloth and bottle tightly. This improves with age.

CUCUMBER CATSUP.

Take twelve cucumbers, lay them an hour in cold water. Pare and grate them. Grate six onions, season with red and black pepper, celery seed, and vinegar. Make it the consistency of jam. Put it in a glass jar, covering with three pints vinegar, salt to taste, and three tablespoonsful black pepper. Keep the jar covered tight, so as to exclude all air.

PEPPER SAUCE (Pickled).

Half peck green tomatoes, one head cabbage, half dozen white onions, half dozen large green peppers. Chop them all very fine. Add quarter pound white mustard seed, half tablespoonful black pepper, one tablespoonful of salt, and one tablespoonful celery seed. Put all in a skillet and cover with the best vinegar. Simmer slowly three hours. Some allspice and cloves will improve it.

TOMATO CATSUP OR SOY.

One peck ripe tomatoes, eight tablespoonsful of mixed mustard, four tablespoonsful salt, two of ground black pepper, half of allspice, and four pods of red pepper. Simmer the ingredients three hours, strain through a sieve, add one quart of vinegar, simmer ten minutes longer. Then pour it into small bottles, cork it tightly, and keep it in a cool place.

ANOTHER RECIPE.

One peck tomatoes, half a dozen onions chopped fine, two tablespoons of allspice, two of cloves, two ounces celery seed, quarter pound salt or more if liked, one pound brown sugar, and one quart of strong vinegar. This is an excellent recipe, and the proportions are always approved.

WALNUT CATSUP.

Early in June take the walnuts, while soft enough to beat to a paste, and to every hundred thus prepared add two quarts or a gallon of vinegar and a handful of salt. Let the liquor stand eight days in a stone jar, stirring it frequently. Then strain it into a tin saucepan, boil it, and skim it well; adding to it ginger, horseradish, mustard seed, a few cloves of garlic, and a little black pepper. Let it boil up once, pour it into an earthen pan, and when cold bottle it, dividing the ingredients between each bottle. The white walnut is best suited for making catsup, but, as that is not found in all districts, the black may be used if gathered while tender enough for the rind of the nut to be pierced with a pin. This is an excellent condiment to fresh boiled fish.

TOMATO CATSUP.

Gather the tomatoes, put them into a skillet covered close until all the juice is drawn out, then wring them hard through a coarse cloth. Season them high with pepper and salt, and boil them well without skimming, adding a few grains of whole pepper, five or six large blades of mace, and the same quantity of cloves. When cold add one third of good vinegar; bottle and cork them well, keeping them in a cool place.

CUCUMBER CATSUP.

Put peeled cucumbers into cold water, grate them, season well with salt, then tie them up in a thin cloth, and let them drain all night. Mix in the vinegar, white mustard and celery seeds, black pepper, and a little sugar. Pour over the cucumbers. When cold it is ready for use.

TOMATO CATSUP.

One gallon tomatoes, one quart vinegar, six pods of red pepper, six tablespoonsful black pepper, six of allspice, two of cinnamon, four of salt, and one of mustard seed. Grind the spices. Boil slowly four hours.

GREEN TOMATO CATSUP.

To one gallon green tomatoes cut fine add one quart finely-chopped onions, one quart good cider vinegar, four pods of red pepper, half a teacup salt, one of mixed ground spices, one cup brown sugar. Stew till reduced one half.

TOMATO CATSUP.

One peck tomatoes, one cup of salt, three tablespoonfuls black pepper, two of cloves, two of allspice, one large pod of red pepper chopped fine, four onions chopped, one teacup brown sugar, twelve whole cloves, and same of garlic. Pour boiling water on the tomatoes to remove the skins; put them into a kettle with one quart of vinegar, and boil two hours; strain through a cullender. and add two tablespoonsful of celery seed. Bottle while hot.

COLD CUCUMBER PICKLE.

Three dozen large cucumbers, eight white onions good size. Sprinkle on them three-quarters of a pound of salt, put in a cullender and drain twelve hours, then take a teacup of white mustard seed, one-half teacup of ground black pepper, mix with the cucumbers and cover with vinegar. Good in three days. Keep it fastened air-tight. Pare and slice the cucumbers, skin and slice the onions.

CHOWCHOW PICKLE.

Cut up fine one large head of cabbage, one dozen onions, one dozen green peppers, two dozen green tomatoes, three roots of horseradish grated, cover with strong salt and water, boil until tender, strain through a sieve. Boil in three pints of vinegar, one-half ounce of turmeric, one-quarter pound of white mustard seed. Pour this hot over the vegetables; when cold add one-half teacupful of mustard mixed, one-half teacup of celery seed. Cauliflower would be very nice added, also salad oil.

TOMATO PICKLE.

One peck green tomatoes sliced thin, sprinkle with salt, let stand one night; slice twelve onions, put with tomatoes, boil in vinegar two hours with spices. Four ounces of white mustard seed, four ounces ground mustard, one ounce of turmeric, one ounce of cloves, allspice, cinnamon, ginger and pepper, one-quarter cup salt, one-half pound brown sugar.

ONION PICKLE.

One peck of white onions (small size), peel them, and for nine consecutive mornings scald with fresh salt water, pouring off the old. The 10th day drain the onions, and pack in jars. Make a dressing of one pound of ground mustard, one cup of oil, one pound of sugar, and enough vinegar to cover well. Let all come to a boil, and pour over the onions. Do not fill your jars too full of the onions, they must have plenty of dressing to make them good, and to keep.

CUCUMBER OR GHERKIN PICKLE.

Choose small but perfect cucumbers not over a finger long. Pack in a stone jar or wooden bucket, in layers, strewing salt thickly between these. Cover the top layer with the salt, and pour cold water enough to cover all. Lay a small plate or round board on them, with a clean stone to keep it down. You may leave them in the brine for a week or a month, stirring up from the bottom every other day. If the longer time, be sure your salt and water is strong enough to bear up an egg. If you raise your own cucumbers, pick them every day, and drop in the pickle. When you are ready to put them up, throw away the brine, with any cucumbers that may have softened under the process, and lay the rest in cold fresh water for twenty-four hours; change the water then for fresh, and leave it for another day. Have a kettle ready, lined with green vine leaves, and lay the pickles evenly within it, scattering powdered alum over the layers; a bit of alum as large as a pigeon egg will be enough for a two-gallon kettleful. Fill with cold water, cover with vine leaves, three deep; put a close lid or inverted pan over all and steam over a slow fire five or six hours, not allowing the water to boil. When the pickles are a fine green, remove the leaves and throw the cucumbers into very cold water. Let them stand in it while you prepare the vinegar. To one gallon allow a cup of sugar, three dozen whole black peppers, the same of cloves, half as much allspice, one dozen blades of mace. Boil five minutes; put the cucumbers into a stone jar and pour the vinegar over them scalding hot, cover closely. Two days afterward scald the vinegar again and return to the pickles. Repeat this process three times more at intervals of two, four and six days. Cover with stoneware or wooden top; tie stout cloth over this and keep in a cool, dry place. They will be ready for eating in two months. Examine every few weeks.

VERY FINE CHOWCHOW.

One head of cauliflower, one quart of very young corn before it has filled at all, not more than a finger long, one quart of celery chopped in small pieces, one quart of very small cucumbers, one quart of large cucumbers sliced, one pint of chopped onions, one pint of very small whole onions, one quart of string beans, very tender, one quart of nasturtions if you can get them, one pint of sliced green peppers. Let all these lie in salt and water a day and night. Then strain them all from the salt and water, put on the fire, and cover with vinegar and water; let them come to a boil. Then have your seasoning ready to pour over the vegetables, after you drain them from the vinegar and and water. Make the seasoning as follows: one-quarter pound of English mustard, one ounce of turmeric, one-half gallon of vinegar, three-quarter pound of sugar, tablespoonful of celery seed, teacup of salad oil, teacup of flour. Mix mustard, turmeric, flour and sugar with the vinegar, into a smooth paste. Cook it very carefully until it begins to thicken. When boiling hot, pour over the vegetables. This pickle I have kept for several years.

WINES.

WINE OF THE FIRST QUALITY.

Carefully pick the grapes from the stems, rejecting all green and decayed berries. Crush them in an ordinary apple crusher; should you desire the wine to be light colored, with delicacy of taste, press lightly in an ordinary cider press. If it is desired to make a red wine, with full body and astringency, mash the grapes and let them stand in a cask or vat, covered with cloth, for twenty-four hours, before pressing. The longer the fermentation of the *mash* and *must* continues the more *astringent* and *rough* the wine will be, and the *sooner* and *lighter* he presses it the less character will the wine acquire, though it will be much more *delicate* and *smooth*. Before filling the vessels they should be perfectly clean and sweet, without the slightest mouldiness. It is best, where wooden kegs or casks are used, to dip a strip of canton flannel in melted sulphur and igniting it, hang it by a wire in the bung-hole of the barrel, and after letting it stand bunged up with the vapor of sulphur in it for an hour or so, rinse well with clean water. The best ripe juice put in a musty barrel will make only a *spoiled wine*. Should the barrel hold twenty gallons put in forty pounds of *grape sugar* or glucose—the best is that made by the Buffalo Grape Sugar Co. from corn starch—that made from potato starch is apt to give an earthy taste to the wine. In no case use *cane sugar*, for the vinous fermentation of cane sugar always produces *rum*, while that of grape sugar produces *wine*.

As soon as the fermentation commences let the skins, seeds, and froth *work out* of the barrel. This is best accomplished by having a tin gutter adapted to a bung piece. As you keep 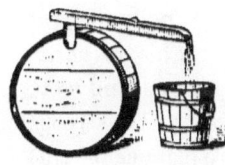 the barrel and bung piece full to an overflow, all the impurities will work out. When clear, the first fermentation may be said to begin. Place the barrel in a cool cellar, and set it up high enough so that it can be drawn out by a siphon into another barrel at will, without disturbing the sediment. Insert in the bung a plug, say four inches long, into the centre of which is placed a tube. It is essential 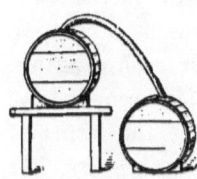 to wax around the bung and tube, so as to force all the carbonic acid gas, that results from the fermentation, through the tube and into the tumbler of water in which the tube is immersed. If the wine is thus put away, say about the 1st of September, the first fermentation will last until about the 15th of October, at which time the barrel must be filled up with juice and bunged up tight. It is well to look at it every two or three weeks, and fill up the barrel. It is essential to success to keep the barrel full, so that as little air as possible shall act upon the surface of the wine. 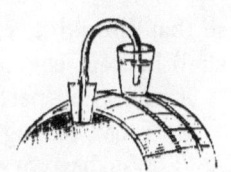 In the Spring, say April, when the vine is again in bloom, the second fermentation will begin.

SECOND FERMENTATION.

All that is necessary to be done is to loosen the bung and let the barrel have vent. The fermentation will be over May 1st, when it will require to be filled again to the bung and tightly closed. By the 15th of June the wine will be settled clear, when it may be bottled for use.

WINE OF THE SECOND QUALITY.

After the grapes are pressed the skins and seeds should be thrown into a stand cask containing the following mixture: Twenty-three gallons rain water, fifty-three pounds grape sugar, one pound crystals of tartaric acid. This is normal wine, as to its proportions of free acid, grape sugar, and water, and will contain about ten per cent. of alcohol, say the strength of claret. Should it be desired to make it stronger, twenty-three gallons rain water, ninety pounds grape sugar, one pound crystals tartaric acid will give the normal wine of the strength of sherry, say seventeen to eighteen per cent. alcohol. Having determined the strength you want, throw in the skins and seeds of, say, three to four hundred pounds of grapes, that is whatever is left after each pressing. It is best to put in the pumice immediately, and thus save the surface of the skins of seeds from the action of the atmosphere. It is essential that the stand cask shall have a floating lid, perforated with half inch holes, so that the skins, which arise when the fermentation begins, shall be kept covered with fluid.

A, Floating perforated lid resting on the fluid.

B, Block resting on the floating lid.

C, Wooden cover; under which is a cloth covering the barrel.

D, An upright piece, reaching to the ceiling of the cellar to fasten the wooden cover down to the barrel.

The violent fermentation in the stand cask lasts about ten days, and as the skins come to the top they must be well stirred up every morning. At the end of ten days the skins will begin to sink, when the fluid may be run off at the tap, and the refuse pressed, barreled, and treated as the juice of the first pressing.

Should you desire to make wine vinegar take twenty-three gallons rain water, fifty-three pounds grape sugar, one pound tartaric acid, and put back the skins and seeds of the second pressing. Treat precisely as you did the second grade wine.

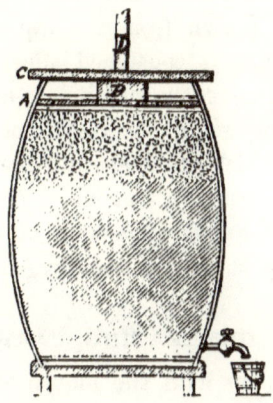

Stir for the first ten days in the stand cask, and when well fermented press again and put the fluid in a barrel, the bung of which is a straw plug, and set in a warm shed until it becomes vinegar.

Having given receipts for the manufacture of wine, it follows that the best foreign modes of preserving it are essential. I therefore quote from John J. Griffen's work, "Chemical Testing of Wines and Spirits," 1866, page 128, London.

"PRESERVATION OF WINES IN PARTLY EMPTY CASKS."

"If a bottle of light wine is opened, and some of the wine is left for two or three days in the partly empty bottle, the oxygen of the air acts upon the acetic ferment, and the wine becomes sour. When wine is cellared in a cask evaporation constantly takes place through the pores of the wood, and air enters by the same passages into the cask to fill the vacuum produced by the evaporation. Unless this air is frequently expelled by the addition of fresh wine all the wine in the cask is liable to turn sour. In places where draught wine is used, and where air must be permitted to enter into a cask, in proportion as wine is drawn from the tap the same difficulty occurs, and if the wine is consumed slowly, the oxygen and the acetic ferments frequently turn it into acetic acid. This is prevented by keeping within the casks a constant pressure of carbonic acid gas, which gas keeps the acetic ferment out of the reach of free oxygen, without which element the acetification cannot occur; for the conversion of alcohol into acetic acid demands a large supply of free oxygen."

APPARATUS FOR GENERATING CARBONIC ACID GAS.

A is a stone-ware jar with the mouth sufficiently large to admit an ordinary champagne bottle.

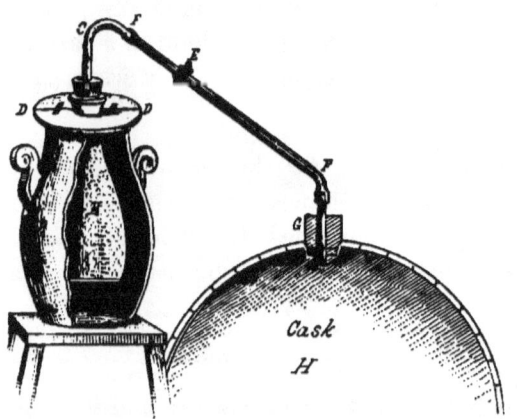

B is a bottle cut off at the bottom (so that it can be suspended within the stone jar to within an inch and a half of the bottom), having a perforated bottom of either lead or wood.

C is a bent glass tube fitted to a cork, which tightly fits the neck of the bottle.

D are two half circles of wood dowelled together so as to enclose the neck of the bottle and hold it suspended within the stone jar A.

C, a bent glass tube that comes through the cork of the bottle B.

F F, an india-rubber gum tube that fits on the glass tube C.

E, a screw clamp that is attached to the gum tube that regulates the flow of gas to the barrel.

G, the bung of the barrel having a glass tube in its centre, to connect with gum tube F F.

Being ready to make the gas fill the bottle B with pieces of broken marble the size of hazel-nuts, and press in the perforated bottom. Fill the bottom of the jar A with pebble stones to a point that the bottle B does not touch it. Fill the jar A about one-half full of diluted muriatic acid, and suspend the bottle B in it by means of the wooden top D D. The carbonic acid gas will arise in the bottle B, and flow down the tube F F into the cask—all these must be air-tight. When the passage of the gas is stopped the gas collects in the bottle B and drives the acid into the outer jar A. When the gas again enters the barrel H the acid passes the outer jar A into the bell jar B, and produces a fresh supply. Any instrument constructed on this principle can evidently be used to keep a constant pressure of carbonic acid gas in a partly empty barrel of wine, and so prevent the access of air and oxygen and the mischief they occasion. This is also applicable to cider, ale, or beer on draught.

Wine does not improve in bottles; besides, for home use, it is a great deal more convenient to draw as wanted from the cask, and to know that what remains in the partly empty cask will go on improving in bulk so long as the air is excluded from it.

GENERAL DIRECTIONS FOR HOME-MADE WINES OTHER THAN GRAPE.

Ripe fruit five pounds, soft water one gallon, grape sugar two and a half pounds, cream tartar two and a half ounces. Ferment in stand keg, and treat same as grape wine. The more ripe fruit and grape sugar in proportion to the soft water the stronger the wine.

BLACKBERRY WINE.

Ripe berries bruised twelve gallons; pour on them six gallons of hot water, let them stand two or three days, stirring occasionally; then strain off the liquor, and to every gallon add two and a quarter pounds of sugar; let it stand and ferment; before it is bottled add half a gallon of brandy. The brandy can be left out if preferred.

CURRANT SHRUB.

Draw the currants as for jelly, and to each pint of juice put one pound of sugar, half a pint brandy, then bottle it up for use.

GERANIUM CORDIAL.
(Very fine; as good as Imported Cordial.)

A handful of rose geranium leaves dried in the shade for several days. Pour over these one pint of alcohol and let it stand for two weeks, sometimes shaking the bottle a little. Strain and add a pound of loaf sugar boiled into syrup with one pint of water. Violets or orange peel can be used in same way. Also fresh mint.

PUNCH.

One gallon New England rum, one pint lemon juice, juice and peel of two oranges, let stand twenty-four hours, then add four pounds sugar, one pint strong tea, four pints water. It can be bottled in a few days.

FISH HOUSE PUNCH.

One gallon New England rum, one gallon brandy, one quart Jamaica rum, five dozen oranges, six dozen lemons, one gallon water, twelve pounds sugar, one quart strong tea. This will keep for years, bottled tight.

PHILADELPHIA FISH HOUSE PUNCH.

One quart brandy, two quarts Jamaica rum, half gill of brandy, one quart lemon juice (about twenty-four lemons), three pounds of sugar, two quarts water. Mix water and sugar, strain lemon juice, and add to syrup. Mix liquors separately and add to above; water to suit the taste. Put in a large lump of ice.

ENGLISH CLARET CUP.

Two bottles of good claret, two of soda water or apollinaris, three pounds of ice, two pounds of sugar, three pints of water, one large lemon, a little cucumber and fresh mint.

BLACKBERRY OR DEWBERRY CORDIAL.
(Medicinal.)

Two quarts blackberry juice, one pound loaf sugar, four grated nutmegs, quarter ounce ground cloves, quarter ounce ground allspice, quarter ounce ground cinnamon. Simmer all together for thirty minutes in a stew pan closely covered, to prevent evaporation. Strain through a cloth when cold, and add a pint of the best French brandy. Soothing and efficacious in the summer complaints of children. Dose, one teaspoonful poured on a little pounded ice, once or several times a day, as the case may require. Whortleberry cordial may be made by the same recipe. Good old whiskey may be used for either in the absence of brandy.

RASPBERRY VINEGAR.

Put one quart of ripe raspberries in a bowl, pour over them one quart of good vinegar, let them stand twenty-four hours, strain through a bag, pour over this another quart of fresh raspberries, and continue to do this for three days; when the last is prepared make it very sweet with white sugar; refine and bottle it.

CURRANT WINE.

Four pounds currants, add a little water, mash them well, and strain through a hair sieve. Then add three pounds sugar to the strained liquor; after it is dissolved strain it again. Should not the juice and sugar measure one gallon add as much water to the currants as will make up the gallon. Mash them over again, put into a clean vessel, leaving room for it to work, and stop it tight.

SUPERIOR PUNCH.

Half gallon whiskey, one pint Jamaica rum, one quart peach cordial from brandy peaches, two pounds sugar, one quart sherry wine, three oranges, sliced, taking out seeds, two lemons, just water enough to dissolve sugar. A large lump of ice about an hour before it is used.

CHAMPAGNE PUNCH.

Four quarts of champagne, one quart madeira wine, two oranges, one lemon, one pound loaf sugar. Just water enough to dissolve sugar. Fill with crushed ice just as you are going to use it.

RATCLIFFE PUNCH.

One quart sherry wine, one quart cherry bounce, one quart peach cordial, one quart whiskey; slice three oranges, one lemon, two pounds of loaf sugar, water enough to dissolve sugar, or one quart of strong green tea is better. A large lump of ice about an hour before it is used. It will keep for months bottled.

EGG-NOGG.

Beat the yellows of two dozen eggs very light, stir in as much white sugar as they dissolve, pour in two glasses of brandy gradually to cook the eggs, two glasses old whiskey, one of peach brandy, two nutmegs, three quarts rich milk; beats whites to a froth and stir in last.

EGG-NOGG.

To make a two gallon bowl of egg-nogg take the yolks of thirty eggs, beat light, adding two and a half pounds of fine sugar gradually. Then pour the liquor on the eggs slowly so as to cook the eggs. Half gallon French brandy or good old whiskey, one quart Jamaica rum, one quart peach brandy; fill the bowl with rich cream. Beat some of the whites very stiff with sugar, putting it over the top of bowl. Grate some nutmeg over the whole.

ONE GALLON ROMAN PUNCH.

One and a half pints lemon juice, the rind of two lemons grated on sugar, half a pint of brandy, one pint of rum, two quarts water, three pounds sugar; a peck of ice will freeze it in summer.

GRAPE WINE.

Put your grapes in a tub, squeeze them until you get all the juice. Put water over the stems and skins, enough to cover them. Beat them well, and strain that with the juice. Then to each gallon of juice add three pounds of white sugar. Mix well, and strain. Let it ferment in an open tub for several days, then put it in a cask, which ought to be full, skim it well first; cork tight; put clay or cement over the bung. Draw it off in February and bottle.

BLACKBERRY WINE.

Take ripe blackberries, mash and press them, strain off the juice, and let it stand thirty-six hours to ferment; skim off what rises. To every gallon of strained and fermented juice add one gallon of cold water, and two pounds of brown sugar. Let it stand in open vessels for twenty-four hours, then skim, strain, and put the juice in a cask and close the bung tight. Let it stand in the cask until March, when the wine must be drawn off and bottled.

CURRANT WINE.

Gather currants fully ripe, take out leaves and hard stalks (need not strip from stems), put in a large tub and mash well; to every gallon of mashed currants add one gallon water, rub through a sieve and squeeze pulp until the juice is entirely extracted. Strain juice a second time, to each gallon of juice and water add three pounds white sugar, stir until mixed, put in clean cask, and leave bung out until the third day, then close it very tight, to stand six months before drawn off to be bottled. The water used with mashed currants should be cold. No matter whether the cask is full or not.

STRAWBERRY WINE.

Put the berries in a large vessel, and mash until all the juice is obtained. Then to one gallon of juice add three pounds white sugar and three quarts water. Strain it well, and put in a demijohn to ferment, with a piece of network tied over the mouth of the vessel. After fermentation it is again strained and tightly bottled for use.

BLACKBERRY CORDIAL.

Half a gallon blackberry juice, two pounds white sugar, several sticks cinnamon, teaspoonful cloves, one of allspice tied in a very thin piece of muslin; put all on to boil for fifteen or twenty minutes. When partly cool add one pint good old whiskey and one pint old apple brandy. Shake together well, and seal your jug. This keeps for several years.

BEER.

Two quarts wheat bran, two and a half gallons water, a few hops, one pint molasses, and one pint of yeast.

EGYPTIAN PUNCH.

Peel eighteen lemons, steep the rinds in one gallon rum or brandy (or equal quantity of each) for thirty hours. Add five quarts water, two nutmegs, grated, three pounds loaf sugar, the pieces of the lemons, and two quarts boiling milk. Stir well, strain through flannel bag until perfectly clear.

GINGER BEER.

Three gallons boiling water, three pounds white sugar, two tablespoonsful cream of tartar, two lemons, one ounce green ginger; put all in a stone jar and pour the water on it. Let it stand until milk warm, and stir in a teacup of yeast. Make about dusk—let it stand all night and bottle in the morning. Throw the corks into boiling water, then squeeze them in a lemon squeezer before putting in the bottles. Tie them down tight.

CURRANT SHRUB.

One gallon juice, add two pounds white sugar, one quart brandy or whiskey; stew the juice and sugar ten minutes, then add the brandy, put in bottles or a jug; when used add water and ice; if not sweet enough add more sugar.

CHERRY BOUNCE.

Fill a demijohn with cherries, and fill up with whiskey, let it stand three or four months, then draw off and sweeten to your taste; this will keep for years, the older the better.

ROMAN PUNCH.

One gallon water, three pounds loaf sugar, one pint old Jumaica rum, one pint brandy, six lemons; freeze and serve in glasses after soup on great occasions, and good any time.

BLACKBERRY CORDIAL.

To a quart of juice take one pound loaf sugar, quarter ounce mace, cinnamon, cloves, and allspice, the spice to be pulverized; boil all together fifteen minutes, and to every pint when cold add one gill of best brandy.

CLARET PEACH CORDIAL.

One pound peaches pared and cut up, one pound sugar powdered and sprinkled on them; boil them for two hours until they are a rich syrup, then strain and add brandy to your taste and bottle it.

GINGER POP.

Two pounds brown sugar, one large tablespoonful of the fibrous part of ginger, half lemon sliced, one dessertspoon of cream of tartar, pour on it two gallons of boiling water, when milk warm stir in one pint brisk yeast; make it in the morning, bottle it at night. It will be ready for use in three days.

APPLE TODDY, No. 1.

Bake twelve sound, red-streaked apples, put them in a stone jar while hot, and mash them well. Then pour on them three quarts of boiling water. Cover the jar close, and let them stand until cool, then add three pints Cognac brandy, one pint Jamaica rum, half a pint peach brandy, sweeten to taste, and let it stand twenty-four hours, stirring frequently and mashing well the particles of apple. Then strain for use. A few oranges improve the flavor.

RATCLIFFE PUNCH, No. 1.

Rub loaf sugar over the peel of six lemons to break the little vessels and absorb the ambrosia of the lemon. Then squeeze out the juice of six oranges and six lemons, removing the seeds; add to it five pounds of loaf sugar (including the sugar rubbed over the peel), and two quarts of water, with five cloves and two blades of mace (in a bag). Simmer this over the stove about ten minutes, making a syrup. This will keep forever. It should be bottled and kept to sweeten the liquors when punch is made. Mix one pint of green tea, a scant pint of brandy, one quart Jamaica rum, one quart champagne, and one teacupful of chartreuse. When well mixed, sweeten to taste with the syrup. Pour it into the punch bowl, in which is an eight or ten pound piece of ice. Slice three oranges and three lemons, and put them also into the punch bowl, removing the seeds. This is delicious.

EGG-NOGG.

Beat the yolks of six eggs and half a pound of sugar together until it froths. Add half a pint of brandy or whiskey, next the whites of the eggs beaten stiff, and then three pints of whipped cream.

COBBLERS.

These can be made of sherry, claret, or Catawba wine. Put four or five tablespoonsful of the wine into a glass with half a tablespoon of sugar; one or two thin slices of orange or lemon may be added. Fill the glass with finely-chopped or crushed ice. Now pour this from one glass to another once or twice to mix well. Then put two or three strawberries in for a garnish. Each glass should be furnished with two straws.

EGG AND MILK PUNCH.

Stir well a heaping teaspoonful of sugar and the yolk of an egg together in a goblet, then add a tablespoonful of best brandy. Fill the glass with cream or milk until it is three-quarters full, then stir well into the mixture the white of an egg beaten to a stiff froth.

MILK PUNCH.

Sweeten a glass of half milk and cream to taste, and add one or two tablespoons best brandy and grated nutmeg.

FRUIT CORDIAL.

Half pint black cherries, quarter pound ginger sliced, half ounce cinnamon, the same of cloves. Put these into a jug with proof spirit. Cork it, and let it stand till autumn. As blackberries, raspberries, or currants ripen add them, always adding sufficient spirit to cover the fruit. In autumn pour off the spirit and cover the fruit with pure water, and let it remain a week or more. Then strain off and mix with the spirit. Sweeten to taste. You may add apple parings or pineapples, but the black cherry is the most important fruit.

BLACKBERRY CORDIAL.

To two quarts of juice add one pound white sugar, half ounce pulverized cinnamon, same of pulverized cloves. Boil all together for a short time. When cold add one pint brandy.

BITTERS.

One ounce gentian, one ounce cardamon seed, one ounce chamomile flowers, some dried orange peel. Bruise all together, and pour on this quantity three pints of good whiskey or brandy. If preferred strain it off after it has stood some time. This is an excellent recipe, and a tablespoonful in a little sugar and water is beneficial occasionally.

REGENT PUNCH.

Take a large cup of the best strong black tea, in which put the rind of two lemons cut very thin; add to this one pint of sugar, three wineglasses of brandy, three of rum, the juice of three lemons and of two oranges, and one quart bottle of champagne. Put in a large lump of ice. For a large quantity measure everything by pints.

CLARET PUNCH.

Pour one quart bottle claret into a bowl or pitcher, add one pint water, sweeten to taste; throw in some slices of lemon. If preferred use no water, only ice.

APPLE TODDY.

One gallon apple brandy, one pint peach brandy, one pint French brandy, one pint Madeira wine, and one dozen apples baked without peeling. Sweeten to taste. About two pounds sugar to this quantity, and just enough hot water to dissolve the sugar.

LEMON BRANDY.

One pint brandy, the rind of two lemons, two ounces loaf sugar, quarter pint water. Peel the lemons, but be careful not to get any of the white pith. Put the rind into a bottle with the brandy, and let them infuse for twenty-four hours, then strain them. Boil the sugar and water for a few moments. Skim it, and when cold add it to the brandy. A dessert-spoonful of this is an excellent flavoring for custards. Oranges may be used in the same manner.

CLARET PUNCH, No. 1.

One gallon claret; three oranges, sliced, taking out the seeds; three lemons, sliced; two pounds sugar; no water; a lump of ice just before using it.

SELIGSON'S HALF AND HALF.

This is an English drink and means half porter, and half ale; we very often use half old and half new, as one may prefer.

SELIGSON'S CHAMPAGNE COCKTAIL.

A champagne goblet, one-third crushed ice, one lump of sugar, a dash of Angostura bitters, slice of orange; fill up with champagne, and stir. Use none but Baker's or the genuine Angostura bitters, as it possesses a certain rich flavor, that no other bitters has.

SELIGSON'S FRAPPED CAFÉ ROYAL.

It consists of three-fourths of a cup of black coffee, one-fourth brandy, frapped in a cooler; sugar to taste. Drink while the mixture is yet in a semi-frozen state. It is very potent.

MENUS.

HOME BREAKFAST.

Fruit,—whatever is in season.
Oat Meal Porridge.   Lamb Chops.   Breakfast Bacon.
Potatoes, Lyonaise.   Hot Rolls.
Cream Muffins.   Soft Boiled Eggs.   Tea and Coffee.

SUMMER BREAKFAST.

Cantaloupes.   Oat Meal and Cream.
Broiled Taylor.   Hash.   Brown Potatoes.
Sliced Cucumbers and Tomatoes.
Broiled Chicken.   French Rolls.
Thin Batter Cakes of Corn Meal.   Turnover Rolls.
Coffee, Tea, and Milk.

WINTER HOME BREAKFAST.

Oranges.
Oat Meal and Cream.   Turkey Hash and Fried Hominy.
Fried Oysters.   Beaten Milk Biscuit.
Flannel Cakes and Maple Syrup.   Coffee, Tea, and Milk.

RATCLIFFE MANOR BREAKFAST.

Oranges.
Oat Meal and Cream.   Broiled Guinea Chicks.
French Rolls.   Claret.
Fried Oysters.   Maryland Biscuit.   Fried Hominy.
Buckwheat Cakes and Fresh Sausage.
Cakes and Maple Syrup.   Tea, Coffee, Chocolate.

BREAKFAST.

Fruit in Season.   Broiled Shad.
Potato Chips.   Claret.   Spring Chicken.
Hot Rolls.   Coffee.
Tomatoes, stuffed with Mushrooms.   Beaten Biscuits.
Rum Omelet.

LUNCHEON.

Grape Fruit.
Cream Lobster.   Potato Croquettes.
Broiled Sweetbreads.   French Peas.
Birds on Toast.   Celery Mayonnaise.
Champagne, Sauterne, or Claret.
Ices.   Coffee.

LUNCHEON FOR SPRING.

Little Neck Clams.   Sherry.
Cream of Chicken, à la Chervreuse.   Asparagus.
Patties of Lobster.   Sauterne.
Partridges, with Tomato and Lettuce Salad.
Claret Wine.
Vanilla Ice Cream, with Strawberries.   Cake.   Coffee.
Crème de Menthe.   Appolinaris, with any course.

LUNCHEON.

Shaddocks.
Cream of Celery, served in cups.
Scalloped Oysters.   Sherry Wine.
Chicken, à la Tartare.
Roman Punch.
Quail.   Celery Salad.   Claret.
Neuchatel Cheese and Crackers.
Biscuits.   Glacés.   Cake.
Coffee.

LENTEN LUNCHEON.

Shaddocks.
Cream of Potato Soup.
Kennebec Salmon.   Potatoes.   Sherry.
   Oyster Patties.   French Peas.
Benedictine.
Devilled Eggs.   Sauterne.
Lettuce and Tomato Salad.   French Dressing.
Crackers and Cheese.   Olives.
Neapolitan Ice Cream.   Black Coffee.
Always serve Appolinaris.

LUNCHEON FOR SIX PEOPLE.
GIVEN BY A CLUB IN WASHINGTON.

Shaddocks	40
Sherry for Bouillon	10
Bouillon	35
Trout	35
Paté Shells	65
Veal	10
Chops	40
Peas	35
Lettuce	5
Tomatoes	25
Cheese	5
Ice Cream	75
Cake	25
Radishes	20
Almonds	20
Candies	20
Wine	35
	$5 00

LUNCHEON.

Grape Fruit.
Bouillon.
Broiled Sardines on Toast.   Potato Chips.
Sweetbreads.   French Peas.   Appolinaris.
Spring Chicken.   Asparagus.
Roman Punch.
Birds on Toast.   Lettuce Salad.   Sauterne.
Cheese.   Crackers.
Ices.
Coffee.

LUNCH FOR BRAIN-WORKERS.

Broiled Striped Bass.   Celery.   Brown Bread.
Apple Sauce.

AFTERNOON TEA.

Russian Tea.
Lettuce Sandwiches, with
Mayonaise Dressing on the Lettuce.
Café Frappé.   Wafers.   Ices and Cakes.
Or Champagne Punch and Cakes.
Salted Nuts.   Peppermints.
Fruit and Glacés.

AFTERNOON TEA.

Russian Tea.   Wafers.   Chicken Salad.
Brown Bread Sandwiches.   Lalla Rookh Punch.
Fancy Cakes.   Salted Nuts.   Fruit.
Candies.   Olives.

CHRISTMAS DINNER.—Decorations Holly.

Celery.   Olives.   Salted Almonds.
Blue Points.   Grand Chateau Yquem.
Green Turtle Soup.   Sherry.
Broiled Pompano with Pommes Duchesse.
Roast Turkey.   French Peas.   Asparagus.   Chateau Lafitte.
Terrapin, a la Maryland.   Champagne.
Roman Punch.
Red Head Ducks.   Fried Hominy.   Currant Jelly.
Champagne.
Celery Mayonnaise.
Burning English Plum Pudding, Brandy Sauce.
Ice Cream, a la Noisette.
Fruit.   Salted Almonds.   Bon Bons.
Cheese.   Crackers.
Black Coffee.
Crème de Menthe, with Crushed Ice.

EASTERN SHORE HOME DINNER.

Oysters on Half Shell.   Turtle Soup.   Sherry.
Boiled Rock, with Egg Sauce.
Potato Croquettes.   Walnut Pickle.   Sauterne.
Roast Turkey.   Cranberries.   Hominy.   Sweet Potatoes.
Ham.   Lettuce Salad.
Bell Fritters, Wine Sauce.
Fruit.   Crackers.   Cheese.   Coffee.   Claret.

HOME DINNER FOR WINTER.

Oysters on Half Shell.   Turtle Soup.
Boiled Fish and Creamed Potatoes.
Fillet of Beef and Mushrooms.   French Peas.   Macaroni.
Lettuce Salad.   Crackers and Cheese.
Cardinal Richelieu Pudding.   Fruit.   Coffee.
Serve Claret and Appolinaris.

SPRING DINNER.

Little Neck Clams.   Sherry.
Cream of Asparagus Soup.
Broiled Shad.   Cucumbers.
Potatoes.   Spring Lamb, Mint Sauce.   French Peas.
Lalla Rookh Punch.
Snipe on Toast.   Sauterne.   Cauliflower Salad.
Strawberries and Vanilla Ice Cream.
Cake.   Fruit.   Roquefort Cheese.   Crackers.
Coffee.   Madeira.

SUMMER DINNER.

Tomato Bisque Soup.   Sherry.
Boiled Sheep's Head.   Cream Potatoes.   Black Walnut Pickle.
Fried Chicken.   Green Corn.
Fried Egg Plant.   Lima Beans.   Punch, à la Washington.
Baked Sweetbreads, Sherry Sauce.   Lettuce Salad.
Tutti Frutti Ice Cream.   Cake.   Cheese and Crackers.
Coffee.   Appolinaris.   Claret Wine.

DINNER.

Oak Island Oysters.   Green Turtle Clear.   Sherry.
Fillet of Pompano.   Pommes Duchesse.   Sauterne.
Saddle of Venison, Currant Jelly.
Chestnut Croquettes.   Chambertin, 1872.
Larded Sweetbreads.   French Peas.
Terrapin, Maryland Style.
Montebello Extra Dry.
Asparagus Salad.   French Dressing.   Cheese.
Claret, Chateau la Rose.
Tutti Frutti Ice Cream.   Maccaroons.   Fruit.
Salted Almonds.   Black Coffee.   Madeira.
Crème de Menthe.

DINNER.

Caviar on Toast.
Oysters on Half Shell.   Sauterne.   Clear Soup.   Sherry.
Lobster Farci.   Cucumbers.
Fillet of Beef, Mushroom Sauce.   Claret.
White Potatoes.   Green Peas.
Lalla Rookh Punch.
Canvas Back Ducks, Currant Jelly.   Champagne.
Salad of Lettuce.
Baba Pudding.   Vanilla Ice Cream.   Coffee.
Crème de Menthe.

COLONIAL DINNER.

English Beef Soup.   Roast of Beef.   Ham in Cider.
Sherry.
Goose, stuffed with Potatoes.
Fried Apples.   Browned Parsnips.   Cabbage Rolls.
Claret.
Spiced Cantaloupe Pickle.
Celery.   Olives.   Buena Vista Cake.
English Hunt Pudding, Wine Sauce.
Toasted Crackers.   Cheese.   Black Coffee.

THANKSGIVING DINNER.

Oysters on Half Shell.   Sherry.
Mock Turtle Soup.   Sherry.
Wild Turkey Roasted, Cranberry Jelly.   Champagne.
Baked Ham, in American Champagne or good Cider.
Sweet Potatoes.
Cauliflower.   Baked Tomatoes.
Macaroni.
Lettuce Salad, with Toasted Crackers and Cheese.
Mince Pies.   Pumpkin Pudding.   Black Coffee.
Crème de Menthe Cordial.

FRIDAY DINNER.

Blue Points.   Cream of Celery Soup.
Broiled Blue Fish.   Sliced Cucumbers.   Cream Potatoes.
Claret.
Soft Shell Crabs.   French Peas.   Celery Salad.   Appolinaris.
Frozen Pudding.
Fruit.   Nuts.   Wafers.   Coffee.

CARDINAL DINNER.—Decorations in Scarlet.

Little Neck Clams.   Crême de Céleri.
Saumon Sauce Homard.   Grand Chateau Yquem.
Cassolettes Financière.
Chevreuil à l'Américaine.   Chateau Lafite, 1875.
Filets de Volaille Périgord.
Punch à la Romaine.   Chambertin, 1875.
Coqs de Bruyère Rôtis.   Salade.   Asperges en Branches.
Savarin aux Fraises.   Glace Renaissance.   Desserts.
Montebello Extra Dry.

SUPPER AFTER THE THEATRE.

Caviar on Toast.   Vermouth Cocktail.
Oysters on Half Shell.   Celery.   Sauterne.
Terrapin, à la Maryland.   Champagne.
Bird on Toast.   Celery Salad.   Champagne.
Individual Ices.   Cake.   Coffee.
Crème de Menthe.

SUPPER.

Blue Points.   Lobster, à la Newburg.   Champagne.
Broiled Pheasant on Toast.
Omelet Soufflée.   Celery Salad.   Crackers.   Cheese.
Ices.   Coffee.

SUPPER.

Chicken Bouillon.
Game on Toast.   Champagne.
Salad.   Toasted Crackers and Cheese..   Coffee.

HOME TEA.

Broiled Chicken.
Hot Rolls.   Rice Waffles.   Coffee.   Tea.
Deviled Crabs.   Tomato Salad.
Peaches and Cream.   Cake.

DIET FOR INVALIDS.

BREAKFAST.

Oat Meal and Cream.   Broiled Sweetbread on Toast.
Cup of Chocolate.

DINNER.

Lamb Chops.   Mashed Potatoes.   Stuffed Tomatoes.
Baked Custard.

TEA.

Stewed Prunes.   Graham Rolls.

COFFEE AND TEA, ETC.

TO MAKE COFFEE WITH MILK.

Take three-quarters of a mill of ground coffee, dampen it with white of egg, and add cold water enough to cover it. Then add one teacupful of boiling water, and set it to boil for *two* minutes. Now pour on this *one* pint of cold fresh milk, let it boil *twelve* minutes, and then stand *five* minutes to settle.

CUBAN COFFEE.

Put three pints of rich sweet milk into a coffee-pot and let it boil. When it is boiling put in a teacupful of ground coffee, and boil it five minutes. Strain and serve it.

TEA.

Put the table teapot near the fire till it is quite hot. Put in the dry tea leaves, and replace the pot, closely covered, near the fire for five minutes. Fill the teapot full of boiling water, and let it stand on the table at least three minutes before pouring out. One teaspoonful of leaves to every pint is about the allowance. In hot summer strong black tea, to which lemon juice and sugar have been added, will be found very refreshing. The tea may be made in the morning, and placed on ice about an hour before using, adding the lemon juice and sugar at table. If ice is left in the tea it weakens it too much.

HOW TO MAKE CHOCOLATE.

Grate one-half pound of Walter Baker's chocolate, and stir on it gradually one pint of boiling water. Mix it to a smooth paste. To this add slowly one gallon of rich milk (new milk is best). When well mixed put it on the fire and let it boil half an hour, stirring all the time, and being careful not to let it scorch. Whites of two eggs, beaten to a stiff icing, season with vanilla, and serve on top the cup of chocolate. The chocolate will not require much more sugar.

TO MAKE CHOCOLATE (for One.)

Take two heaping tablespoonsful of Walter Baker's chocolate, grated; mix it into a paste with cold water, then add one pint of boiling milk. Let it come to a boil. A great improvement is the white of an egg beaten stiff and placed on top of the chocolate after it is poured in the cup. If you wish chocolate for more than one person, the whites of four eggs are enough for a gallon, and if you prefer it thicker put four spoonsful of chocolate to a pint of milk.

GOOD BOILED COFFEE.

One teacupful ground coffee already cleared. Mix with a little cold water, then add one quart of boiling water and some eggshells. Let it come to a good boil. When done add about a tablespoonful of cold water, and let it stand a few moments before pouring off and sending to table.

FRENCH COFFEE.

Allow a tablespoonful of the best Java or Mocha coffee; place it when ground in the biggin, and pour a teacup of boiling water over it to every spoonful of coffee; let it drip slowly on the stove.

FOR INVALIDS.

CHICKEN BROTH.

Wash half the breast and one wing of a tender chicken. Put it in a saucepan with one and a half pints of water, a little salt, and a tablespoonful of rice or pearl barley. Let it simmer slowly and skim it. When the chicken is thoroughly done take it out of the broth. Serve the latter in a bowl with light bread or a fresh cracker.

IRISH MOSS JELLY.

Wash two handsful of carragreen or Irish moss through two or three waters, then drain, and pour on it three pints of boiling water. Let it simmer until the moss becomes a complete pulp, then strain it and sweeten to taste. After this add the juice of two large lemons. Do not eat until cold. Sea moss, blanc mange, and tapioca jelly, given among the desserts, are good for invalids.

SAGO.

Pick and wash the sago, and to prevent the earthy taste, which renders it so unpleasant, soak it in cold water for an hour or two. Pour off the water, add more, and boil it gently until it becomes clear. Sweeten it with loaf sugar, and add wine and spice if approved.

BEEF TEA.

Cut about one pound of lean beef into small pieces, put them into a wide-mouthed bottle, such as a pickle bottle, cork it tightly, and place it in a pot of cold water in which there is a saucer of cold water at the bottom. Heat it gradually, then let it boil slowly two or three hours when all the juice will be extracted. Now pour off the juice, season it with salt carefully, as it requires very little. When cold skim off all the globules of fat.

HOW TO PREPARE AN UNCOOKED EGG.

Beat well the yolk and a teaspoonful of sugar in a goblet, then stir in one or two teaspoonsful of brandy, sherry, or port wine. Add to this mixture the white of the egg, beaten to a stiff froth. Stir all well together. It should quite fill the goblet. If wine is not desired flavor the egg with nutmeg, but it is very palatable without any flavoring at all.

PANADA.

Break in pieces some stale loaf bread and put them in a saucepan. Cover them with cold water, and leave them an hour. Then set the saucepan on the fire and add salt, butter, and sugar to taste. Let it simmer about an hour, then add two yolks of eggs beaten with two tablespoonsful of wine.

ICELAND MOSS.

Take one ounce Iceland moss, wash it, and boil it in one quart of water until it is reduced to a pint. Then strain it, and add one pound white sugar and the juice of two lemons. It is very palatable and can be used as freely as desired. This is excellent for a cough.

EGG WATER.

Take white of an egg, put it in a pint of cold water. Add a small pinch of soda. Beat it up well, and keep in the ice. This is an invaluable receipt for a baby with delicate stomach, just let her drink it whenever she wants water. It is also good for a grown person, with a few drops of lemon juice.

BARLEY.

Take two ounces of barley and wash it in cold water. Then boil it in half a pint water for a short time, and strain it. Pour over it four pints boiling water, and let it boil down to two pints. Then strain it again. Sweeten this if desired.

LEMON SPONGE.

One pint water, one ounce isinglass, the grated rind of one lemon, and half a pound loaf sugar. Let it simmer for half an hour, then strain it through a fine sieve. When nearly cold add the juice of three lemons and the white of one egg. Whisk all together until thick and white.

CORN MEAL GRUEL.

Take half a pint of sifted corn meal. White corn meal is the only kind fit to use in making gruel. Moisten it with cold water, and stir it in one and a half pints of boiling water, and add salt to taste. Stir it well, so that there will be no lumps in it, and let it boil an hour.

PANADA.

Toast a slice of stale bread, break it in a pint bowl, add a small lump of butter, two wine glasses full of sherry or Madeira wine, a few cloves and allspice, one dozen raisins, nutmeg and sugar to taste; fill the bowl with boiling water and cover it closely. To be eaten in five minutes.

GRAPE JUICE.

To three quarts of fresh, ripe, juicy grapes, freed from the stems, put one quart of water, *no* sugar. Let it come slowly to a boil, and when the whole mass is boiling hot strain the juice through cheese cloth. Then return liquor to the fire, and as soon as it arrives at boiling point again, can it. Use glass jars to put it in.

"We use Virginia Waukesha Lithia Water entirely, and find it a wonderful water, especially in all Kidney troubles, and also for Rheumatism and Headaches. We are never without it. It is a great regulator, and certainly possesses invaluable properties."

"Horsford's Acid Phosphate is the best tonic for Dyspepsia, and having used it in our family for several years, find it invaluable in cases of Malaria, and also Insomnia. We recommend it most highly.

"I recommend Armour's Extract of Beef as decidedly the best on the market. It not only gives to soups a zest and flavor which are very hard to obtain in any other way, but it is also a most convenient and satisfactory article to have in the sick room. It is not mawkish or nauseating; but possesses a nice Roast-Beef flavor and is unquestionably a pure Essence of Beef, concentrated.

"There are times when *predigested* nourishment is invaluable, and I know of nothing better than Armour's Nutrient Wine of Beef-Peptone when one is enfeebled or debilitated. I have had personal experience of its value in my family and cannot say too much in praise of it."

CANDY.

MOLASSES CANDY.—TAFFY.

None but the best molasses should be used, the poorer kinds will not candy. The boiling syrup should be stirred frequently, from the first, to prevent burning, and, after it becomes thick, it will be necessary to stir constantly. Try it by dropping a little into a cup of cold water, or by setting a small quantity out of doors to cool. It is done when it can easily be pulled, or when, if chewed, it does not stick to the teeth. It will make the candy less brittle and whiter if, ten minutes before taking it off, cooking soda be added in the proportion of an even teaspoonful to a gallon of molasses.— Take out a cupful of the syrup and mix the soda well in. Then take the kettle from the fire and stir the mixture into the syrup. It will bubble up, and vigorous stirring will be needed to keep it from boiling over. Return to the fire and stir steadily until done, which ought to be in about ten minutes. For sugar taffy—to three pounds of sugar allow half a teacupful of water and half a cupful of vinegar. Set on the back of the stove until the sugar is dissolved. Then bring it forward and let it stew steadily until done, which may be determined in the same way as with the molasses. Do not stir the candy while stewing, as so doing makes it turn back to sugar. If you do not wish it hard and brittle, add an even teaspoonful of soda in the same way as with the molasses taffy only don't stir it. In pulling taffy it is a mistake to oil the hands. The candy will be nicer if instead you wash your hands occasionally with cold water, drying them perfectly afterwards. Use fresh butter or olive oil for greasing the pans into which you pour the candy to cool.

MOLASSES CANDY.—From Vassar College.

One cup molasses, two cups sugar, one tablespoonful of vinegar. Mix and boil for ten minutes. When done add a lump of butter and a teaspoonful of vanilla, or any other flavoring; to be pulled until light.

COCOANUT AND CHOCOLATE CARAMELS.

Cocoanut candy is made by taking two pounds of sugar to an ordinary cocoanut. Add the milk of the cocoanut to the sugar, with a little water, if the milk is less than a small teacupful. Stew until it ropes when poured from the spoon, then stir in the cocoanut, which you should have already grated, and pour into buttered pans. When cool, break into pieces—a process which will be facilitated if, when the candy is cool, but not cold, you score it half through with a knife. and nut candy can be made in the same manner by substituting nut kernels for the grated cocoanuts. For cream candy allow a cupful of rich cream to three pounds of sugar, and stew until the syrup candies when dropped into cold water. Then flavor with vanilla, lemon, or what you like, and pour into buttered pans to cool, or pull the candy as you prefer. Another recipe for cream candy, without the cream, requires two cups of granulated sugar, half a cup of water, a piece of butter the size of a walnut, two teaspoonfuls of vanilla. Do not stir while boiling. When done pour on buttered plates, and when cool pull it until white.

There are many recipes for chocolate caramels. The following will be reliable: To a pint of milk add three pounds of sugar and a half pound of butter. Let the mixture come to a boil, when add a half a pound of chocolate scraped fine. Let it boil until quite thick, stirring all the time. It will be better if you mix the chocolate smooth with a cupful of boiling milk before adding it to the whole quantity. When done, flavor with lemon or vanilla, and pour into buttered pans. When nearly cold cut into small squares. A delicious fruit candy is made by adding chopped raisins and figs to a syrup made by stewing two pounds of sugar with the juice of two lemons, or, if lemons are not at hand, with a cupful of vinegar flavored with essence of lemon. Dried cherries and any firm preserves may be used instead of the raisins and figs. For cream chocolates, take one pound white sugar, a teacupful of water and half a pound of chocolate. Scrape the chocolate and set it on the back of the stove to melt into a paste. Boil the sugar and water together for ten or fifteen minutes, then take off and beat rapidly until it is creamy; flavor to taste, then roll into small balls, a teaspoonful to each ball, and dip in the chocolate until covered. For this you can use two forks, handling the balls carefully. Lay them on buttered paper to cool.

BARLEY SUGAR, AND BURNT ALMONDS.

The following recipe for barley sugar, a favorite candy with the English children, is taken from an English magazine: One and a half pounds of fine loaf sugar should be broken into small lumps and boiled over the fire with a pint of water. It should be skimmed carefully till it looks like glue, and when dropped into cold water becomes brittle and will snap. The juice of a lemon and six drops of essence of lemon should now be added, the sugar boiled up just once, and then the bottom of the pan should be placed in cold water till the first heat has subsided. The preparation should then be poured upon a marble slab, which has been slightly smeared with butter. It will, of course, spread out, but it should be drawn together with a knife, and keep as much as possible in a lump. As soon as it is cool enough to handle, pieces about the size of an egg may be cut off, rolled to the form of round sticks, and twisted slightly, as barley sugar usually is bought. These should be put on an oiled sheet and left till they are cold and stiff, when sugar should be sifted light over them.

For burnt almonds take a pound of almonds and bleach by scalding in hot water, when the skins will easily slip off. Dry them and warm them slightly. Three-quarters of a pound of sugar should now be boiled with half a pint of water, till the surface looks like large pearls or globules, when a few drops of prepared cochineal, a few drops of vanilla, or any other suitable essence, and the almonds should be thrown in and all stirred gently together with a wooden spoon, to detach the sugar from the bottom and sides of the saucepan. The almonds should be kept from sticking to the pan, and should be thoroughly turned over and over, so that they might be well coated, or, as it is called, "charged," with sugar. As soon as they give out a cracking noise the pan should be removed from the fire and still gently stirred, until the sugar has the appearance of being grained almost like sand, when almonds, sugar and all should be turned upon a wire sieve and covered with paper for five minutes.

At the end of that time the almonds should be picked out and the grained sugar put again into the sugar-boiler with just enough water to dissolve it, and when it is again boiled to the point it had before reached, the almonds should be thrown in again and stirred until they have received another coating, being careful only to keep them entirely separate.

CARAMELS.

One and a half cakes of Walter Baker's chocolate, three pounds brown sugar, half a pound butter, one cup cream, one bottle vanilla. Boil until very thick, stirring constantly. Pour in buttered tins or plates. To test when it is done drop a little from a spoon into a cup of ice water. If it hardens it is done.

CARAMELS.

Quarter pound Walter Baker's chocolate, beaten or grated, quarter pound butter, one teacup of milk, one and a half pounds of brown sugar. Put it on the fire, and stir without stopping for twenty minutes, then pour into a greased dish to cool.

CARAMELS.

Half a cake Walter Baker's chocolate, one pound brown sugar, a cup of syrup, a cup of cream, and a piece of butter the size of an egg. Boil about twenty minutes.

COCOANUT CARAMELS.

One large cocoanut grated, two pounds white sugar, half a pint cold water, the two latter stewed slowly. When it begins to harden stir the cocoanut in and let it boil a few minutes. Season with vanilla or rose water.

CHOCOLATE CARAMELS.

Two pounds of New Orleans brown sugar, one-quarter pound of Walter Baker's chocolate, one cup of rich cream, butter the size of an egg. Boil the sugar and milk, and beat it *hard* (*don't stir*) all the time it is cooking. When it comes to a boil, then add the grated chocolate and let it boil five minutes, then take it off and add a tablespoonful of vanilla, beating it hard for five minutes. Pour it on buttered pans. *Never stir* it, but beat hard.

CARAMELS. (Ashby Recipe.)

Six ounces of Walter Baker's chocolate (not sweet), one and a half pounds of dark brown sugar, quarter pound of butter, half pint of cream. Vanilla to taste.

CARAMELS. (Very Fine.)

One cake of Walter Baker's chocolate, three pounds of sugar—one and a half of brown, one and a half of white—

half pint of cream as rich as you can get it, one teacup of butter. Flavor with vanilla. Cook about twenty minutes.

TAFFY.

One quart New Orleans syrup, one pound light brown sugar, lump of butter, three cups shellbarks. Any nuts may be used.

EVERTON TAFFY.

Two cupfuls of sugar, two cupfuls of molasses, one cupful cold butter, grated rind of half lemon. Boil over a slow fire until it hardens when dropped in cold water. Pour thinly into tins well buttered, and mark into little inch squares before it cools.

CHOCOLATE CANDY.

One pound white sugar, half pint cream, quarter pound Walter Baker's chocolate, a small piece of butter. Season with vanilla, and boil it until stiff. Drop it in cakes with a spoon.

CHOCOLATE CARAMELS.

Half pound grated Walter Baker's chocolate, half pound butter, half pint milk, three pounds brown sugar, half bottle vanilla. Stir well, and cook for thirty minutes. Do not add the vanilla till just before taking off the fire.

CREAM CANDY.

Take three pounds of loaf sugar and put them in a kettle with half pint of cold water, and one pint sweet cream or rich milk. When it is heated add a heaping spoonful of butter, and just before it boils add two tablespoonsful of strong vinegar. Let it boil a few minutes only; just before taking it off the fire add one and a half teaspoons of vanilla. It can be pulled or not, as desired, and is much better after being kept a week.

WHITE TAFFY CANDY.

Six pounds white sugar, half pound butter, one teaspoonful cream of tartar. Boil until it cracks, pour out, and pull till light and white. Flavor with vanilla.

MOLASSES CANDY.

Three cups molasses, one of sugar, a piece of butter the size of an egg, and one tablespoonful of vinegar. Boil twenty minutes, stirring constantly. When it has boiled eighteen minutes add half teaspoonful soda.

COCOANUT CARAMELS.

Grate a medium sized cocoanut. Take one and a half pounds of sugar, a piece of butter the size of an egg, one cup of milk, and milk of the cocoanut. Stir all together and cook about twenty minutes, not too hard. Butter the pans and cut in squares.

PLAIN CANDY.

Three pounds sugar, quarter pound butter, half pint cream; put all together in a kettle, and let it melt slowly without coming to a boil. After it is melted let it boil twenty minutes. Flavor as you like.

CHOCOLATE DROPS.

The Cream.—Boil two cups of sugar, and one and a half cup of milk (or water) for five minutes. Add two teaspoonfuls of vanilla, then beat it for half an hour until stiff enough to hold; then make it into balls. Now take half pound Walter Baker's unsweetened chocolate, grate it and steam it over the tea-kettle. Drop the balls of cream when hard, one at a time, into the hot chocolate, using two forks at a time to take them out; scrape off the cream that drips from it, and place the balls on a buttered dish. Keep in a cool place.

SUGAR CANDY.

Six cups sugar, one cup vinegar, one cup water, one tablespoonful butter, put in at the last with one teaspoonful soda dissolved in hot water. Boil without stirring half an hour or until it ropes, or hardens in cold water. Pull it white with the tips of your fingers. This is a very nice simple candy for children. Flavor as you like.

CURING, CANNING, ETC.

RECIPE FOR BEEF BRINE.

Four gallons of water, six pounds of salt, two ounces saltpetre, six and a half pounds of brown sugar; boil these together, and skim the liquid as it boils. Pour it over the beef when the liquid is cold. The beef must be previously rubbed with salt, and the bloody brine allowed to run off. This should be done two or three days before the brine is poured over the beef, which it should cover.

PICKLE FOR BUTTER.

Half a pound salt, one ounce saltpetre, half a pound sugar, to three quarts of water. Scald and skim the pickle; when cold pour it over the butter.

TO CURE SHAD.

Strike the shad as you would herrings, then put it on a board, with a stone on it to press it down. Let them remain three days, then take them out and wash them in brine. Drain them well. To every hundred shad add one pound saltpetre, one pound brown sugar, mixed well together with as much alum salt as you think proper. In packing put alternate layers of shad and salt.

TO CURE BEEF HAMS.

To two pounds of meat take three ounces saltpetre, four ounces brown sugar, one pint fine salt. Mix well together. Rub the meat thoroughly all over, and lay it by for twenty-four hours, then salt it down in an open tub, or on a shelf, to let it drain, with two quarts fine salt. Let it lie fifteen days, then hang it up. If you prefer to put it in pickle, do so after it has lain four or five days.

TO CURE PORK HAMS.

To every 1000 pounds of pork put three quarters bushel of salt, two and a half pounds brown sugar, and two and a half pounds saltpetre, half a gallon of molasses. Mix all together, and rub on well, first hams, then shoulders, and then middlings. Keep in salt four weeks, then hang them up, and smoke them occasionally, for four or five weeks, with green hickory wood.

TO MAKE GOOD SAUSAGE MEAT.

To every fourteen pounds of meat cut fine take three ounces of salt, two ounces black pepper, half pint sage, one ounce saltpetre, a very little red pepper, and spices if you like (eighty cloves and quarter ounce allspice).

SAUSAGE MEAT.

Twenty-five pounds lean meat, two and a half pounds leaf fat, two and a half pounds chine fat, six ounces salt, five ounces pounded sage, five ounces of pepper. Cut the meat and fat in small pieces, mix it well with the salt, sage, and pepper, and grind in chopper.

SAUSAGE MEAT.

For fifty-one pounds sausage take twenty-seven pounds fillet, twenty-four pounds chine fat, three quarter pounds salt, six ounces sage, three ounces pepper, a small teaspoonful saltpetre, the same of red pepper, and the same of cloves pounded fine. Mix all these well together, and add it to the sausage meat. If necessary pass the meat through the chopper twice.

TO PRESERVE BUTTER FOR WINTER.

Take equal quantities of salt, saltpetre, and fine loaf sugar, well mixed. When packing the butter allow one ounce to every pound of butter. Put thick cloths on the top. This will keep till late in spring.

TO CURE BEEF.

To forty-five pounds of beef take two quarts coarse salt, one pound brown sugar, one teaspoon saltpetre. Mix all well together, and rub the meat thick with it. Keep rubbing it on until all is gone. Let it lie for two weeks, then take it out, pour boiling water over it, and hang it up in a dry place.

ANOTHER RECIPE.

Take six pounds alum salt, half pound brown sugar, half ounce saltpetre, four gallons water. Boil these ingredients until they are dissolved, taking off the scum as it rises. Let this get quite cool, then pour it on the meat. Do not take more meat than the pickle will cover.

TO CURE BACON.

One thousand pounds meat, half bushel of salt, one pound saltpetre, and eight pounds brown sugar. Mix all well, and rub the meat hard with them, on both sides of the piece. From four to five weeks is sufficient for the meat to take salt. Every ten days take the meat out, expose it to the atmosphere half an hour, then wash it in the pickle it has made. It is better to dip the meat in water, and wipe it with a coarse cloth before hanging it up to smoke. All meat ought to be secured from the fly before the first of March by smoking. Smoke with hickory and decayed wood so as to occasion a smother. After rubbing, meat should be put in casks where it makes its own pickle.

IMPORTANT TO BUTTER MAKERS.

A method in practice among the best butter makers in England for réndering butter firm and solid during the hot weather is as follows: Carbonate of soda and alum made into powder are used for the purpose. For twenty pounds of butter, one teaspoonful of carbonate of soda, and one of powdered alum, mixed together at the time of churning, and put into the cream. The effect of this powder is to make the butter come firm and solid, and give it a clean, sweet flavor. It does not enter into the butter, but its action is upon the cream, and it passes off with the buttermilk. The ingredients of the powder should not be mixed together until required to be used, or at the time the cream is in the churn ready for churning.

BEEF PICKLE.

Four gallons spring water, four ounces saltpetre, six pounds alum salt, one and a half pounds brown sugar, and one ounce of potash.

CANNED SALMON.

California canned salmon is a great success in canning. It is very nice for breakfast heated, seasoned with pepper and salt, placed on thin slices of buttered toast, with a cream dressing poured over all. For dinner it is excellent with any fish sauce.

CANNED TOMATOES AND OKRA FOR SOUP.

Throw ripe tomatoes into boiling water, then peel them. Put them into a bell metal kettle and boil them. As the water rises dip part of it off, or it will require a long time to reduce the tomatoes so as to can them. Boil until almost ready for table use. In the meantime wash the okra, cut it crosswise, drop it into boiling water, and let it boil half an hour, skimming it several times. Dip it up with a perforated ladle, drop it into the tomatoes, and let all boil half an hour. Then put in tin cans, and seal them up while hot.

TO SEAL PRESERVES.

Beat the white of an egg, take tissue paper the size you require, and dip it into the egg, wetting the paper on both sides. Then cover the jar, carefully pressing it securely round the sides.

TO CAN TOMATOES.

Pour boiling water on the tomatoes till you can easily peel them. Then put them in a kettle, and cook down till the water from the tomatoes is nearly out. Can while hot, and seal immediately.

TO PREPARE RENNET.

Take the stomach from the calf as soon as it is killed. Do not wash it, but hang it in a dry, cool place for four or five days. Then turn it inside out, slip off all the curd nicely with the hand, fill it with a little saltpetre mixed with the necessary quantity of salt, and lay it in a small stone pot. Pour over it a small teaspoonful of vinegar, and sprinkle a handful of salt over it, covering it closely to keep it for use. Never wash it; that would weaken the gastric juice, and injure the rennet. After it has been salted six or eight weeks, cut off a piece four or five inches long, put it in a large mustard bottle, or any vessel that will hold about a pint and a half. Put on it five gills of cold water, and two gills of rose brandy. Stop it very close, and shake it always before using. A tablespoonful of this is sufficient for a quart of milk. It must be prepared in very cool weather, and if well done will keep more than a year.

TOMATOES FOR BROILING. (Very fine.)

Take nice large smooth tomatoes. Cut them in half right through the centre. Then put them in your baking pan with the cut side down, with very little water. As soon as they get *hot*, put them carefully in new *tin* cans, which also must be very hot. Seal them up at once, they are as good as fresh.

TO CLEAN CALF'S HEAD AND FEET.

These directions are, of course, for those who live in the country, and butcher their own meats. As soon as the animal is killed have the head and feet taken off, wash them clean, sprinkle some pounded rosin all over the hairs, then dip them in boiling water, and take them instantly out. The rosin will dry immediately, and they may be scraped clean with ease. The feet should be soaked in water three or four days, changing it daily. This will make them very white.

HOW TO MAKE VINEGAR.

To four quarts rain water put one pound of coarse brown sugar, or one pint of molasses. Boil it well and skim it; pour it into a tub, and add one quart of rain water to each gallon of the above, then take a slice of well raised bread, toast it brown, and cover it well with yeast, put it in a tub, cover it with a cloth, and let it remain four or five days to work, then pour it off into a good cask. Roll up a sheet of white paper and put it in the cask for mother. Let it stand four or six months. If not sour enough add one gallon of whiskey. To keep vinegar put in all slops of tea, brandy, wine, lemonade, and scum of preserves.

HORSERADISH VINEGAR.

Half pound scraped horseradish, one ounce of minced eschalot, one drachm cayenne pepper, and one quart vinegar. Put all the ingredients in a bottle, shaking frequently for a fortnight. When steeped well, strain and bottle for use. It is good in two weeks.

HOW TO MIX MUSTARD.

Ingredients.—Mustard, salt, and water. Mustard should be mixed with water that has been boiled and allowed to cool. Put the mustard in a cup with a pinch of salt. Add the water gradually, and make it into a smooth paste. You can make it as thin as you like.

RECIPE FOR PRESERVING CORN.

Cut the corn from the cob, uncooked, pack it down in a jar in alternate layers of salt and corn. When the jar is tightly packed put a thick layer of salt on the top, and tie a thick piece of cotton over the jar. Cover it and set it away in a cool place. Before using the corn in winter it must be soaked an hour in warm water to extract the salt, and then boiled in fresh water.

TO PRESERVE ORANGES WHOLE.

With a sharp penknife take off the outer skin of the orange as thin as possible. Boil the fruit in water until you can puncture the skin with a straw. Make a small hole in the fruit at the stem with the handle of a teaspoon; take out all the seeds, being particular that none are left. Make a syrup of two pounds of sugar to one pound of fruit. Boil the syrup and take the scum off. Boil the fruit in the syrup until the oranges look clear and transparent.

TO PREPARE SYRUP FOR PRESERVES.

To every pound sugar allow one gill water, and let it stand till dissolved; to every twelve pounds allow half ounce Russian isinglass. Dissolve it in a little boiling water. Put it in with the sugar. When cold place it on the fire, let it boil, skimming constantly, till no more scum will rise. The syrup is then ready for any fruit you may wish to preserve.

BEEF PICKLE.

Five gallons of brine, strong enough to bear an egg, one gallon of boiling lye. Let it stand until clear and cold, not strong. Add one pound brown sugar and six ounces of saltpetre. Mix all well, and pour it on the meat. This is good for pork also.

SAUSAGE.

Six pounds lean fresh pork, two pounds fat fresh pork, twelve teaspoonsful powdered sage, six of black pepper, six of salt, two of powdered mace, two of cloves, and one grated nutmeg. Grind the meat, fat and lean, in a sausage mill. Mix the seasoning well; taste it to be sure all is right, and pack it down in stone jars, pouring melted lard on top. If you wish to make link sausage prepare the intestines as follows: Empty them, cut them in lengths, and lay them in salt and water for two days; then turn them inside out, and let them soak one day longer. Then scrape and rinse them well in soda and water; wipe them and blow into one end, having tied up the other with a little twine. If they are whole and clear stuff with the meat; then tie them up and hang them up in the cellar.

TO KEEP GAME FROM TAINTING.

Draw them as soon as they come into your possession. Rinse with soda and water, then with pure cold water. Wipe them dry, and rub them lightly with a mixture of fine salt and black pepper. If you must keep them for some time put in the cavity of each fowl a piece of charcoal, and hang them in a cool dark place with a cloth thrown over them.

TO BROWN FLOUR.

Spread some flour on a tin plate, set it upon the stove or in a *very* hot oven, and stir it continually after it begins to color until it is brown all through. Keep some always on hand as it is always coming in use. Put it away in a closely covered glass jar, and shake it every few days to keep it light and prevent it from lumping.

THE BEST MODE OF KEEPING BUTTER.

Have the butter well washed. Work it three times, then have ready a pickle made by the recipe given before, and have some corn shucks prepared as follows: When they are dry remove the ear of corn carefully, then scald the shucks. Let them lie in the sun until dry. Meanwhile work the butter into the shape of ears of corn, and when the shucks are dry dip them in ice water, then open them carefully and place the butter inside, and fold the layers of the shucks nicely over. Then tie them up tight and put them in the pickle; put a heavy weight over it, and keep it covered with the pickle. This butter, if prepared properly, I have kept a year.

TO CURE CORN FOR WINTER USE.

Take nice sugar corn about the month of September. Remove the first layer of shuck; then have ready a tight barrel. Pack the corn in tightly, standing it on end, and pour over it a strong brine, strong enough to bear an egg. This brine should be boiled and well skimmed, but not poured over the corn until cold. Place a heavy weight on the corn to keep it under the brine. Cover closely. It will be good until spring, and tastes like fresh corn. It can be boiled on the ear just as it is packed.

TO CURE PIG'S FEET FOR SOUSE.

As soon as the feet are cut off have them scraped clean. This can be done by dipping them first in hot lye, removing the hair and the hoofs; then have some whitewash ready heated. Dip them in it, and scrape off at once with a knife. Now wash them through two waters, after which put them in clean cold water, and let them lie until next day. Then change the water, and the third day wash them well, and put them on to boil. When done have ready a pickle made of strong salt and water, with some meal in it, and flavor it with a little vinegar. This pickle must come to a boil, and when cold pour over the feet, after they also are cold. This will keep them sweet for weeks. They are nice washed off and eaten cold, or cut in half, sprinkled with flour, and fried in boiling lard.

TO MAKE LARD.

Take the leaf fat, wash it off with warm water, remove the skin, and cut the fat in small pieces. Put one quart water in a large pot, and dissolve in it three teaspoonsful of bread soda. Then fill up the pot with lard and set it on the fire. Stir it constantly to keep it from scorching. When the cracklings are a light brown, and commence to sink, the lard is done. Strain it through a coarse cloth; put it in tin cans or stone jars, and tie it up tight. No salt is used with the soda, and I have found, from long experience, that soda is the better of the two to use. Meat fat is prepared the same way. It is best to keep it separate. The butcher's fat requires no water, as it has to lie in water twenty-four hours before it can be cooked. Put more soda to it than to lard.

i

MISCELLANEOUS RECIPES.

HOW TO COOK A HUSBAND.

First catch him. Many good husbands are spoiled in the cooking. Some women go about it as if their husbands were bladders and blow them up. Others keep them too much in hot water, while others freeze them with icy indifference and freezing coolness. Some smother them with constant contention, hatred and variance, and some keep them in hot pickle all their lives. These women always serve them up with tongue sauce. Now it cannot be supposed that husbands will be tender and palatable if cooked in this way, on the contrary, they are tart, tough and snappish—actually good for nothing. If, however, cooked by the following recipe they are prime and delicious. Get a large jar, called the jar of faithfulness (which all good wives keep on hand), place your husband in it, and set him near the fire of conjugal love, let the fire be pretty hot, but especially let it burn clear, and above all let the heat be constant. Cover him with affectionate kindness and confidence, garnished with modest and becoming familiarity and spiced with amiable pleasantry, and if you add a few sweet kisses and other confectionaries, let them be accompanied with sufficient portion of secrecy mixed with prudence and moderation. And let the whole conjugal life be seasoned with love and devotional piety. We would advise all good wives to try this recipe and realize what an admirable dish a husband makes when properly and discreetly cooked.

TOMATOES SERVED FOR LUNCHEONS AND DINNERS IN THE WINTER INSTEAD OF FRESH ONES.

Take one quart can of best tomatoes, put them on and let them come to a boil, then strain through a strainer, and have half a box of Chalmers' Gelatine dissolved well and pour on the tomatoes. Season only with little salt. Put in moulds the shape of tomatoes, then put on ice; they will turn out whole and look just like tomatoes. You can then cut them open very carefully, so it will not spoil the looks of the tomatoes, and fill them with chopped celery, seasoned with mayonnaise dressing. You can, in fact, put any kind of salad in them you please. Serve them on leaves (white) of lettuce with cheese and crackers. *Very fine.*

SICILIAN SORBETTO.

Peel and mash one quart of mellow peaches. Add to them one pint of strained orange juice. Boil together one pound of sugar and one quart of water for five minutes. When cold add this to the fruit mixture. Turn into a freezer, pack and turn slowly until the dasher is hard to move. Make a meringue with the white of one egg and one tablespoonful of sugar. Stir into the sorbetto, repack and stand aside for at least two hours.

BISCUITS TORTONI.

Beat the yolks of six eggs with a half cup of powdered sugar. When very light add four tablespoonsful of maraschino and one tablespoonful of kirschwasser. Stand in a basin of hot water over the fire and beat constantly for five minutes. Be careful not to curdle the eggs. Take from the fire, stand in a basin of ice water and beat until cold. Stir in carefully one pint of whipped cream and one teaspoonful of vanilla. Fill paper cases with the mixture and sprinkle the top with grated and sifted macaroons. Put in a freezer in layers with letter paper between. Take out dasher, but leave on cover and handle to keep straight. Pack with salt and ice, cork in the lid, cover with a piece of carpet and stand aside.

INDELIBLE INK.

A stick of nitrate of silver dissolved in soft water. Keep the solution in a vial wrapped with dark paper and in a dark place to exclude light.

HOW TO USE THIS INDELIBLE INK.

Wash the linen to be marked with a solution of carbonate of soda, and let it dry. Then write with the solution of nitrate of silver, and place the linen in the sunlight.

HOW TO REMOVE INDELIBLE INK STAINS.

Dust the spot of indelible ink with cyanide of potash, and moisten the linen with water. In five or ten minutes wash the linen with soft water, and the ink stain will disappear.

RECIPE FOR COLOGNE.

One ounce oil of bergamot, one drachm oil of nutmegs, twenty drops of oil of cloves, half ounce oil of verbena, one ounce tincture musk, one gallon of alcohol. Mix and shake well.

REMEDY FOR POISON.

A dessertspoonful of made mustard, and mixed in a tumbler of warm water, if drunk immediately, is a simple but efficient remedy for poison. It acts as an emetic, and being always easily procured can be used in any case where one is required. This simple antidote may be the means of saving many a fellow creature from an untimely end.

OPODELDOC.

Fill a vial half full of whiskey, put in broken gum camphor and let it dissolve, then add castile soap scraped fine (other good mild soap will answer). Shake the vial well, and when the soap is dissolved and the mixture becomes thick it is ready for use. The proportions of camphor and soap are matters of guess or judgment.

COLIC DROPS.

One teaspoonful of magnesia and one of paregoric, half a teaspoonful of rhubarb, one teaspoonful of mintwater, and four tablespoonsful of cold water sweetened with loaf sugar. Dose for a child two weeks old one teaspoonful. Repeat if necessary in fifteen or twenty minutes.

STAINING FLOORS.

One gallon linseed oil, one pound Spanish brown, two pounds sienna powder, one ounce litharge, half an ounce lampblack. Boil the mixture, and add one pint of turpentine. Apply with a brush like paint.

RECIPE FOR RESTORING COLOR.

Take one pint soft soap, two tablespoonsful of spirits of turpentine, one tablespoonful of hartshorn. Put these into five gallons of rain water, and wash as ordinarily. This is particularly nice for worsted goods.

MUCILAGE FOR ENVELOPES.

Quarter pound of gum-arabic, one pint boiling water, and a piece of borax as large as a walnut. Put it into a large mouthed bottle when thoroughly mixed. Shake it occasionally for three or four days. After it is corked, if the weather is hot, a tablespoonful of alcohol will prevent mould.

TO CURE A FELON.

Take the yolk of an egg with an equal amount of home-made soft soap, and the same quantity of common salt; add one teaspoon of spirits of turpentine. Mix well, and apply the poultice on going to bed. If the felon be so far advanced as to render lancing necessary, then apply a new one after lancing, as before.

SMALL-POX REMEDY. (Very fine.)

One grain sulphate of zinc, one grain foxglove (digitalis), half a teaspoonful sugar; mix all with two tablespoonsful of water. When thoroughly mixed add four ounces of water. Dose.—A spoonful every hour. For a child smaller doses according to the age. This remedy is also good in scarlet fever.

BONESET FOR A COUGH.

Pour one and a half pints of water on a ten cent package of boneset. Let it steep by the fire ten or fifteen minutes, then strain it. Sweeten it with two and a half coffee-cupsful of loaf sugar, then add half a pint of Jamaica rum, and bottle it. Dose for a child one teaspoonful before each meal; for a grown person a sherry glassful.

TO COOK PUDDINGS IN BOILING WATER.

Wet and flour the cloth before putting in the pudding. In tying it leave room enough for the pudding to swell. If cooked in a mould, do not fill the mould quite full. Never let the water stop boiling. As it wastes away in boiling replenish the kettle from another containing boiling water. It is better to cook puddings (plum puddings as well) in a steamer than in boiling water. The principle is just the same, and there is no water soaked.

FOR CLEANSING LACES.

Pour a little pure, clear alcohol into a china bowl, or other deep vessel that can be covered to prevent evaporation, into which place the lace to be cleaned. Leave it some time, till the dirt has softened and settled at the bottom. Then, with perfectly clean fingers, rub the lace gently in the liquid till all the stains have disappeared. If they do not come out let it soak longer. After rubbing squeeze the lace as dry as possible. Take one piece at a time while damp and pull it out with the fingers, picking out the edge very carefully with the nails. It should be damp while handling it. When the meshes are all opened lay the lace between the leaves of a book, and press it till entirely dry, taking care to fold it in and out among the leaves, so as not to crease it. If the lace is very much soiled rub it gently in soapsuds before using the alcohol. In such cases do not rinse it. Black lace can be beautifully renovated this way.

RECIPE FOR SOFT SOAP.

Fifteen ounces of castile soap, thirty ounces sal soda, six drachms of pulverized arrow-root. Put these ingredients into six quarts of hot water that has just come to a boil. When these are dissolved add fifteen quarts of cold water, and let the whole come to a boil. The soap is then done and is fit for use as soon as cold. The castile soap should be scraped fine and the soda pounded. A teaspoonful of hartshorn added to the soap used will remove tar, paint, or grease spots from cloth.

AN EXCELLENT MIXTURE FOR WASHING CHINA, GLASS, OR SILVER.

Fill a stone jar with alternate layers of any good laundry soap, shaved very thin, and of washing soda. When the jar is full, pour over the mixture cold rain water. Let it stand a few days until it jellies. Put one tablespoonful to a pan of hot water when needed for use.

HARD SOAP.

Six pounds soda, four pounds lime, four gallons water. Mix in the pot till quite hot, but do not let it boil. Let this settle. Put in seven and a half pounds of grease, and let it simmer till soft. Then add the soda, lime, and water, and let it boil two hours, not longer. While boiling feed with soda water. Put in half a pint of salt fifteen minutes before the boiling is done. It must be stirred all the time while boiling. If the lime is very strong two and a half pounds will be enough. The sediment of the soda and lime will do for whitewash.

HARD SOAP (without Boiling).

Dissolve one box lye over night in seven pints of warm water, and in the morning add six pints liquid grease. Stir for three-quarters of an hour, *all one way.* Pour it into moulds, and cut it out the next day. A small piece of beef tallow added will make it finer.

HARD SOAP.

Put one box of saponifier into three gallons of water; knock off the end, and let the box boil until it empties itself; add four and a half pounds soap fat, and let it boil two hours and ten minutes. Then add a small half pint of salt, and let it continue boiling thirty-five minutes longer. Then add half a gallon of hot water, and let it come to a boil. Take the tub in which the soap is to be put, and pour a tumblerful of cold water round the sides and bottom of it to keep the soap from sticking. Let it stand all night, and cut it out in the morning.

TO CURE A GATHERED BREAST.

To half pint linseed oil add half pint brandy, a piece of castile soap as large as a walnut, a piece of mutton tallow and beeswax. Stew them together, and when cold spread it on brown paper, and apply it to the breast. To be kept on until all hardness is dispersed. Cocoa butter is very fine also.

COUGH MIXTURE.

Syr. tolu, three ounces; aquæ font., one ounce; potassa bromide, three drachms; acid hydrocyanic dilute, and sol. morphia Maj., each thirty drops. Mix. Dose—Teaspoonful every four hours.

TO EXTRACT THE SALT FROM LARD.

For medicinal purposes, lard which is free from salt is often required. In order to extract the salt put a tablespoonful of lard in a tin cup, and pour on it a pint of boiling water. Set it aside to get cold. The lard will be found in a cake on the top, and the salt which it contained will remain in the water.

A PRETTY EXPERIMENT.

An acorn suspended by a thread within half an inch of the water in a hyacinth glass will in a few months burst, and throw out a root, and shoot upward with straight and tapering stems, covered with beautiful green leaves.

A PRETTY CENTRE PIECE.

Take a goblet from which the stem has been broken off, and sew tightly round it a piece of coarse flannel, wet it, and put as much flaxseed on it as will stick to it. Place this in a saucer of water, and replenish it as often as it commences to dry up. The tumbler will soon be thickly covered with green, and is a very pretty ornament to a table.

TO CLEAN WHITE SATIN SLIPPERS.

White satin slippers can be cleaned by scrubbing well with a brush, castile soap, and rain water. Then put in the sun to dry, after stuffing the toes with cotton.

COSMETIC SOAP.

Take one pound castile soap, or any other nice old soap, scrape it fine, and put it on the fire with a little water. Stir till it is a smooth paste; pour into a bowl; when cold add lavender water or some kind of essence. Beat with a silver spoon till well mixed; thicken with corn meal, and keep in small pots. Cover tight, for the air will make the soap hard.

TO CURE A FELON.

As soon as the part afflicted begins to swell, wrap it with cloth saturated with lobelia.

EXCELLENT LIP SALVE.

Take one teacupful of fresh butter just churned, and half a pound beeswax. Mix well, and boil until dissolved. Strain and put it into a mould. This salve cures the worst chapped hands and lips in one night.

POISON OAK CURE.

Bathe the affected parts long and well in sulphur and cream; in half an hour wash well in salt water. Repeat this twice a day. Three or four applications will cure.

LEMON FOR A COUGH.

Roast a lemon very carefully without burning it. When hot through cut it and squeeze it in a cup, and sweeten it to taste. When the cough is troublesome take a dessertspoonful. It is excellent.

A FINE RECIPE FOR A COUGH.

Boil flaxseed in water till it becomes slimy, then strain, and sweeten with rock candy powdered as fine as possible. Season with the juice of fresh lemons. Take a wineglassful whenever the cough is troublesome.

SCALDS OR BURNS.

If a scald or burn is not deeper than the outer skin make an ointment of sulphur and lard stiff enough to spread on a cloth, or scraped Irish potato is good.

CURE FOR A COLD.

A very great relief for a cold in the head is to inhale spirits of ammonia every few minutes, or camphor. Take three teaspoonsful of paregoric when first taken at night.

ITEMS.

One teaspoonful vinegar in one pint *limestone* water, will antagonize all its ill effects upon the bowels of those who are unaccustomed to it.

As much powdered alum as will rest on a dime, stirred in a pail of water, clears it in five minutes.

To keep oranges, lemons, and apples, wrap them close in pepper, and keep cool and dry.

Thaw frozen fruit and vegetables in cold water.

Cranberries covered with water will keep for months in a cellar.

A good remedy for a burn is dry soda rubbed on the blister.

Colors can be set in goods by dissolving one tablespoonful of lead in two gallons of water, and letting them stand all night.

THREE WAYS OF CLEANING BLACK SILK.

One teaspoonful ammonia and one of turpentine in one pint of warm water.

Boil an old black kid glove in a quart of water till it is reduced to one pint.

Take a coffee-cupful of water and the grounds of coffee mixed with a little bluing.

Always sponge the silk on the right side, and iron on the wrong. It is always well to roll silk after cleaning on a broom-handle or round stick. A kid glove of any color will clean a silk of a similar color. If you have not one of the same color use a white one. After boiling in a quart reduce it, as before mentioned, to a pint, and keep it at that quantity until nothing but the threads are left of the glove.

TRICÓPHORUS FOR THE HAIR.

One and a half ounces of castile soap, half ounce of fine cantharides, forty drops of lemon oil, forty drops of bergamot oil, one pint of best alcohol. Apply to the scalp once a day.

TO SET COLORS IN CALICOES.

Three gills of salt to four quarts boiling water. Put the dresses in while hot, and leave them till cold. Another way is, to take one teaspoonful of turpentine, and one of hartshorn, put in the quantity of water required to wash a dress.

MORE ITEMS.

A brass kettle should always be cleaned with a little salt and vinegar before using it.

One pint lime, one pint salt, and three gallons of water will keep eggs for winter use.

Stair rods can be cleaned by dipping a cloth in coal and rotten-stone, and rubbing them well. Then rub off with another cloth or a piece of paper.

If you wash matting in salt and water it will keep it from turning dark.

A NICE PAINT FOR PAVEMENTS.

One gallon flour paste, not very thick, two pounds Venetian red. Mix this thoroughly, and apply it to the pavement with a whitewash brush.

FLOOR POLISH THAT IS USED AT MT. VERNON.

One pint of linseed oil, one of soft soap, one-half pint of turpentine, one-half pound of beeswax, two ounces of yellow ochre, if you want it light; if dark, the same quantity of brown Spanish. Melt all together, stir well, apply *hot* with a woolen cloth. Rub hard and quickly *immediately* with a dry woolen cloth. Very fine.

CURE FOR THRUSH, OR SORE MOUTH.

Three tablespoonsful of honey, two teaspoonsful of bolamenia, one of borax, and half a teaspoon of burnt alum. Put all in an eggshell, and let it get hot. Do not stir it till it begins to rise in the shell, then stir it till it falls.

HOP POULTICE.

Place a sufficient quantity of fresh hops to make two poultices in a saucepan, and add enough vinegar and water, in equal parts, to keep it from burning, so that when sufficiently hot for use the hops will only be moist. When ready to be put in the bag sprinkle in a little meal. Have the poultice a little warmer than the body, put it in the flannel bag, and as soon as cool replace it with another. A piece of flannel should be laid over the poultice to prevent the clothes from getting soiled.

CAMPHOR BALL.

Four tablespoonsful sweet oil, one hundred and twenty grains of white wax, one hundred and twenty grains spermaceti, six and a quarter grains camphor. Put all in a cup on the fire until dissolved.

TO RESTORE COLORS.

Hartshorn will restore colors taken out by acids. It may be dropped on any garment without injuring it.

TO REMOVE SPOTS FROM CARPETS.

Dissolve a small quantity of ammonia in some rain water, and wash the spots with it.

TO TAKE MILDEW OUT OF LINEN.

Rub the spots well with soap, then rub in well some scraped chalk. Lay the article upon the grass, and when dry renew the soap and chalk. This will remove mildew in two applications. Javille water will remove most any stain, but it must be washed *at once*.

ANOTHER RECIPE.

Rub over the spots the juice of a raw tomato, and then sprinkle them with salt. Lay the article in the sun, and repeat the application until the spots disappear. This is almost infallible.

TO REMOVE SPOTS IN FURNITURE.

Spots may generally be removed by rubbing them quick and hard with flannel wet with the same thing which made the stain. The very best restorative is pulverized rotten-stone and linseed oil.

TO DESTROY BED-BUGS.

Add one ounce quicksilver to the whites of two eggs well beaten, and apply with a feather. If the vermin are in the walls fill up the cracks with verdigris, green paint.

TO RESTORE COLOR TO IVORY-HANDLED KNIVES.

When they become yellow rub them with nice emery or sand paper. It will effectually restore their whiteness and take out the spots.

ESSENCE OF VERBENA (Cologne).

Take rectified spirits of wine, half drachm otto of verbena, one drachm otto bergamot, quarter ounce tincture tolu. Mix all together and it is ready for use.

CROUP MIXTURE.

One and a half drachms chlorate of potash, two ounces syrup of squills, one drachm pulverized ipecac, two ounces spring water. Mix all together. Dose—Two teaspoonsful every half hour.

TO CURE FRECKLES.

Two drachms of Sal-ammoniac, with an ounce of German Cologne; the solution mixed with a pint of distilled water. Apply two or three times a day.

CURE FOR RHEUMATISM, NEURALGIA, ETC.

Half ounce sweet oil, half ounce alcohol, half ounce oil of turpentine, half ounce oil of peppermint, half ounce opodeldoc, and half ounce of laudanum. Warm the mixture, and rub the part affected gently with the hand.

REMEDY FOR DIPHTHERIA.

To inhale the fumes of slacked lime is an excellent remedy in diphtheria. Put some lime in a teacup, and with a funnel inhale it.

FOR WHOOPING COUGH.

Take about half an ounce chestnut leaves to one pint water. Let it come to a boil, then pour the whole into a teapot without straining. Drink occasionally—either cold or warm—as much as the patient will through the day and at bedtime. Children like it even without sugar, which it is best not to use. It may be given also to infants. Burn a cresoline lamp always at night.

CHALK MIXTURE.

To half a pint arrow-root gruel put half an ounce prepared chalk, one teaspoonful powdered cinnamon, brandy and sugar enough to make it pleasant. The child should eat it frequently when the bowels are disordered.

FOR EAR ACHE.

Take a clove of garlic or onion and toast it till it is soft. Then dip it in sweet oil and insert it in the ear. In a short time the pain will cease. Then insert some cotton to keep out the cold.

CURE FOR A COUGH.

Take one package each of boneset, horehound, mullen, and yarrow; boil them in two quarts of water. Strain it, and add one pound brown sugar, and boil to a syrup. Dose.—One tablespoonful as often as required.

TO CURE A CONSUMPTIVE COUGH.

One gill of gum turpentine, one quart of Holland gin, one-half pint of clear honey. Mix well, stand twenty-four hours. Dose.—Take six (or more if necessary) teaspoonsful a day. I have seen some wonderful cures from using this.

SORE EYES.

For inflamed or weak eyes bathe them in a weak solution of salt and water, just sufficiently strong to taste slightly saline, and to be sensible to the eye. If there is much pain add a few drops of laudanum or Pond's Extract.

PRICKLY ASH.

Pour three pints boiling water on one ounce prickly ash, and boil it down to a quart. Let it cool, then strain it, and add a pint of the best whiskey. Commence with half a wineglass half an hour before each meal, and increase the dose to a wineglassful. Excellent remedy for cough.

TONIC TO PREVENT CHILLS.

One pint whiskey, half a pint water, three ounces Peruvian bark, fifteen drops of oil of cloves, forty drops of Fowler's Solution. Dose.—Three-quarters wineglassful for thirty days, before breakfast. This is excellent.

TO CURL TUMBLED FEATHERS.

Hold them over the heated top of the stove, not near enough to burn; withdraw, shake them out, and hold them over it again until curled.

TO CLEAN STRAW MATTING.

Wash with a cloth, dipped in clean salt and water, then wipe dry at once. This prevents from turning yellow.

FLOOR STAIN.

One pound of burnt umber ground in oil; mix this with boiled linseed oil, enough to color well without thickening the oil. Rub this mixture well into the wood with a woolen cloth, wiping with another cloth until the stain ceases to come off. Mix one gallon of turpentine with one pound of wax, shaved up, let it stand all night. Next day rub on the floor with a woolen cloth.

TO MAKE THE BEST TEA.

Scald your teapot, then allow a teaspoonful for every two cups; have the water boiling on the table, put the tea in the pot, then add the boiling water. Let it steep about five minutes. Sliced lemon and sugar for those that prefer it, but true lovers of good tea never take lemon, and often no sugar. Some persons prefer cream with it.

TO CLEAN BLACK LACE.

Half cup rain water or very soft spring water, one teaspoonful borax, one tablespoon spirits of wine. Squeeze the lace through this three times, then rinse in a cup of hot water, in which a black kid glove has been boiled. Pull out the edges of the lace until almost dry; then press it for two days between the leaves of a heavy book.

TO STOP THE FLOW OF BLOOD.

Bind the cut with cobwebs and brown sugar, press it on like lint, or, if you cannot procure these, with the fine dust of tea. When the blood ceases to flow apply laudanum.

COLOGNE WATER.

Sixty drops of oil of lavender, sixty of bergamot, sixty of oil of lemon, sixty of orange flower water, and one pint of alcohol. Cork and shake well.

ANTIDOTES TO POISON.

If you have taken corrosive sublimate, half dozen raw eggs, after mustard and water. If laudanum, a cup of very strong coffee. If arsenic, first the emetic, then half cup sweet oil or melted lard.

HAIR TONIC.

Sixty grains of quinine in one quart of bay rum, and rubbed in the scalp every day. Very fine.

TO WHITEN AND SOFTEN THE HANDS.

Use lemon juice and glycerine—two-thirds glycerine, one-third lemon juice. Use every night after washing the hands. Rub it in well.

FOR CHILDREN TEETHING.

Tie a quarter of a pound of best wheat flour in a thick cloth, and boil it in one quart of water for three hours. If water boils away add more. Then remove the cloth, and expose the flour to the air or heat until it is hard and dry. Grate from it, when wanted, one tablespoonful, which put into half a pint of new milk, and stir over the fire until it comes to a boil, when add a pinch of salt and a tablespoonful of cold water and serve. Or, brown a tablespoonful of flour in the oven, feed a few pinches at a time to a child, or mix with water and give it. Will stop summer complaint in children often when everything else fails.

MAIDS OF HONOR.

There are some delightful little cakes, fit for the gods, or at any rate for afternoon tea, which go by the quaint name "maids of honor."

At one Fifth-avenue mansion they are considered a great delicacy. The recipe, by the way, has been in this family for generations. It descended possibly from the time of Queen Elizabeth; the making of these cakes was one of the occupations of the virgin Queen's ladies in waiting.

The night previous to making these cakes cut a piece of rennet about four inches square, wash off the salt carefully, wipe the rennet dry, and put it in a cup of warm water to soak. Early in the morning stir the rennet water into a quart of milk and set it in a warm place until the milk becomes firm, and put on ice; when quite cold, put the curd into a sieve and drain it dry, crumbling it fine in your hands. Have ready two ounces of sweet almonds, two ounces of bitter almonds, blanched and pounded in a mortar to a smooth paste and mixed, as you proceed, with rosewater, to prevent their oiling. Grate upon lumps of loaf sugar the yellow rind of three lemons, then squeeze the juice of the lemons over the sugar and let it dissolve. Mix in a deep pan the crumbled curd, with three-quarters of a pound of butter cut up and three-quarters of a pound of powdered sugar. Stir the curd, the butter and the sugar together till very light, adding a wine-glass of brandy, the almonds and the lemon, also grate in a small nutmeg. Beat well together the yolks of eight eggs, then add gradually to the other ingredients, finishing with a tablespoonful of farina and beat the whole thoroughly. Have ready some puff paste, with which you line small patty pans, then fill with the mixture, and sift powdered sugar over each cake. Put in a hot oven and bake thoroughly.

BUTTERLESS SAUCE.

Scald half a gill of milk; mix half a pint of powdered sugar with the yolks of two eggs and add to the boiling milk. Stir until the mixture is as thick as boiled custard. When cool flavor, and just before serving whisk in lightly the stiff whites of the eggs.

COLD CREAM SAUCE.

Beat together a cup of sugar and half a cup of butter; add a cup of cream. Stir all to a thick, even liquid; flavor with lemon or vanilla and place on ice until ready to serve.

EVERYDAY SAUCE.

A pint of boiling water, a heaping teacup of sugar, a tablespoonful of butter, a pinch of salt and a tablespoonful of corn starch dissolved in cold water. Boil half an hour. Season with nutmeg, or flavor with a tablespoonful of currant jelly liquefied in a tablespoonful of hot water.

FOAMING SAUCE.

Melt a teacupful of sugar in a little water, let it boil; stir in a glass of wine and whisk in the well-beaten whites of three eggs. Serve at once.

HELPS FOR HOUSEWIVES.

Use lemon juice and salt to remove iron rust, ink, and mildew on white goods.

After blood stains have been well saturated with kerosene, wash in cold water.

For a burn, apply dry flour, and then bind it up in raw cotton saturated with sweet oil.

No receptacle for soiled clothing, even if handsomely decorated, should be kept in a sleeping apartment.

Soak glass globes in hot soda water, then wash hard in lukewarm ammonia water, and rinse in cold water.

When an eider-down comfortable has got hard and lost all its elasticity, hang it in the cool, balmy sun for a few hours, and all the life will come back to it.

Handsome parlor vases are usually filled with some such ingredient as sand to weight them and prevent the light porcelain from being brushed off the mantel-piece.

Whiten yellow linen by boiling half an hour in one pound of fine soap melted in one gallon of milk. Then wash in suds, then in two cold waters with a little bluing.

The best way to remove mildew stains from leather-covered chairs is to rub the leather well with a clean, soft and very dry cloth. Then apply a rag moistened with pyroligneous acid.

If you want your pie crust to come out flaky and nice, and not take up the juice of the fruit or other filling, brush the under crust with the partly-beaten white of an egg before putting the filling in.

Don't let the baby suck its thumbs. Interesting as this habit is, it is the cause of broad, flat thumbs in after life.

The German custom of making infants' sleeves an eighth of a yard longer than the arms is an excellent preventive.

This is said to be a certain cure for a felon, if you apply in time: Take equal parts of gum camphor, gum opium, castile soap and brown sugar. Wet to the consistence of paste with spirits of turpentine and bind on the felon with a soft linen cloth.

A delicious toilet powder for the body is made by mixing two packages of violet rice powder, four grains of powdered musk, five drops of oil of sandalwood and two ounces of powdered orris. After mixing spread in the sun for several days to dry out.

In cleansing hairbrushes use cold water and soda. Dissolve the soda in the cold water and then shake the brush around in it, rinsing off as soon as the bristles look clean. Stand the brush up on the end of the handle to dry, and don't put it in the sun or near a hot stove.

The best of all rules for successful housekeeping, and making both ends meet, is to "pay as you go." Beyond all countries in the world, ours is the one in which the credit system is the most abused and most used. Passbooks are the bane and pest of domestic economy, a perpetual plague, vexation and swindle.

To clean the railing of banisters, wash off all the dirt with soap and water, and when dry rub with two parts of linseed oil and one of turpentine. If the odor of turpentine is objectionable, use two parts of sweet or cotton-seed oil and one part of alcohol, but the mixture of linseed oil and turpentine is more desirable.

Mothers are nearly always to blame if the baby's ears stick out. Never tie anything behind a child's ears like bonnet strings or hat elastic. Always lay the baby flat on its ear when sleeping. In extreme cases, a skeleton cap should be worn, but a silk handkerchief drawn over the top of the head, down over the ears and tied securely under the chin, answers the same purpose.

By putting lace handkerchiefs in warm water in which are a few drops of ammonia, and using castile soap, they are easily washed and made a beautiful, clear white. Then do not iron, but spread the handkerchief out smoothly on marble or glass, gently pulling out or shaping the lace. Just before it is entirely dry, fold evenly and smoothly and place under a heavy weight of some kind, and you will find handkerchiefs lasting thrice as long as before.

Irons are pretty sure to gather rust this weather and cause a good deal of bad temper in the laundry. Heat them hot, then run them forcibly over a flannel cloth that has a liberal sprinkling of salt on it. This will remove every bit of the rust—be sure and rub the edges also—then run the iron over a greased cloth or a cloth that has a little white wax or beeswax on it, then treat it to a vigorous rubbing on a perfectly clean white cloth.

If the top of the oven insists on being too hot for pastry or bread, put a pan of water on the grate above the bread that is baking too brown. If the grate has been removed to make room, take a big sheet of the common brown wrapping paper, fold it and lay over the bread or pies or whatever it may be. If that is not at hand use a newspaper. Fold it to as many thicknesses as necessary. The thicker it is the more protection it will afford from the too-hot oven. Of course, it will brown and crisp, but you have only to be careful about slipping it out when it has answered its purpose.

For shampooing get five cents' worth of powdered castile soap, the same quantity of borax; add to them a tablespoonful of alcohol, the beaten yolk of an egg and a pint of hot water. Put this in a bottle and cork. There is sufficient for three or four shampoos, as it only takes a small quantity applied to the scalp to cause a good lather, which must, however, be carefully rinsed out with several basins of warm water. Some people hold the theory that thorough combing is more beneficial to the hair than brushing, as the latter seems to make it come out more, but, like everything else, it is a matter which depends on the hair, as well as the brusher, and, consequently, depends on the judgment of each individual.

A very pretty work a great many energetic women are trying now is that of making their own bead portieres. The Japanese shops sell bamboo and strings of beads, so that one can make curtains to harmonize perfectly with each room. For instance, I saw a charming effect produced by a portiere of green beads used between a dining-room and a small conservatory adjoining. You have no idea how exquisite the plants and flowers looked through this transparent screen of green. Gold beads give a sunshiny effect, and portieres of solid pink or blue beads are dainty in the extreme. A friend who has recently returned from Japan tell me that the curtains strung in patterns are made by having the designs drawn on large pieces of paper and laid on the floor, and then the beads are strung on just as we would trace out the lines in making lace.

When you are paring apples for sauce or pastry, wash them well first. Take the parings and cores, and put them in a pan of water on the stove, and cook till all are tender. Then squeeze the juice through a jelly cloth, and put it in a wide-mouthed jar, with a pound of sugar and a gill of good liquid yeast to a gallon of juice. Let the liquid stand near a warm stove for a month, the mouth of the jar covered with a thin cloth, so that the air can get to the liquid, and bugs and flies cannot. By that time you will have a gallon of splendid vinegar. Pour off a third or more of it in another jar, to settle, and after add to the first jar the juice of your fruit parings every day if you like, pouring off a part of it every week or two, for immediate use. In that way you can keep a perpetual supply on hand, and you can be sure that it will not eat up your pickles or the lining to your stomach, as some of the vinegar that you buy does.

BEIGNETS d'ABRICOTS.

Make a batter as follows: The whites of three eggs beaten lightly and two tablespoonful of potato flour, with the same quantity of powdered sugar and an ounce of melted butter well mixed together. If too stiff, add a small cupful of milk. Make the batter some time before it is required for use. The apricots should not be too ripe; they need not be skinned, but should be cut in quarters, and the stones removed. Well cover each piece with the batter and drop them into clear boiling fat, fry to a light golden brown, drain, cover with powdered sugar and serve hot.

Beignets of peaches, apples, and oranges are made with the same batter. Apples are pared and cored, then cut through to make rings (oranges are divided by the natural divisions). French cooks add a little olive oil to the batter, in place of butter, and water instead of milk. The specialty of the batter thus made is that it clings to whatever is immersed in it and swells into crisp coating.

GREENGAGES GLACÉS.

Boil half a pound of lump sugar with a tumblerful of water. Throw into the syrup some ripe greengages. Let them cook in this until they show signs of breaking, when take them out. Boil the syrup again until it is half reduced in quantity. When it has become cold, dip each greengage into it to become thoroughly coated, and roll them in castor sugar. Set them out separately on sheets of white paper.

FRUIT CHARLOTTE.

Dissolve a packet of lemon jelly in water, add to it a little more sugar and the strained juice of a fresh lemon. Have ready a fancy mould and place a small jam jar in the middle to preserve a hollow centre. Put a weight inside this to keep it in place. Pour a little jelly around this jar, then set the mould on ice for the jelly to solidify. As soon as it will "bear," place a mixed row of ripe raspberries, currants, stoned cherries, &c., or ripe sliced peaches; then pour in more jelly, and when that is set repeat the fruit, and so on until the mould is full. When quite solid, stand the mould in hot water for a minute, to enable it to turn out well, put a little water also inside the jam jar, that you may slip it easily out of its place. Turn the jelly out on a glass dish and fill up the centre with a little cream whipped with white of egg and sugar.

GOOD REMEDY FOR RHEUMATISM.

Drink at least a pint of hot water three times a day, about an hour before eating, and take half small teaspoonful of bread soda after each meal.

"Chalmers' Gelatine is the best for purity and strength in the market, and I recommend it most cordially."

"I recommend the Electro-Silicon as the very best polish for silver, having used it for years."

"Brown's Iron Bitters is a fine tonic for adults and children."

SUNDRIES.

PEACHES IN THE CHAFING-DISH.

(Recipe given by the Chef of " The Inn of William the Conqueror," at Dives, in Normandy, France. Very fine.)

Make a syrup with port wine, wine of cyprus (if not attainable use muscat, or other sweet white wine) and syrup of currants; throw your peaches with skins on into the syrup and boil for twenty minutes. Add rum and kirsch. Put in the chafing-dish and serve hot from it.

CORN MEAL PUDDING BREAD.

One pint of meal, sift before measuring, one pint milk, half pint hot, not boiling, water, two eggs, two tablespoonsful lard, one teaspoonful salt. Pour the hot water on the salt and meal. Mix well, then add other ingredients. Beat the eggs light, melt the lard and pour in last. Pour in a well-greased pan and bake one hour. Be sure that the stove is hot or the meal settles.

WILD DUCKS.

The best way to cook wild ducks is to put them in a very hot pan with no water. Let the stove be very hot. Seventeen minutes will cook a blackhead, and twenty a redhead or canvas-back. This is long enough for epicures.

STEWED SWEETBREADS.

Put them on after they have been blanched, so as to draw out the blood, and remove the sinews, cover with water, just enough to cook them; add several blades of mace. When tender, which will not take long, pour some of the water off, if there is too much for a nice gravy; add a good-sized lump of butter, pepper, and salt, and a cupful of rich cream; a teaspoonful of flour rubbed with the butter. Serve hot with slices of lemon.

BEST TEA PUNCH.

Two pints strong green tea freshly made, one quart bottle champagne, half pint curaçoa, half pint brandy, the grated rind of two lemons and the juice of three, a large orange, sliced, taking out the seeds. Sweeten to taste. Either freeze or serve with crushed ice.

HOW TO CROWN SOUPS.

Take quarter pound brown sugar and put it in a pan over the fire. Let it melt and add about a pint of water. Let it boil, and allow an ironspoonful to a tureen of soup; a little sugar improves soup. This will keep in a bottle corked tight.

GENERAL DIRECTIONS FOR BOILING.

Always have the water boiling hot for puddings, and keep it boiling, don't let it stand. Always immerse any meat to be boiled in boiling water. Poultry is much improved by soaking several hours in skimmed milk, as it makes them white. Let them simmer over the fire a long time, keeping them closely covered. A small piece of bacon and some parsley put inside of the fowl improves it. Some like an onion. A good-sized turkey must boil two hours and a half; chickens, if young, one hour and a half. Always have the water boiling hot for fish. They do not take long to boil, and you can ascertain when they are done as then the bones leave them easily.

PUMPKIN PRESERVE.

Ten lemons, half a pound ginger, green or dried, to twelve pounds of fruit. Three-quarters pound of sugar to one pound of fruit. Lay the pumpkins in the sugar until a syrup is formed, and boil as for other preserves. If the ginger is too strong lessen the quantity.

TOMATO MARMALADE FOR WINTER SOUP.

Peel one bushel of ripe tomatoes, add one peck of gumbo cut up fine, one pint of sliced onions, two teacups of salt, three-quarters cup of fine black pepper. Boil five or six hours, until thick, then put in tin cans and seal *hot*. Very fine.

PARFAIT AUX FRAISES.

Press a quart of fresh strawberries through a fine sieve. Sprinkle over fine pulverized sugar to taste. Whip in a bowl with an egg whisk a quart of *double* cream until it is a stiff froth; stir in the strawberry pulp; put in mould and pack away in ice, without further stirring.

Parfait of peaches, raspberries or bananas, made in the same way.

STRAWBERRY ICE CREAM.

Boil one quart of sugar in two quarts of water half an hour, making a syrup. Let it get quite cold. Mash three boxes (a short three quarts), of strawberries, so that all the strawberries are broken and they are mashed rather fine. Add the cold syrup; freeze, stirring hard half an hour. If two or three quarts are made, the cylinder form of the ice cream machine looks very well. In this case, take out the dasher when the cream is frozen and smooth the cream into shape at top, when packing away; or, the cream can be packed away, pressed into another mould. Serve with whipped cream around the mould.

Raspberry Ice Cream, made as last receipt, is especially good.

FELICIA'S APPLES.

Pare and take out cores of good cooking apples, leaving them whole. Boil them in sweetened water. When the apples are done, take them out and let the water boil down to half quantity. Flavor with anything (Felicia's mixed lemon and vanilla extracts, half and half), and add a little corn starch to thicken slightly. Pour this over the apples, or dish in which they are to be served. Bake in oven giving a little color. Serve with cream.

STUFFED PEPPERS.

Take either green or red peppers, cut off the top, scoop out the inside. Chop up some veal very fine, add salt, a little of the inside of the peppers, some butter, chopped parsley and a little cream. Stuff the peppers with this, put a little lump of butter on top and a few cracker crumbs. Heat thoroughly and serve hot on a napkin.

BONED TURKEY.

To bone a turkey, lay the bird on its breast on the table, and with a sharp knife make a clean cut down the length of the back. Without cutting through the skin cut towards and disjoint the wings. Then cut towards and disjoint the thighs, leaving the wing and thigh bones in the flesh. Now proceed to cut all the flesh from the carcass of the bird, keeping it entire and being careful not to cut through the skin. When it is all removed lay its skin down upon the table and take out the wing and thigh bones without cutting through the skin.

GALANTINE OF TURKEY.

For galantine of turkey put the carcass over the fire in four quarts of cold water, with a bouquet of herbs, an onion, peeled and stuck with ten cloves, a carrot and turnip, peeled, and bring it to a boil, skimming it clear. Either make a forcemeat of one pound each of fresh veal and pork, finely minced, or use an equal quantity of nice sausage-meat unflavored with sage, or chicken may be used. Season the forcemeat highly with a teaspoonful of mixed ground cloves, nutmeg, mace and allspice, a teaspoonful of salt and a saltspoonful of pepper. Add to it a glass of sherry or madeira wine and one raw egg for each pound of the forcemeat, also one-quarter of a pound of larding pork, the same amount of cold tongue, cut in one inch dice, and mix it thoroughly. Lay the flesh of the turkey on the table skin down; put the forcemeat on it and fold the turkey up over it in the form of the bird. Roll it tightly in a strong clean cloth, tie it with tape in the centre and near the ends of the roll; fasten the ends firmly with strong twine, taking care to make the roll compact and secure. Put the turkey into the water containing the carcass, and boil it slowly for three hours, replenishing the stock with boiling water, so as to have the turkey entirely covered with it. When the turkey has boiled three hours take it up, remove the cloth, wash it in cold water and tie the turkey up again in it; put it between two platters under a heavy weight, and let it stand over night to cool. Strain the stock in which it was boiled, and let that stand over night so that all the fat can be removed. Remove all the fat, put the stock over the fire, add to it two ounces of gelatine dissolved in a pint of cold water, and clarify it as for consomme. Strain it through flannel until perfectly clear; pour it into two shallow moulds; color one dark brown with caramel, and cool until the jelly is firm. Lay the galantine, or boned turkey, on a dish, and garnish it with the jelly cut in fanciful shapes. Serve it cold.

ORANGE OMELETTE.

For orange omelette grate the yellow rind and squeeze the juice of one orange; beat the yolks of three eggs to a cream and add the orange rind and juice to them, with two teaspoonsful of powdered sugar; beat the whites to a stiff froth. Meantime have a clear, smooth frying-pan on the fire heating, with a piece of butter as large as a chestnut. When the pan is hot put the omelette into it, lift it constantly from the bottom of the pan with a fork, piling it in the middle. When it seems nearly done pile it at one side of the pan; hold a hot dish close to it, and turn it out lightly and quickly. Dust it with powdered sugar and serve at once.

OMELETTE SOUFFLÉE.

For omelette soufflée mix to a cream three ounces of powdered sugar, the yolks of two eggs and a teaspoonful of vanilla essence; beat the whites of four eggs to a stiff froth; gently stir the yolks and sugar into the whites; put the mixture by the tablespoonful on a buttered gratin dish or soufflée pan and bake it golden brown in a moderate oven, dusting it with powdered sugar when it is half done; serve it the instant it is done or it will fall.

BARBECUED HAM.

Put into the dish one tablespoonful of butter, one of tomato catsup, one of wine. When boiling, put in one thin slice of boiled ham. As soon as boiling hot, serve.

CHINESE EGGS.

Cut hard-boiled eggs into thin slices; put one tablespoonful of butter in the dish with one tablespoonful of flour; mix and add a half-pint of milk; stir until boiling; add egg, half teaspoonful salt, dash of pepper; when hot, serve.

SAUTED OYSTERS.

Drain twenty-five fat oysters, put one tablespoonful butter in chafing-dish, when hot turn in the oysters. When gills curl season with salt and pepper and serve.

CURRY OF OYSTERS.

Put one tablespoonful butter, one teaspoonful curry powder, one of onion juice in the dish; when hot add twenty-five oysters, and three tablespoonsful stock. When boiling, serve.

LOBSTER NEWBURG.

Cut a boiled lobster into pieces about one inch square. Put into the chafing-dish one tablespoonful butter, one tablespoonful flour, mix. Beat yolks of two eggs, add one gill of cream, stir until boiled; add lobster, heat, season, add four tablespoonsful sherry and serve. Chicken, shrimp and terrapin may be served same.

BAKED TOMATOES WITH CORN.

Scoop out the inside of tomatoes as for a "farci," cutting out a small round piece at the stem end. Remove the seeds and replace the pulp with some corn grated from the cob and well seasoned with butter, pepper and salt. Bake in a pudding dish and send them to the table in the same dish when well browned.

HOW TO PREPARE POTATOES.

Potatoes go very nicely with fish, and this is the way to prepare peeled or boiled potatoes: Thoroughly wash the required number of potatoes and peel them very thin, and lay them in cold salted water; while the potatoes are being peeled, put some water in a saucepan over the fire, with a level teaspoonful of salt to about a quart of water; after the potatoes are peeled, put them into the boiling water and boil them until they are tender enough to be pierced easily with a fork; then drain them, put over them a clean towel folded several times, set the saucepan on a brick on the back of the stove, where the potatoes will keep hot without burning, and let them stand until they are required for use.

BAKED SWEETBREADS.

Blanch some sweetbreads as already directed; score them deeply on the top, lay them in a buttered baking-pan, season them with salt and pepper and squeeze over two or three the juice of a sour orange, quickly brown them in a hot oven; transfer them to a hot dish, pour over them the drippings from the pan, and garnish them with sour orange slices; serve them hot.

HOW TO BROIL A BEEFSTEAK.

First scrape the surface of the steak with the back of a knife to remove any bits of bone remaining after cutting it; then trim off the tough outer skin and all gristle and excess of fat, the natural proportion of fat being about one-third the steak; wipe the steak with a damp cloth, but do not wash it, because that would detract from its flavor and nutriment; place the steak on a gridiron, close to a very hot fire, and quickly brown on both sides. When it is brown on both sides season it with salt and pepper, and finish cooking it to the desired degree. About fifteen minutes at a very hot fire will cook a steak an inch and a half thick, medium rare; twenty to twenty-five minutes will cook it moderately well done. When it is done to desired degree put it on a hot platter, season it with salt, pepper and butter, and serve it at once.

FRIED BEEFSTEAK.

Follow first the directions given in the recipe for broiled beefsteak for preparing the steak for cooking. Put over the fire a frying-pan, and let it get hot enough to sizz when the steak is put into it. Put the steak into the pan, set it over the hottest part of the fire and brown it as fast as possible, first on one side and then the other. When the steak is brown on both sides, move the frying-pan to where the steak can cook to the desired degree without burning. When the steak is done transfer it to a hot dish, season it with salt, pepper and butter, and serve it at once. A steak cooked in this way has all its juices preserved, and in some respects is nearly as good as a broiled steak. This method of cooking a beefsteak is often desirable, because an open, broiling fire is not always available.

PINEAPPLE PUDDING. (Fine.)

Line a dish with rich pastry, peel and grate a large pineapple; weigh the pineapple after it is grated and allow an equal weight of sugar and half the weight of butter. Mix the butter and sugar to a cream, beat in the yolks of five eggs, then add the grated pineapple and half a pint of cream; last of all, beat the five whites to a stiff froth, mix them lightly with the other ingredients, put the mixture into the pastry-lined dish, and bake the pudding in a moderate oven until the pastry is done. Serve it hot.

SHADDOCKS FOR LUNCHEON.

Cut in baskets, keep the baskets in the ice chest until wanted. Fill a short time before serving with small pieces of the inside (freed from the partition skins), sweetened. Just before serving partly cover the tops with small pieces of ice and a spoonful of Maraschino. It is very good without liquor. Tie a little bunch of flowers or leaves at side of handle with ribbon.

TIMBALE OF BEEF,
OR ANY OTHER MEAT—VENISON, VEAL, ETC.

One pint of meat pulp put through the machine five or six times, or sieve if one has no machine. Cook to a paste one cupful milk and a scant cupful of bread crumbs. Beat very light three whole eggs together, mix all together, and put through sieve; season with salt and pepper, and fry in pans with a little onion.

SARDINE FRITTERS.

Drain from the fishes as much of the oil in which they were preserved as you can. Carefully remove the skins and the backbone; if large divide in two; otherwise replace the halves after taking out the bone, sprinkle a little lemon juice and cayenne over them, and dip into a light frying batter—allow a small dessertspoonful for each fish. Fry in boiling fat, drain on blotting paper, and serve at once with a garnish of parsley.

SAUSAGE ROLLS. (From Mrs. President Harrison.)

Take half a pound of sausages, parboil them and remove the skins, and cut each sausage in two. Take some good light paste, roll it out to an eighth of an inch thick, cut into square pieces, roll up the pieces of sausage in the paste, slightly moisten the edges and press the ends together; brush the rolls over with the yolk of egg and bake in a quick oven. The remains of pressed beef, or roast beef and ham, seasoned with spice, pepper, salt, and a pinch of finely-chopped herbs, and then moistened with an egg and made into small rolls, can be substituted for the sausages.

PRUNE PUDDING.

Cook one cup of prunes until soft in as little water as possible, and rub through a colander. Beat the whites of five eggs to a stiff froth and add to the prunes. Mix a half cup of sugar and a half teaspoonful of cream of tartar thoroughly and sift into the prunes. Put in a baking dish and bake a few minutes in a moderate oven to cook the egg. Serve with a custard made as follows:

Custard.—Put one pint of milk into a double boiler to scald. Beat the yolks of four eggs until light. Add to them two tablespoonsful of sugar. When the milk is scalded pour it into the egg mixture, then pour the whole back into the double boiler. Bring to the scalding point, remove from the stove and add one teaspoonful of vanilla. Stand away to cool.

FIG LAYER CAKE.

Put half a cup of sugar and one cup of water in a saucepan, stir until the sugar is dissolved, then add one pound of figs chopped fine. Stew all together until the mixture is soft and smooth. Take from the fire and cool. For the layers.—Cream, half cup of butter, add very gradually one and a half cups of sugar, beating until the whole is light and creamy. Then add, little by little, one cup of water and two and a half cups of sifted flour. Beat thoroughly until all the flour is beaten in smoothly, then stir in two teaspoonsful of yeast powder. Have ready the whites of four eggs beaten to a stiff froth. Stir these in carefully and add one teaspoonful of flavoring extract. Bake in three layers. Spread the fig mixture between the layers and on top put an icing as follows:

Gelatine Icing.—Put one tablespoonful of gelatine in a bowl with one tablespoonful of cold water; let it soak ten minutes. Add two tablespoonsful of boiling water; stir until dissolved and add enough pulverized sugar to make it the proper consistency to spread. Flavor and spread the icing on the cake, then stand in a cool place to dry.

NUT DROPS.

Cream, half cup of butter, adding little by little one cup of sugar, beat well. Add half a cup of water, stir until well mixed, then add one egg well beaten. Sift two and a half cups of flour, add to the mixture and stir until smooth. Then add one cup of nuts chopped fine, stir them in thoroughly, and add one teaspoonful of yeast powder. Mix well; drop on buttered tins and bake until brown.

ECLAIRS.

Put one cup of water into a saucepan, add two ounces of butter, and when it boils hard throw in one cup of flour. Stir rapidly until it forms a ball and leaves the sides of the pan. Take from the fire and stand aside to cool. When cold stir in four eggs, unbeaten, one at a time. Beat the whole vigorously. Put this batter into a pastry bag and press out on well-buttered tins, making the eclairs about five inches long and placing them two inches apart on the tins. Bake for about a half hour in a quick oven until perfectly light. Make an incision in one side and fill with the following mixture:

Filling.—Put one cup of milk in a double boiler. Beat four eggs and four tablespoonsful of sugar together until light, add one tablespoonful of cornstarch; mix thoroughly. Stir into the scalding milk; stir until the mixture is thick and smooth and stand aside to cool. Add one teaspoonful of vanilla just before filling the eclairs.

Icing.—Take two ounces of cocoa melted with two ounces of pulverized sugar and stir until it makes a paste. Dip the bottom of each eclair into this and set aside to harden. Eclairs may be filled with whipped cream or preserved fruits and iced with fruit icings if desired.

RUM FRUIT.

One quart of Jamaica rum, seven pounds fruit, seven pounds sugar. Put one pound strawberries in a stone jar, sprinkle over one pound granulated sugar, then pour over the quart of rum. Put a plate over the fruit to keep it under the rum. After three days put in another pound of fruit and another pound of sugar. Each time you add fruit stir from bottom with silver spoon. A nice combination—strawberries, raspberries, currants, cherries (stoned), bananas, peaches and pineapples. When finished pack in stone jars.

SALMON SANDWICH.

Spanish onions chopped fine, and mixed with twice the quantity of canned salmon, is a fine filling for a sandwich to be eaten at bedtime. Season with salt, red pepper, and a little vinegar.

SARDINES.

Sardines are excellent mixed with the chopped pulp and grated yellow rind of lemon. Season with pepper and salt and spread on hot toast or toasted crackers. Two lemons for one small can of sardines.

A NEW WAY OF COOKING LIMA BEANS.

If, when you are dining out, you receive lima beans that have a delicious yet unfamiliar flavor, you may conclude that they are cooked after a new fashioned recipe, with cocoanut milk and lemon juice. The beans are first boiled in the usual way, that is, rapidly in boiling water for a quarter of an hour, and then more slowly fifteen minutes longer, drained and cooled. After that the outer covering is removed without breaking the beans, and they are covered with cocoanut milk, and allowed to simmer eight minutes. Season just before dishing with salt to taste, a tablespoonful of butter, and a teaspoonful of lemon juice. The milk is prepared by pouring a quart of boiling water over a grated cocoanut. Stir vigorously, and when the water begins to cool, squeeze and press out of the nut all the fatty substance possible. Strain through a cooking-napkin. Mrs. Gibson used the top layer of this milk, which is like a cream, for some salad-dressings. The milk beneath is the part used on the beans.

AMATEUR SURGERY.

There are times when a simple thing in amateur surgery goes a great way towards easing pain. On New England farms the women all know what to do with a cut or burned finger.

The materials for the operation are always close at hand. Under the shell of every egg there is a white gelatinous film that is in itself a perfect skin. If the cut is not very large a piece of this film, fresh and wet, laid over the wound, will prevent soreness and in a great measure hasten the growth of the new skin.

The film adheres closely, keeps out all foreign matter, and draws the edges of the wound together. It will not come off easily, and another advantage that women will appreciate is that it does not show.

There is a woman in New York who has another simple remedy for cuts and burns. When a member of the family has a burn or cut she drags forth a bottle of shellac varnish and industriously paints the wound. The varnish, drying, acts in the same manner as the egg film, and at the same time is almost as invisible. The remedy is an old one in carpenter shops, and has been proved by use to be an efficacious one.

MISCELLANEOUS.

In case you have no benzine or alcohol at hand cologne will be found just as effectual in removing grease spots.

A delicious way of serving the common small chestnuts is to roast them, then shell, sprinkle with sugar and cover with rum, which must be lighted and allowed to burn until all the alcohol is consumed.

Black lace will resume much of its pristine beauty if washed in thick suds made of tar soap. The lace must be allowed to dry without rinsing, as the tar imparts a slight stiffness, which is very desirable.

Crackers prepared as follows are nice to serve with soup or bouillon or for a Sunday night tea. Saltines or water crackers should be slightly buttered, sprinkled with grated cheese and thoroughly browned in the oven.

Home-made marrons glaces may be prepared by boiling the chestnuts until thoroughly cooked, then dipping them into a syrup of sugar and water, such as is used for crystallizing cherries and walnuts.

Cinnamon almonds are new and delicious, and are made the same as the salted nuts, omitting, of course, that condiment.

Soapsuds are said to be excellent for making plants grow and blossom, on account of the potash contained therein.

GOOD WHITEWASH.

When oil paint cannot be afforded for fences and outhouses, a good whitewash will look well and durable. The following wash is excellent.

Take a clean barrel that will hold water. Put into it half a bushel of quicklime, and slake it by pouring over it boiling water sufficient to cover it four or five inches deep, and stirring it until slaked. When quite slaked, dissolve it in water, and add two pounds of sulphate of zinc, which may be had at any of the druggists, and one of common salt, and which in a few days will cause the whitewash to harden on the woodwork. Add sufficient water to bring it to the consistency of thick whitewash.

To make the above wash of a pleasant cream color, add three pounds yellow ochre.

For fawn color add four pounds umber, one pound Indian red, one pound lampblack.

For grey or stone color, add four pounds umber and twenty-one pounds lampblack.

The color may be put on with a common whitewash brush, and will be found much more durable than common whitewash.

A SURE CURE FOR CORNS OR BUNIONS.

Keep them wrapped in *oil silk* all the time, so as to exclude all air.

COMPLEXION WASH.

If there should be any ladies who are afflicted with any defect of their complexion, they may make a wash which should be applied morning and evening. It is not immediate in giving a white, painted look, but a week's use of it will prove that it is better than any of the so-called beautifiers. Take one fluid ounce tincture benzoin, and turn it slowly into eight ounces of rose water, shaking it all the time. Then take one ounce pure glycerine and one teaspoonful of borate of soda and stir them together, adding one ounce of emulsion of bitter almonds. Stir these well together, and add them slowly to the rose water and benzoin, shaking all well. If this should smart the skin, add water to it until it does not. This is the famous Egyptian wash known and esteemed so highly, and is most excellent. The face, neck, hands and arms should be washed with tepid water and rubbed dry. This, then, should be applied with a sponge all over, letting it dry on the skin. It will leave a soft, clear, satiny surface, smelling deliciously refreshing and pleasant. Wrinkles and discolorations disappear gradually, and even pittings, as there is a peculiar process going on as long as it is used. The application forms a sort of transparent varnish on the skin, which cracks and peels off in microscopic particles, not visible to the eye, and each bit that comes off carries just so much of the outer skin with it, and so, imperceptibly, a delicate new skin is exposed, and the old clogged pores are set free and the sluggish circulation in the face is invigorated, and six months' conscientious use of this will restore to the most faded woman a fresh and blooming complexion, without the use of any cosmetic. Some ladies might not like the polished smoothness it gives, but such could dust a little rice powder or Récamier powder over it. Many gentlemen have found it a very soothing and refreshing application after shaving. A bottle of the proportions mentioned above would cost, made up by a druggist, about one dollar, and it would last a year, and prove invaluable all the time for moths, freckles, tan, sunburn and chapped skin, to say nothing of wrinkles and that general withered look that is so annoying to those who care for their appearance. Its emollient and healing qualities are remarkable.

"I can recommend most highly the 'S. and W.' Brand of Tomatoes and Sugar Corn put up by Chas. T. Wrightson, as

I have visited his factories and know he will have nothing but what is first-class. I use his tomatoes and think them very fine."

"The Queen Anne Cream prepared by the Bertha Company will be found a most valuable food for skin, muscles and nerves. *It is not a cosmetic.* Having used this myself I can recommend it to all, even children who have delicate nerves. It is very strengthening.

"I consider Sexton's Grand Heater, the very best stove in use to-day. I have had two of them in constant use for twenty years, and find them invaluable for heat and safety.'

"The Cresta Blanca Souvenir vintages are the very finest American wines on the market to-day, and are fully equal to the finest imported wine. So decided by the best connoisseurs of wines in this country."

"I recommend Madame Harriet Hubbard Ayer's Récamier Toilet Preparations as being very pure and beneficial.

"I consider Brown's Iron Bitters the very finest made, and a wonderful tonic for malaria and nervous prostration. I have used it for years,—always receive great benefit from it."

The best baking powder made is, as shown by analysis, the "Royal."

Gnus Edsan

Com'r of Health, New-York City.

I regard the Royal Baking Powder as the best manufactured.

Marion Harland,

Author of "Common Sense in the Household."

ROYAL BAKING POWDER CO., 106 WALL ST., NEW-YORK.

Pure OLIVE OIL

is almost unknown and unobtainable in this country. If you insist upon getting the genuine brand,

LAUTIER FILS, *IN GRASSE, near Nice (France)*,

you will receive not only a genuine and pure oil, but at the same time the best obtainable; pressed in Mr. L. F's factory from own grown Olives, packed and shipped in original bottles and tins. This oil has NO EQUAL in quality. Obtained highest awards at all exhibitions. Leading chemists from all over the world testify to its purity. Used in high-class hotels and clubs here and abroad.

WHOLESALE AGENTS:

GEO. LUEDERS & CO.,

NEW YORK: 218 PEARL STREET.

CHICAGO: 90 LAKE STREET.

Eighth Avenue Bank,

EIGHTH AVENUE AND 23D STREET,

NEW YORK.

Capital, $100,000.   Surplus, $5,000.

WOLSTAN R. BROWN, President.   ANDREW McLEAN, Vice-Pres.
FLOYD S. PATTERSON, Cashier.

Transacts a general Banking business. Individual and family accounts are solicited. A room has been provided especially for ladies with private windows to the banking departments.

THE
Virginia Waukesha Lithia Springs Water,
STAUNTON, VA.

One of the few to which was awarded a Medal and Diploma of the Great World's Fair at Chicago.

Nature's Own Remedy for

Diabetes, Bright's Disease, Calculi and other Diseases of the Urinary Organs; Dyspepsia, Torpid Liver, Constipation, Gout, Asthma, Malaria, Insomnia and all Maladies marked by Poverty of Blood, Torpor of Secreting Organs, or Nervous Debility.

DAVIS A. KAYSER, Proprietor,
STAUNTON, VA.

Joel Gutman & Co.,

IMPORTING RETAILERS AND JOBBERS OF

Silks, Cloaks, Velvets, Dry Goods,

Linens, Curtains, Millinery, Laces,

Hosiery, &c.

112-122 North Eutaw Street.

Huyler's Bonbons — AND — Chocolates.

Specialties in Favors and Confections in Choice Colors for Dinners and Luncheons.

1119 F Street, Cor. 12th,   WASHINGTON, D. C.

Candies Carefully Packed and Shipped to all parts of the Country by mail or express.

M. V. & L. A. CUMMINS,

Ladies' Hair Dressers and Hair Cutters,

SHAMPOOING A SPECIALTY.

813 14TH STREET, N. W.   WASHINGTON, D. C.

AMERICAN AND EUROPEAN PLANS.

ABSOLUTELY FIRE-PROOF.

THE BERTHA COMPANY,
Skin and Hair Specialists,
406 Park Ave.

Are Baltimore's authority on Head, Hair and Face Treatments.

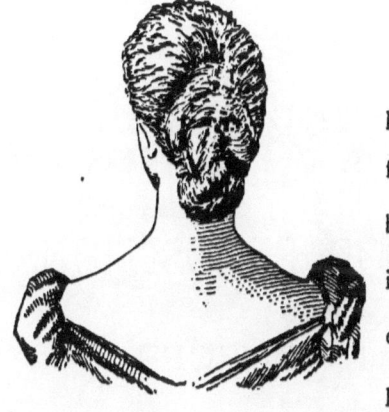

They have [15] remedies put up with full directions for home use, that have been in use for 30 years, improvements being made every year until they are perfect.

The Principal of The Bertha Company is the most renowned Specialist for the head and face in America, being a practical woman with a perfect knowledge as to handling the hair; can in one treatment prevent what would take years to cure.

Heavy folds in the face or white hair can be restored by curing the nerve.

SEND FOR BLUE BOOK.

WALTER BAKER & CO.,

THE LARGEST MANUFACTURERS OF

Pure, High Grade Cocoas and Chocolates

ON THIS CONTINENT, HAVE RECEIVED

HIGHEST AWARDS

FROM THE GREAT

INDUSTRIAL

— AND —

FOOD EXPOSITIONS

IN EUROPE

AND AMERICA.

Unlike the Dutch Process, no Alkalies or Dyes are used in any of their preparations. Their delicious

BREAKFAST COCOA,

is absolutely pure and soluble, and *costs less than one cent a cup.*

SOLD BY GROCERS EVERYWHERE.

WALTER BAKER & CO.,
DORCHESTER, MASS.

SEXTON'S IMPROVED NEW BALTIMORE RANGE.

With Horizontal Boiler and Hot Air Attachment. The latest and best.

This Range is a perfect baker. Economical in the use of fuel, is heavy and durable. The most desirable Range in the market.

SEND FOR TESTIMONIAL BOOK.

S. B. SEXTON & SON,
Manufacturers of Fire-Place Heaters, Furnaces and Ranges.

Store, 23 E. Lombard St.   Foundry, 511 to 527 W. Conway St., Baltimore, Md.

Indigestion

Horsford's Acid Phosphate

Is the most effective and agreeable remedy in existence for preventing indigestion, and relieving those diseases arising from a disordered stomach.

It acts as a general tonic and vitalizer, promoting digestion, and quieting and restoring the nervous system to healthful vigor.

Physicians of all schools testify to its great value, and prescribe it freely with excellent results.

Descriptive pamphlet free.

Rumford Chemical Works,

PROVIDENCE, R. I.

HUTZLER BROTHERS,

212-214-216-218 N. HOWARD STREET,

THE LEADING DRY GOODS HOUSE OF

BALTIMORE.

MAIL ORDERS RECEIVE PROMPT ATTENTION.

BARTON

IMPORTER OF

Gowns, Wraps, and Materials,

405 North Charles St.,

Baltimore.

BRAND.

Tomatoes AND Sugar Corn.

UNEXCELLED IN QUALITY.

ASK YOUR GROCER FOR THEM.

PACKED BY

CHAS. T. WRIGHTSON,

EASTON, MD.

A Woman's Life

to be happy must be a healthy one. The many causes of ill health need not be enumerated here, but suffice to say that thousands of women living to-day who were broken down—either from diseases peculiar to their sex—raising children—overworked, or worn out by the multitude of household annoyances, were cured by the great strengthening medicine, **Brown's Iron Bitters**—it is pleasant to take—will not stain or injure the teeth as all other iron medicines will. **Brown's Iron Bitters** is specially recommended for weak and suffering women, nursing mothers and weak and puny children. **Have you never tried it for yourself?**

White Plains, Ga., June 29, 1894.

About nine or ten years since I was broken down in health and suffered from **Extreme Nervousness.** Also, about that time severe neuralgic pains would afflict different members of my body; sometimes the pain would be in my eyes and head, sometimes in my hands, and often in my shoulders and neck. I used many remedies but found none so good as Brown's Iron Bitters. I have used a few bottles each year since then, always with good effect. I have often advised others to take the Bitters, and know of seven different families who use and praise Brown's Iron Bitters from having my experience given them.

Yours truly,

MRS. VILLA H. MAPP.

John N. Matthews & Co.

TEAS, WINES, GROCERIES,

Cor. Garden and Biddle Streets,

BALTIMORE, MD.

Armour's Extract of BEEF

BEST AND MOST ECONOMICAL STOCK FOR SOUPS.

SEND ADDRESS TO
ARMOUR & CO CHICAGO
FOR
LITTLE BOOK OF RECIPES, FREE.

Armour's

VEGETOLE.

ONE POUND OF VEGETOLE WILL DO THE WORK OF TWO POUNDS OF ANY OTHER SHORTENING. MAKES LIGHT AND WHOLESOME PASTRY.

Armour's Celebrated BUTTERINE.

ARMOUR'S IS THE MOST PERFECT BUTTERINE MADE.
NO WORRY ABOUT THE UNCERTAIN FLAVOR OR PRICE OF BUTTER ONCE YOU START BUYING THIS.

Armour's

BEST IN THE WORLD
☆ ARMOUR'S ☆

STAR HAMS AND BACON
NOTHING FINER MADE.

Chafing Dishes in Gorham Electro Plate

Consisting of CHAFING DISH AND COVER,
STAND AND LAMP, HOT WATER PAN,
AND CUTLET DISH (if wanted).

These dishes are made in a variety of sizes and are both oval and round in form, polished silver finish with ivory handles. Illustrations and prices sent by mail on application to

J. E. CALDWELL & CO.,
902 CHESTNUT STREET,   PHILADELPHIA.

A copy of a most useful book of directions, containing one hundred recipes for the Chafing Dish will be given free, to every purchaser of a dish, or may be had separately by mail. Price $1.00.

For Good Pastry, use
Lea's "Pastry" Flour.

For Good Bread, use
Lea's "Best" or Clifton FFF.

Also Manufacturers of all Grades of

Wheat and Corn Products.

THE WM. LEA & SONS CO.,
WILMINGTON, DEL.

Have you tried

Burchell's Spring Leaf Tea?

Enjoy a pure, fragrant, delicious Tea—so readily and certainly prepared; a veritable household comfort—

At 50 cents a pound.

N. W. BURCHELL,

1325 F Street,

Send for Sample.   WASHINGTON, D. C.

Seligson's

→ 1884 ←

IMPORTER AND WHOLESALE DEALER IN

Wines, Cognacs, and Whiskies,

Sole Agent for Passadena California Wines,

Fine Cigars a Specialty,

1200 and 1202 Pennsylvania Avenue, N. W.,

WASHINGTON, D. C.

Compliments of

Seligson's.

Telephone Call 1638.

Overland Monthly,

EDITED BY
Rounsevelle Wildman.

Established 1868.

The only Magazine on the Pacific Coast.

Its literary matter represents the best thoughts of such writers as Hjalmar Hjorth Boyesen, Charles Warren Stoddard, Edith M. Thomas, Joaquin Miller.

Its illustrations show in the best style the glories of the Pacific Coast.

It is a pictorial history of the Great West. It covers the whole basin of the Pacific, including China, Japan, and Corea. You want it, so does your family.

One Sample Copy, 10c. Single Numbers, 25c.
Yearly Subscription, $3.00.

All Postmasters are authorized to take subscriptions.

Overland Monthly Pub. Co.

SAN FRANCISCO, CAL.

All women require some.   Some women require all.

The Récamier Toilet Preparations.

Yes, my little dear, and so do thousands of other mammas.

They are used by the most famous and most beautiful women in the world. Among others, Her Royal Highness the Princess of Wales, Mesdames Patti, Bernhardt, Langtry, Clara Louise Kellog, Lillian Russell, James Brown Potter. They are recommended by physicians and clergymen. They will preserve a good skin and cure a bad complexion.

Récamier Cream—for tan, sunburn and all skin diseases, and for the nursery.

Récamier Balm—a liquid beautifier pure and simple.
Récamier Moth and Freckle Lotion.
Récamier Powder—stays on and does not make the face shine.
Récamier Depilatory—guaranteed to remove superfluous hair permanently, without pain or inflammation on or after application.
Récamier Wrinkle Specific—the successful tissue builder.

On receipt of address will forward free of charge sample of Récamier Powder and Circular.

If your druggist has not our preparations in stock, you may obtain them by addressing

HARRIET HUBBARD AYER,
RÉCAMIER MFG. CO.,
131 West 31st Street, N. Y.

Mutual Reserve Fund Life Association.

E. B. HARPER, President.

1881
HOME OFFICE:
MUTUAL RESERVE BUILDING,
Cor. Broadway & Duane St., N. Y.
1894

60 % Dividend Saved in Premiums. 60

The total cost for the past 13 years for $10,000 Insurance in the Mutual Reserve amounts to less than Old System Companies charge for $4,500 at ordinary life rates—the saving in premiums being equal to a cash dividend of nearly 60 per cent.

35 MILLION DOLLARS SAVED IN PREMIUMS 35

THE MUTUAL RESERVE, by reducing the rates to harmonize with the payments to widows and orphans, and by judicious economy in expenses of management has already *saved* its Policy-holders more than *Thirty-five Million Dollars in Premiums.*

THE ELOQUENCE OF RESULTS.

Number of Policies in Force, over 85,000
Claims paid every 60 days, approximates $500,000
Bi-monthly Income exceeds 750,000
Reserve Emergency Fund exceeds 3,820,000
Total Death Claims Paid exceeds 20,500,000
New Business Received in 1893, over 64,000,000
New Business, January to December, 1894, ... 70,346,730
Total Insurance in force exceeds 280,000,000

EXCELLENT POSITIONS OPEN in its Agency Department in every Town, City and State, to experienced and successful business men, who will find the *Mutual Reserve the very best Association they can work for.*

Further information supplied by any of the Managers, General, or Special Agents, in the United States, Canada, Great Britain, France and Sweden. Correspondence with the Home Office invited.

Any Lady,

Who is not conversant with the various uses of our Yeast for Plain and Fancy Vienna Baking, by mailing to our address 25 tin-foil wrappers with our YELLOW LABEL AND SIGNATURE attached, shall receive by return mail, in care of her grocer, free, our "HANDY BOOK FOR HANDY PEOPLE," containing recipes for all kinds of Baking and Fancy Dishes, and either of our beautiful Banners entitled "Little Sunshine" or "Little Sweetheart." These Banners are works of art and would grace the walls of any home in the land.

FLEISCHMANN & CO.,

Original Manufacturers of COMPRESSED YEAST.   CINCINNATI, OHIO.

☞ Send your grocer's name and your own address in full.

Blout's

Millinery Establishment.

The latest and finest productions of Foreign and Domestic Markets, in Round Hats and Bonnets together with a complete stock of Millinery belongings always on hand.

I. L. BLOUT,

710 Seventh Street, N. W.,   WASHINGTON, D. C.

Established 1872.

Prepared Especially for Family Use.

Chalmers' Gelatine.

Absolutely Pure
and
Without Odor.

Healthful.

Superior to that
made from
Calves-foot.

Nutritious.

PACKET MAKES TWO QUARTS OF RICH SPARKLING JELLY.

CHALMERS' GELATINE

Is the very best made, and costs the least money.

Endorsed by Eminent Chemists, Chefs, Cooking Lecturers and Physicians.

ABSOLUTELY PURE.

Requires no eggs to clarify. Contains no acid, so you need use no alkalies.

Insist on your Grocer giving you

CHALMERS' GELATINE,

FACTORY:—Williamsville, N. Y.

The Heinekamp
Upright Pianos

have attained every requirement in tone, touch, durability and style.

We respectfully refer to the following persons and institutions who have them in use.

The Randolph Harrison School,	-	Baltimore.
Miss Carter's School,	- -	- Catonsville.
Sisters of Notre Dame,	- -	Baltimore.
Norwood Institute, -	-	- Washington, D. C.
Augusta Female Seminary,	-	- Staunton, Va.
Mrs. Hon. C. H. Gibson, -	-	- Easton, Md.
Hon. W. L. Wilson,	- -	Charlestown, W. Va.

and hundreds of others.

Wm. Heinekamp & Son,
6 E. Baltimore Street,
BALTIMORE, MD.

Gold Medal Paris Exposition, 1889.

Cresta Blanca Souvenir Vintages.

* *

HIGHEST AWARD WHEREVER EXHIBITIONS HAVE BEEN MADE.

* *

CRESTA BLANCA is situated a few miles south of the town of Livermore, Alameda County.

It was specially selected on account of soil and climatic conditions which gave promise of the highest possible excellence in wines of the Sauterne and Claret types. No mistake was made in this selection, for to-day Cresta Blanca wines compare favorably with the finest vintages of France and are served to the guests of all the leading hotels, restaurants and clubs on the Pacific Coast.

Only a limited quantity is made annually. No expense is spared in the making and care of the wines, and when ready for consumption they are carefully bottled.

Parties ordering these wines should see that the words **CRESTA BLANCA** are on every bottle. A new brand of wine has lately been put on the market and is being sold by one of the leading grocers and other unprincipled parties as Cresta Blanca or Wetmore's wines. Such wines should be refused if Cresta Blanca wines are ordered.

All orders should be sent to

CHAS. A. WETMORE,

Livermore, Alameda County,

319 Pine St., San Francisco.   CALIFORNIA.

"Old Virginia" Brand

High Grade Preserves, Jellies, American Jams, Ketchups, Sauces, Mince Meat, and finest Table delicacies.

Prepared from Famous Old Virginia Home-made Recipes.

Quality Guaranteed.

Ask your Grocer for them.

Write for Illustrated Catalogue.

Trade Mark Patented.

GEO. K. McMECHEN & SON CO.,
Preservers. Wheeling, W. Va., U. S. A.

Westport=on=Lake Champlain.

This pretty village lies on the slope of the natural terrace which encircles the great Northwest Bay, on the New York shore of Lake Champlain. This place has been known for many years as the eastern gateway of the Adirondacks, the great highway leading through Elizabethtown and Keene Valley, to the Au Sable Ponds, Lake Placid, and the high peaks of the range. The Westport Inn, the Over-the-Way, the Gables, and the Elm Cottage are all attractively located and will accommodate one hundred and fifty guests. The parlor, music room, and fine large dining room of the Inn are airy and pleasant, the chambers and bath rooms thoroughly well furnished and the sanitary arrangements excellent. The service is most efficient, and the table is spoken of in the highest terms of praise. There is a good livery stable under the patronage of the Inn and many beautiful and picturesque drives. There are two tennis courts—golf links will be added this season, and there is a boat house connected with the Inn. The wide piazzas command a fine view of the Adirondack foot hills in the west and the great chain of Green Mountains in the east. The Lake excursions are numerous, fine great steamers touching here four times daily, giving opportunity for trips to Ticonderoga, Crown Point and the Au Sable Chasm. The remarkable and unusual features of Westport are the wonderful supply of water and the health record, both of which are unsurpassed. The Westport Mountain Spring bursts from the side of the range at the rate of one million gallons a day and is noted for its temperature and purity.

ROUTES TO AND FROM WESTPORT.

Westport is very accessible, it being only eight hours from New York via the N. Y. Central and Del. & Hud. Railroads, also eight hours from Boston via Fitchburg & Cen. Vt. Railroads, and four hours from Montreal. The Inn will continue under the skilful management of Mrs. O. C. DANIELS, and will be open from June 1st to Oct. 15th.

TERMS—$3.00 to $4.00 a day. Weekly Rates, $12.00 to $21.00 according to location and time occupied. Apply for floor plans.

Baltimore, Chesapeake & Atlantic Rwy. Co.

RAILWAY DIVISION.

Direct route from Baltimore to Ocean City: Maryland's celebrated and only Seaside Resort, situated on the Ocean in Worcester County, 30 miles south of the mouth of Delaware Bay, and is conceded to be the finest and safest beach for bathing on the coast.

Steamer leaves Pier 4½ Light St. Wharf, Baltimore, Md., connecting at Claiborne with Railway for McDaniel's, Harper's, St. Michael's, Riverside, Royal Oak, Kirkham, Bloomfield, Easton, Bethlehem, Preston, Ellwood, Hurlock's, Rhodesdale, Brookview, Ralph, Vienna, Barren Creek, Hebron, Rock-a-walking, Salisbury, Waliston, Parsonsburg, Pittsville, New Hope, Whaleyville, St. Martin, Berlin and Ocean City.

STEAMERS.

CAMBRIDGE.	IDA.	CHOPTANK.	TANGIER.
TIVOLI.	ENOCH PRATT.	KENT.	MAGGIE.
AVALON.	CHOWAN.	POCOMOKE.	HELEN.
JOPPA.	TRED-AVON.	EASTERN SHORE.	

The above Steamers run to all the celebrated and most desirable resorts on the Chesapeake Bay, both on the Eastern and Western Shores.

Leave from Piers 3 and 4 Light St. Wharf, Baltimore, Md., on the several lines as follows:

CHOPTANK RIVER LINE.

For Tilghman's Island, Corners, Easton, Double Mills, Oxford, Bellevue, Travers, Kirby's, Cambridge, Oyster Shell Point, Secretary, Wright's, Choptank, Windy Hill, Hog Island, Dover Bridge, Kingston, Turkey Creek, Two Johns', Williston, Lyford and Denton, at 8 P. M. daily, except Sunday.

NANTICOKE RIVER LINE.

For Deal's Island, Roaring Pt., Bivalve, Tyaskin, Sandy Hill, Lewis, Athaloo, Vienna, Riverton, Sharptown, Truett's, Woodland and Seaford, at 5 P. M., every Monday, Wednesday and Friday.

WICOMICO RIVER LINE.

For Wingate's Pt., Deal's Island, Roaring Pt., Dames Quarter, Mt. Vernon, White Haven, Widgeon, Collins, Quantico, Fruitland and Salisbury, at 5 P. M., Tuesday, Thursday and Saturday.

PIANKATANK RIVER LINE.

For Sampson's, Blackwell's, Harcum's, Timb's, Reed's, Harding's, Harvey's, Eubank's, Byrdton, Grace Pt., Chase's, Palmer's, Little Bay, Jackson's, Crickett Hill, Callis, Fitchett's, Warehouse, Conrad's, Green Pt., Bland's and Freeport, at 5 P. M., every Tuesday and Friday.

Leave from foot of South St., Baltimore, Md., on the several lines as follows:

POCOMOKE RIVER LINE.

For Crisfield, Tangier, Finney's, Onancock, Shelltown, Pitt's, Cedar Hall, Rehoboth, Powell's, Pocomoke City, Mattoponi and Snow Hill, every Tuesday and Friday at 5.30 P. M.

MESSONGO RIVER LINE.

For Ford's, Crisfield's, Finney's, Onancock, Chesconessex, Hunting Creek and Messongo, at 5.30 P. M. every Monday and Thursday.

OCCAHANNOCK RIVER LINE.

For Crisfield, Harborton, Evan's, Bogg's, Cedar View, Nandua, Concord, Reed's, Davis, Miles, Shield's and Rues, 5.30 P. M. every Wednesday and Sunday.

For the running schedule of the above lines see advertisement in the Baltimore and County papers.

For further information apply to Agents of the Company, or address General Offices, Baltimore, Md.

B. L. FLEMING,
Genl. Frt. & Pass. Agent.

WILLARD THOMSON,
General Manager.

HENNEGEN, BATES & CO.,
JEWELERS AND SILVERSMITHS,
13 E. Baltimore Street.

Importers of Diamonds,
and Special Dealers in
English Hall Clocks,
with the celebrated Tubular Chimes.

HENNEGEN, BATES & CO., Baltimore.

Established 1837.

JOHN MURPHY & CO.,
PUBLISHERS,
44 W. Baltimore St., Baltimore, Md.

As the largest Publishing House in the South, we offer the best facilities for the distribution of books.

Just Published.

Social-Official Etiquette of the United States. By MRS. M. V. DAHLGREN. An explanation of the forms and usages that prevail in Social and Official circles at Washington; and that govern Society everywhere. It is a complete record of that which has been of usage in social life at the Capital of the Republic; and it makes clear decisions on all points of Etiquette hitherto debatable. A Handsome 12mo. Volume. Gilt top. Price, *$1.00*.

Memories of the Social and Professional Life of John E. Owens, Comedian. By HIS WIFE. Containing 20 fine Illustrations of Mr. Owens in character. One Volume. Octavo. Cloth. Second Edition. Price, *$2.50*.

A Marriage of Reason. By MAURICE FRANCIS EGAN, of the University of Notre Dame. 12mo. Cloth. Price, *$1.50*.
"A story which is at once good, wholesome, bright and melodramatic."

ORDERS BY MAIL RECEIVE OUR BEST ATTENTION.

Bromo = Seltzer

CURES ALL

HEADACHES AND NEURALGIA,

NERVOUSNESS AND NERVOUS DEPRESSION,

RESULTING FROM

OVER BRAIN-WORK, ALCOHOLIC EXCESSES, &C.,

BY ACTING GENTLY UPON THE

STOMACH AND NERVOUS SYSTEM.

PLEASANT! PROMPT! HARMLESS!

CONTAINS NO ANTIPYRINE, NO MORPHINE, NO COCAINE.

10, 25 AND 50 CENT BOTTLES.

SOLD EVERYWHERE.

www.ingramcontent.com/pod-product-compliance
Lightning Source LLC
Chambersburg PA
CBHW032001300426
44117CB00008B/855